The Terrible Fitzball

The Terrible Fitzball:

The Melodramatist of the Macabre

Larry Stephen Clifton

Bowling Green State University Popular Press
Bowling Green, OH 43403

Entertainment and Leisure Studies
General Editors
Ray B. Browne
Michael T. Marsden

Contents

Acknowledgements

I wish to thank Southern Illinois University for the grant used in researching and formulating this work and my graduate study committee, Professors David Stevens, Christian Moe, Marvin Kleinau, Alfreds Straumanis, and Tom Eynon, for the faith shown in me. In addition, I wish to express my esteemed gratitude to Pat Browne, Director, and to Kathy Hoke, Managerial Assistant, of the The Popular Press, for accepting and converting the manuscript into an acceptable format. To all of these, and to those who have helped and influenced me in the past, I humbly offer my gratitude and favor. Also, I would like to thank my father, S. Hollis Clifton, for his illustration of Edward Fitzball, which was gleaned from a nineteenth-century drawing.

Dedication

To My Mother
Whose Love Now
Comes From Heaven's Hill,
And My Father,
Whose Love
On Earth Brings
Comfort Still

"The Terrible Fitzball"
From <u>Thirty-Five Years</u>
<u>in A Dramatic Author's Life</u>
(1859)

Introduction

Since man first attempted to define himself artistically, the macabre has mystified him and played an important role in the exploration of mind, body, and spirit. From the earliest of recorded literature discovered in Egypt, *The Precepts of The* (2500 B.C.), a papyrus on the mystical and practical wonders of life and death; and *The Book of the Dead* (4266-2000 B.C.), a treatise about the afterlife; to modern mystery yarns and horror tales, the fantastic and the eerie have enchanted man in his creation of artistic lore. Homer's *Iliad* and *Odyssey*, Shakespeare's *Macbeth*, Goya's "May 3, 1808," Mussorgsky's "Night on Bald Mountain," and James Whale's cinematic adaptation of Mary W. Shelley's *Frankenstein* are samplings of how quite different modes of art have expressed the universal quest for the grotesque and the harrowing in life and in fancy. At the center of these artworks is the *sensational triad*. As I have coined the term, and as will be established in Chapter II, the sensational triad is the vivid implementation of horror-terror, crime, and madness as concepts for artistic purposes. Man's proclivity for enjoying the unknown and the gruesome has been the basis for the artistic realization of the triad.

This "art of the macabre" has been rejected often as either demoralizing or repugnant. Yet, aspects of the sensational triad have endured in art as they have endured in life. The triad is merely a reflection of that which is morbid in life. Through metaphor and symbol, the sensational triad becomes an artistic voyage into all that is dark and wrenching about the human condition. It was the nineteenth-century English melodrama that proved the most conducive for the triad's particular type of stylistic thrills and chills. There was a reason why this was so. Of all the arts, the theatre was the most viable because that medium was less discriminating in reaching the greatest number of people. One did not have

1

2 The Terrible Fitzball

to be rich to buy a ticket, and one did not have to be literate to understand the action on stage. The theatre was the egalitarian entertainment forum, as television, cinema, and community theatre are today. The minor playhouses, many located in areas where the lower classes lived, were the choice locales for attracting viewers used to *sensationalism* in everyday life.

Edward Fitzball was an English dramatist whose literary output was versatile and prodigious. His forte was the sensational and fantastic melodrama, in the Grand Guignol tradition, which captured man's imagination. To understand Fitzball, one must know his chaotic society, which was experiencing the throes of the Industrial Revolution; comprehend melodrama as drama and as theatre; and consider the genre's linkage to romanticism, its parental literary school, as the dominant fashion in the arts during Fitzball's era. An artistic populist, via his vocation as a "hack" dramatist, Fitzball was very much influenced by the types of people coming to the theatres that engaged his talent and the distinct environment that produced them. His terrifying monsters and villains may have been emblems for the real dangers and anxieties faced by his patrons daily in London's unbalanced society of fear, crime, and toil.

Fitzball was able to create his role as a populist by working as a "hack" for numerous playhouses in London. His role as hack and as dramaturge, a more esteemed title, embraced writing new plays, rewriting other works as adapter, and assessing dramas for production. It may be implied that Fitzball was swamped with dramaturgy in all of its manifestations. The sensational triad proved itself accommodating for the insatiable craving for plays by the audiences of the time. They used the theatre as a haven from their laboring "sweat shops" and Fitzball's plays as vehicles for journeys into lands of enchantment and adventure. Fitzball's exploitation of the spectacular merely whetted the appetites even more for his brand of chaotic delight.

In chronicling the nineteenth-century as a great age for theatre, Freedly and Reeves praise Fitzball as a contributor to the great spectacles at some of London's finest theatres. Fitzball was popular theatre personified (556). Oscar Brockett has more to add.

Edward Fitzball (1792-1873) had dramatized a number of Sir Walter Scott's novels before turning to original compositions; soon his nautical melodramas rivaled those of Douglas William Jerrold. He is now especially remembered, however, because he initiated the vogue of melodramas based on actual crime. His *Jonathan Bradford*; or, *The Murder at the Roadside Inn* had an initial run of 160 nights, a record not broken until 1860. One of the most prolific playwrights of the century, Fitzball continued to turn out plays until his death. (*History* 458)

These excerpts signify the brevity given by theatre historians generally to the career of a prolific dramatist, whose plays numbered some 170 and spanned the gamut of genres: tragedy, comedy, operas, burletta, numancia (sea drama), and the melodrama in all of its categories (horror, domestic, adventure, and mystery). All of Fitzball's drama, however, had the aura of melodrama about it. But to dismiss him as just another mediocre hack is to deny Fitzball's gifts as a writer and champion of a particular sort of drama, attractive as popular entertainment to the people. In addition to being a dramatist, he was a novelist, poet, librettist, and romanticist.

By understanding the sensational triad, as both an artistic and psychological manifestation, Fitzball's type of popular theatre will emerge as a cathartic and enjoyable entity. Fitzball was stimulated by his surrounding society, and the society was enthralled and educated about itself—even if metaphorically and symbolically—by the lurid declarations in Fitzball's plays. Artistically deft, theatrically assured, and dedicated to the principles of romantic literature, Fitzball's melodramas, upon study, reveal genuine craftsmanship. His conceits of the uncanny, fanciful, and the dreadful somewhat resembled the flights of fancy held by such esteemed artists as Poe, Coleridge, and Baudelaire. However, these three writers' excursions into the morbid were definitely of a more philosophical nature, which continues to challenge modern interpretation. Fitzball's journeys into the macabre seemed always to have been pronounced by the dramatist with his tongue planted firmly in his cheek. For Fitzball laughter seemed always a dimension of his grotesquerie, thereby yielding the happy ending as a consistent and customary denouement. While the above writers of the period dealt with the macabre, only Fitzball's horrors were subject to the courageous will of the hero, with a victory over them assured. For Poe the sensational triad wrecks man; for Fitzball the triad is a challenge to be overcome by the hero. The fall of the curtain for Fitzball was not only a signal to end the play; it was also a signal to end the villain's capers. Unlike the above poets, Fitzball worked within a theatrical style that commanded happy endings. His patrons would not have had the time, or the temperament, to endorse any overt inspection into the macabre as a depression of the soul.

Yet Fitzball, like the above poets, had his concern for mankind's dilemmas. Even if philosophically unsuccessful, he did write some interesting social-thesis plays, although they were clearly melodramas, with all of the excitement and trappings of that genre. Perhaps out of his range, Fitzball's efforts were, nonetheless commendable.

4 The Terrible Fitzball

The Questions to be Answered

Fitzballian drama and theatre, in retrospect, have more to offer, as creative and telling art, than a hero fighting a villain. The macabre elements in Fitzball's more harrowing plays addressed society as much as they addressed dramaturgy and theatre. With this broad idea in mind, there emerge the following questions: 1) How did the sensational triad reflect a cultural phenomenon occurring in Fitzball's society; 2) How did Fitzball utilize classical dramatic concepts as a force in his dramaturgy; 3) How did Fitzball treat the sensational triad as a dominant factor in his more exemplary plays of the macabre; and 4) How may Fitzball be evaluated today? Because the answers to these questions will touch upon so may issues, both artistic and social, it will be necessary to put melodrama within a defined, historical context. Brief though this will be, Fitzball's social and artistic era must be understood in order to appreciate his dramaturgy.

Melodrama as an Historical Aesthetic

To understand Fitzball as an author, we must first understand and define the type of play he wrote. Beneath its superficial simplicity, melodrama, upon examination, emerges as a dramatic form replete with an individual, literary mission and guided by a distinct theatricality. As the most popular genre, it has also been the most abused, privy to every type of theatrical quack and bastardized artistic license. As a result, the common reaction to defining melodrama may be either condescension or bewilderment. To the uninformed, the genre is more ersatz than art. James Smith's classic example confirms the dilemma:

What is melodrama? In 1913 William Gillette confessed that when he questioned "really intellectual people, none of them appeared certain." The situation has not changed. Ask a musician, or a literary scholar, or even that convenient abstraction, the man in the street, and you will get three very different answers. (1)

In a possible defense of this definitional quagmire, it may be that the universality of the genre lies more in an emotional appeal, than in a purely intellectual calculation. Emotionally charged, melodrama has always been better suited to feeling and watching, than in defining and pondering, as a genre. Most of the great playwrights have penned melodramas, as such, sometime during their careers. In fact, several plays, when reassessed, have been labelled melodramas, or at least melodramatic. For our purpose, a definition must be made.

The melodrama of the nineteenth-century had a particular prescription to it. Certainly Fitzball's concoctions of horror, adventure, mystery, and domestic crises contain a formula that struck knowingly at the viewer's emotions. If the genre met with critical debate—and Fitzball's plays most assuredly did—it was usually with critics unaware of melodrama's somewhat esoteric rules and formulas, which operated out of a segregated logic. In short, melodramatic theatre often did not share the conventions of the other genres. With the melodramatist free to use any logic available in exploiting the emotions of the audience, the critic may have been put off in this game of dramatic wits, inasmuch as he was looking for a conventional logic on stage; on the contrary, the melodramatist had the prerogative of doing what he would on stage for his own intentions. The critics may have been victimized by an affective fallacy.

For Fitzball his works were destined for spectators unconcerned with standardized judgments of drama: they wanted thrills. And melodrama put a high priority on audience acceptance, which always changed into money in the box-office. Melodrama's assault upon the emotions made the audience aware that fancy, not life, was being shown. However, paradoxically, the viewer was mesmerized into seeing life. The power of the melodrama aesthetic lies in the viewer living the action seen in the medium. The deception of the aesthetic mind, in making it accept absurdity as logic, has always been the stimulus behind melodrama. Eric Bentley, in *The Playwright as Thinker,* confirms this declaration in discussing the attraction of the modern melodrama *The Children's Hour.* Yet, this conclusion is true for all melodrama, even especially for the lurid works of Fitzball. For Bentley the style of theatre matters little; it is the effect that is important:

Thousands have gone to *The Children's Hour* and come away fondly believing what they have seen is life; they have not realized that here too the familiar stock figures, the type characterizations, have been presented before them in modified form. (10)

It is melodrama's manipulation of the emotions which makes the viewer forget that he has seen it all before, only in another dramatic manifestation of the same stock plot and characters. With this considered, Frank Rahill defines this elusive, complex drama.

Melodrama is a form of dramatic composition in prose partaking of the nature of tragedy, comedy, pantomime, and spectacle, and intended for the popular audience. Primarily concerned with a situation and plot, it calls upon mimed action extensively and employs a more or less fixed complement of stock characters, the most important of which are the suffering heroine or hero, a persecuting villain, and a benevolent comic. It is conventionally moral and humanitarian in point of view and sentimental and optimistic in temper, concluding its fable happily with virtue rewarded after many trials and vice punished. Characteristically, it offers elaborate scenic accessories and miscellaneous divertissements and introduces music freely, typically to underscore the dramatic effect. (xiv)

As one may deduce, the classic melodrama, while giving its creator a certain latitude in composition, held fast to several dictates. In Fitzball's case, all of his staged chaos and frenzy were a carefully plotted circumstance, with a moral purpose the chief objective. In melodrama we know that the ending must be just, but that does not prevent emotionalism from surging. As we shall see in analyzing Fitzball's plays, the denouement is expected; it is the steps leading to the conclusion which taxes one's emotions and imagination. The strategem, used by the melodramatist for effect, is no haphazard whimsy. In the chapter about melodrama's relation to Aristotles' elements of drama, it will be shown that Fitzball, a model for the artistic melodramatist, was cognizant of the classical elements and adapted them carefully.

In his book *Playwriting*, Smiley has concluded that the melodrama, in the hands of capable artists, could become a drama of power (47). J.S. Trewin, in *The Pomping Folk of the Nineteenth Century,* indicates that, historically, melodrama had attracted a following simply because of its staged horrors. Although there were differing types of melodrama, ranging from the domestic to the macabre, this statement would account for the macabre melodrama's draw from a people quite used to real horror. Being offbeat, the horror play created fanciful metaphors and semblances of hope, as the hero was seen battling villains and escaping death. Thereby, the empathic and purgative rationales (the Aristotelean conclusions) were maintained in the genre. Writes Trewin:

In spirit, however, melodrama was clearly the product of the Gothic extravagance which gripped a Europe loved by the Age of Reason, and which found architectural and antiquarian as well as literary form. In England the link between the Gothic novel was established by the career of Mathew "Monk" Lewis...with a Gothic melodrama, *The Castle Spectre,* in 1787. He thus established a standard for sensationalism which presented a serious challenge to his rivals. There could be no turning back for English melodrama after the appearance of *The Castle Spectre*...Inevitably the finest achievements of German Romantic drama made little appeal to the bloodthirsty audiences of the English theatre. (*Pomping Folk* 109)

Obviously, then, Fitzballian sensationalism had been preceded by that of Lewis and others; therefore, before Fitzball wrought his type of luridness on the stage, playgoers had already succumbed, and willingly, to theatrical horrors. Simply put, the macabre melodrama encouraged man's latent desire to enjoy the dreadful as entertainment. Even the ghastliness of the guillotine became a type of theatre action: the aristocrat was the player and the crowds, the audience. The horror melodrama evidenced that its romanticism lay in graphic sensationalism and frenzied piquancy.

Romanticism as Thought and Art

From 1798, with the publication of Wordsworth's *Lyrical Ballads*, to 1870, romanticism flourished as England's dominant literary fashion. Unshackled from Neoclassicism's cleaving to misapplied, classical rules, romanticism sought to inspire its artists and viewers with creative and human freedom in morality, ethics, and socialization. To mention the likes of Shelley, Byron, and Keats was to declare total liberation. Likewise, classic melodrama followed that robust theme of the morality play: the pitting of evil against good. In all of melodrama, including the chaotic world of Fitzball, the human will is tested. Romanticism was the aesthetic liberation of the artist," an ecstatic exploration of what the creative imagination might produce in the spiritual and emotional modes of expression. Adroitly, melodrama physicalized for audiences, unable to read the thoughts of a Shelley or Wordsworth, the hope, excitement, and worth of human dignity and will. The very gist of the genre was the conquering of tyranny by faithful determination. The generic bombast of the form and spectacle in production did not lessen that noble purpose. Melodrama put romanticism within everyone's reach, educated or not. Romantic drama echoed Eliot's idea of what man needed most: "a kind of faith that issues from despair" (Davidoff 78). Romanticism and melodrama were the fuel and fire of creative freedom.

A middle-class attitude, romanticism spoke against any bureaucracy or hierarchy that intimidated the human spirit. With feudalism over and education on the rise, the middle class began to assert itself over injustice. Faced with the insidious Industrial Revolution—a symbol of social and psychological bondage—romanticism attacked the socio-political chains that forced upon the average man sweat shops, low wages, and a demeaning way of living.

Martin Day illuminates the exacerbating conditions foisted upon the powerless slaves in the Industrial Tyranny of the 1800s:

8   The Terrible Fitzball

The crowded cities and the growth of unsightly, dirty, noisy industrialism stimulated the wish for escape. We were accustomed to the Industrial Age and to an extent have mitigated some of its distressing features, but the romantics were just experiencing its first onrush and understandably were aghast. (*English Literature: 1660-1837* 326)

The economic problems of the working class were one of the targets for reform by the romantics. Paid hardly any wage for their toil, the ordinary laborers looked to romantic drama as one of their limited forms of respite. Romanticism's criticism against economic injustice added fuel to the movement's political involvement. Chartism, a romantically inspired, socialistic philosophy, aimed at equity for all of man, by establishing a utopian and democratic form of government, was short lived. Nonetheless, romantic literature endorsed this stance. Classic melodrama instilled such an ideology, especially in the hero's battling the ruthless bureaucracy, typified by the villain who was often a rich bureaucrat himself. A comment was made by the melodramatist about the corruption of power thrown upon the commoner. The theatrical fall of the villain gave the viewer a vicarious victory over any personal dominator. David Thompson cites the literature of the time thus socially concerned:

Distinguished literary men and women concertedly turned their attention to social evils that the middle of the century saw in a new era of "social literature." Thomas Hood's "Song of the Shirt," Mrs. Brownings "Cry of the Children," Mrs. Gaskell's *Mary Barton,* Charles Kingsley's "Yeast" and "Alton Locke," and Thomas Carlyle's "Chartism" and "Past and Present" are all literary by-products of the Chartist commotions. (863)

To the layman, it may seem strange to include melodrama, especially the Blood-and-Thunder style of Fitzball, within the perspective of social consciousness. However, it is very appropriate. Romanticism was most involved in man's whole being as a free entity, and melodrama, being romantic literature, had much the same value system. Such was the reason for the polarization between good and evil, the free and the tyrannical. Melodrama's obviousness notwithstanding, the conquering of the right over the wrong symbolized the victory of the downtrodden over domination. For example, John Walder's *The Factory Lad* (1832) dramatized the revolt of workers against the hated mechanization of their plant. The factory is burned in retaliation against the evil boss. There is a hint of this play in Gerhart Hauptmann's *The Weavers,* perhaps the classic play of revolt by the working class, in 1892. The style of the two plays notwithstanding, romanticism and realism, the theme is constant:

virtue over oppression. So powerful was this theme that Hauptmann was awarded the Nobel Prize for *The Weavers* in 1912.

Another "social thesis (conscience) play," that reflected the melodramatist's concerns, was William Pratt's *Ten Nights in a Barroom* (1858). The amusing title notwithstanding, and despite melodrama's innate exaggeration—often done so that spectators in the back rows of large theatres could hear and see the play well—the theme of the drama, alcoholism and social oppression, was poignant and present. This play is subsumed within romanticism's plea for human dignity. To dismiss such works as so much Delsartian (the acting style of the age) ranting is to miss the thrust of the playwright's intention. Booth comments on melodrama's social character: "Such manifestations are a part of the class bitterness of much nineteenth-century melodrama. In many ways, melodrama is a true social reflection of its times" (*Villain* 29). Fitzball's contribution to this category will be shown. Although melodrama was, firstly, entertainment, this rationale did not exclude melodrama's having serious overtones. If the genre is accurately judged, many a serious melodrama has made contributions to social consciousness.

Another aspect of romantic literature was religion. Although largely pantheistic, the romantics dreamed of brotherhood on earth. The melodramatic hero and heroine were usually quite devout, calling for divine help consistently, when in the clutches of the atheistic heavy. Religious himself, Fitzball made spiritual battles as adroit as any physical altercation. Spiritual crusades were dramatic gems.

The last tenet of romanticism was the Coleridgean slogan of the viewer's "willing suspension of disbelief." In short, the viewer had to imagine that the romantic art he was seeing was actual; he could not use secular logic to enjoy romantic literature, especially the melodrama, which taxed one's imagination to the hilt. Such a mental task was the strength and glory of melodrama and all of romantic art. To escape the drudgery of their sordid lives, the audience of the melodrama had to call upon that mechanism of needed recreations. David Thompson makes a final case for the fairyland aura of romanticism: escapist entertainment was almost the sole pleasure that the displaced throngs had. Hence, melodrama was as much therapeutic as it was joyful:

These urban population were still mostly country-bred, with the traditional outlook and character of country folk. Their children too often reared in the slum conditions, which resulted from the shoddy houses rushed up to accommodate the new comers, were a phenomenon. (12)

Touting economic, social, and moral justice for man, romanticism's entertainment value advocated the heady themes of sensitivity, nostalgia, mysticism, and a religious communion between God and man. The emergence of romanticism into melodrama cannot be denied, for in a classic melodrama there resided the best intentions of its philosophical source, even if the genre were bombastically produced. The literary school and its drama were, in the last analysis, inspired by human liberty and happiness.

Melodrama in Composition and Form

We may now take a glimpse into the complex nuances of the genre penned by Fitzball and his peers in nineteenth-century England. In *English Melodrama*, Michael Booth asserts that this Romanesque *belles lettres* was more than fluff; indeed, its imagination exploited life:

Drawing its materials from everywhere—history, the sea, crime, military life, the village, city streets, robbers, bands, Gothic castles, fashionable drawing rooms—an endless list of subject matter—melodrama presents it through extremes of action, farce, morality, character, and emotion in framework of fast, short, and rapidly changing scenes mounted with a maximum of sensation and scenic effects. Melodrama has…a variety of content within its rigid pattern. (39)

Although melodrama did offer certain social themes for scrutiny beneath its zealous action, the patrons of melodrama, unconcerned with a laborious and tedious drama of significant, social consequence, cheered the *morality play* aura, in which good vanquished evil, through allegory and symbolism. In fact, it may be possible to interpret the melodrama in the four classic modes of biblical interpretation offered by Origin in the third century: literalism, allegory, analogy, and topology. Because most melodramas were fictional accounts, the last three methodologies of representational, spiritual, and moral deductions are quite feasible, especially with Fitzball, who contended with the personifications of good and evil (i.e. The *Devil's Elixir*). Such interpretations were certainly beyond the grasp of the ordinary viewer, but such insight adds credence to the moral judgments inherent in all classic melodrama: the morality play syndrome.

Booth goes on to acknowledge that melodrama is the dramatic form which expresses the reality of the human condition, as we all experience it most of the time (*English Melodrama* 11). Truthfully, most of us may not fight hideous demons in a cosmic duel, but man does look at life oftentimes in a black or white issue, the scope of melodrama's dichotomies. We fight against evil in all of its guises, from an oppressive employer, to a crooked politician, thus carrying out the theme of the genre. Booth muses over the need for battle in melodrama:

Here the battle lines between good and evil are sharply drawn; indeed, the stage struggle between the two is about as old as English drama itself. (Elizabethan and Jacobean tragedies were)...a rich source of melodrama, containing almost everything melodrama does except for elaborate mechanical spectacle and happy endings...they are crammed with villains, distressed heroines, revengeful ghosts, domestic agonies, inflated language, and physical sensations. (*English Melodrama* 39-40)

Booth's recollections have much to do with acting, an art of keen importance in the melodrama, and an art which will be discussed at some length later in the study; the acting bravado emerges as one of the most fascinating qualities about Fitzballian fare, to be sure. Melodrama's closest kin is tragedy, but both are different. Aristotle commented in *The Poetics* (fourth century B.C.) that tragedy was a complete, serious action of a certain magnitude, that it was "embellished" in language and "several kinds of artistic ornaments," and that a *katharsis*, purging the audience of pity and fear, would be evoked (Aristotle 240). As for plot, the sage called it "the soul of tragedy," the animating principal (Aristotle 247).

The reason that the definition of tragedy has been given here—and will be referred to throughout the study—is that serious melodrama takes tragedy and transforms the definition of Aristotle to suit its own purpose, which is taking the august principles of tragedy and accentuating the *body* and not the *soul*. Hence, a type of *wonderful exploitation* emerges, void of the inner torments of the soul-searching in *Lear* or *Hamlet*. Melodramtic tragedy is the enlargement of serious issues to a contrived pitch. Simply put, a melodramatized version of *Macbeth* would put more emphasis on the gore, horrors, crime, and battles than on Macbeth's wonder about his own damnation. Booth explains well: "To be sure, melodrama is responsible for a great deal of popular trash, but this does not mean that all melodrama is trashy. Like any other genre, it affords a wide range of excellence" (*English Melodrama* 11). In melodrama, the *hamartia* is accentuated on the outside for public gasps and thrills; in tragedy, it is the spiritual degeneration that is all important. The morality play syndrome remains always in the melodrama; the eternal battle between good and evil continues unabated.

No matter how fantastic the plot may be, the audience was likely to empathize with the characters in a tangible setting that offered an identifiable essence of reality. By touching man's creative, imaginative, yet realistic, frame

12   The Terrible Fitzball

of mind, the great melodramas of the nineteenth-century caused the allurement which Michael Booth regards as indispensable for the total theatre experience:

> Inspired by a view of man that regarded him as innately virtuous, endowed with a strong moral sense, and capable of perfectibility through an appeal to his emotions, sentimental comedies and tragedies alike are full of ringing moral sentiments, put into the mouths of generous heroes...Emotional situations are exhaustively exploited. Pity is a favorite, and much is made of pathos and distress; both in tragedy and comedy the playwright is chiefly concerned to wring tears from the audience. Perfect and wicked traits are personified in dramatic characters. Prose dialogue is often as inflated and artificial as are emotion and characters. (*English Melodrama* 41)

It was melodrama's grandiose, if now quaint, use of dialogue that helped give the genre theatrical precision and historical interest. Generations of actors trained their voices to make the melodrama powerfully spoken before the viewer. Sir Henry Irving's strong presence in *The Bells,* for example, promoted vocal power. One may glean this from the dialogue itself. Ashley Dukes reflects on the spoken word enhancing the dramatic style:

> In living theater, the dramatist, like the actor, surrenders himself to some measure to gain his freedom. He gives himself to the stage of form and colour, of winged words and surging harmonies. The spoken word is not dogma, but a litany. It is not a principle, but a foundation. (41)

It is ironic that the English melodrama was not perfected by the stars of romantic literature, its poets. The great poets-cum-dramatists produced lukewarm plays. Coleridge's *Remorse* (1813), Shelley's *The Cenci* (1819), and Byron's *Werner* (1822) are examples of mediocre dramas, although *The Cenci* is occasionally revived. The Victorian theatre prospered because, as in Shakespeare's day, theatre and drama were left to professionals in the field. The shoddy and inept writer quickly faded through commercial pressure. The hack, for all of his hurry and insecurities, kept the theatre solvent, stressing that the theatre was as much an economic concern as it was an artistic one. With Fitzball, this challenge, while often frustrating, suited his economic-artistic slant. Booth notes the situation of the professional dramatist in the 1800s:

> In the nineteenth century, however, not a single great poet or novelist made any kind of dramatic reputation for himself. The fact remains that the nineteenth-century drama is essentially the work of men of the theatre rather than men of literature and culture. The writing of melodrama was left to hacks. (*English Melodrama* 47)

Victor Hugo had given his novel theory in the "Introduction" to his play *Cromwell* (1827). Herein, he asserted that drama, to be reflective of life, must juxtapose that which was ugly and repulsive in life with that which was beautiful and attractive, inasmuch as both essences were involved in the dual nature of man. While such a declaration seems mild when read today, one must remember that dramaturgy had thus far been under the yoke of the neoclassicists, pedants who, although voicing Aristotle's theories about tragedy, had misinterpreted many of the sage's principles. Hugo sent the theatrical world reeling, causing a disruption between liberal and conservative elements. Romanticism in dramatic theory had begun the undoing of neoclassicism. With Fitzball's plays so rich in the demonic and the lovely, it is little wonder why Fitzball became fond of dramatizing Hugo's works. The two were philosophically and, to a degree, creatively similar. Gassner and Quinn's musings about Hugo imply much about the maverick Fitzball:

Hugo's historical dramas have been called irregular, pseudoclassical tragedies of lyric couplets. Despite his fondness for banal trappings of *melodrama*—outlaw heroes, wistful heroines, traitors and assassins, poisons and a secret passageways—he could exalt in passionate verse his lyrical themes of the suffering and joy of love, honor, and patriotic ride. Perhaps his most distinguishing trait as a playwright is the conception of life as a series of paradoxes and antitheses of moral character. He employs disguises to heighten the contrast between reality and appearance and arranges characters in startling contrasts. Sometimes he is attracted by ambivalent forces within a single character. Yet his characters are always unreal. He sees the propensities for good or evil, their embodiment of the ideal or the real, in theatrical and lyrical—rather than truly dramatic—terms. The plays remain, in the last analysis, little more than acted poems. (437)

While this synopsis of Hugo's style may befit him and Fitzball, in many respects, Fitzball's plays are much more "than acted poems." The *Dichtung* in Fitzball's mind is a swirling fantasy, partly childish dream, and partly looming nightmare. Amidst the Victorian turmoil of industrialization, as a vocational dynamic, and science squaring off against religion, as a philosophical dynamic, Fitzball used the grotesque as entertainment to make man relax and as symbol to make him ponder. Following Brunetiere's advice that art is "a spectacle of the will striving toward a goal and conscious of the means it employs" (Davidoff 82), Fitzball used the drama as a lurid voluptuary (that is, as a larger-than-life approach to the theatre) to draw audiences into its clutches. If this were so, then Fitzball was the personification of that tenet.

14 The Terrible Fitzball

It is a grand and beautiful sight to see this broad development of drama wherein the plot moves on to the convulsion with a firm and unembarrassed step, without diffuseness and without undue compression; of a dream, in short, wherein the poet abundantly fulfills the object of art, which is to open to the spectator a double prospect, to illuminate at the same time the interior and exterior of mankind: the exterior of their speech and their acts; the interior, by asides and monologues: to being together, in a word, in the same picture, the drama of life and the drama of conscience. (Gassner and Quinn 396)

Conclusion for Study

Wrote Hugo, "Form is nothing without the spirit; with the idea it is everything" (Gassner and Quinn 437). This "Introduction" has served three purposes. One, melodrama may be noticed as a very spirited form, based upon a deeply moralistic idea. Two, it is plausible to presume that Fitzball's theatre of the macabre is a worthwhile subject for scholarly pursuits. And, three, the artistic, social, and psychological constituencies of melodrama warrant investigation as to why this genre remains popularly enduring. Implicit in all of this was Fitzball's contribution to both art and theory. Although novel and speculative, Fitzball's horrors on stage struck a symbolic chord with his disorderly society, whose people faced serious problems daily. Fitzball's fame with audiences, and managers of the numerous playhouses employing him as a dramaturgy, coincided with his philosophy of making drama amusing and educative, the standard dictum of the melodrama. The captivation of Fitzball lay in his transference of amusement into the most lurid of dramatic situation. J.O. Baily aptly demonstrates that the Gothic play, a Fitzballian hallmark, created chilling thrills for the imaginative mind. Fitzball would have agreed.

The aim of the Gothic play was to provide thrills by creating terror through suggestions of the supernatural. Setting and atmosphere played an important part in the proper mood. The villain is the dynamic character....The play is haunted by evil forces. (23)

This study will demonstrate that the sensational triad was an aesthetic methodology for Fitzball and that, as a classic melodramatist, Fitzball's style had a unique flair for fantastic amusement. The study will also conclude that the forgotten Fitzball would easily fit into mainline entertainment today.

J.O. Bailey's summation of melodrama is a remainder of Fitzball's doctrine of wondrous, thrilling, and poetic escapism.

The common factor in the melange of melodrama was the taste of the people. Melodrama satisfied their desire to escape monotony through vicarious excitement of thrilling entertainment, and yet to see their lives portrayed on stage. There was, of course, an idealizing tendency with a sentimental faith in poetic justice. Every melodrama presents a conflict between virtue and vice...the peculiarity of this theme (from the other serious drama) in melodrama is that virtue is overt conformity to the image of conduct fostered by Sunday Schools. The characters of melodrama were chiefly symbols of virtue and vice, personifications of moral qualities rather than complex people. Action was vigorous...required spectacular scenery...was episodic in structure ...I fairly vibrated to the thrills of pulsating music and the bursts of heroic music... melodrama was able to survive because it expressed a vital force in the common people. Its sentimentality rested upon their simple idealism. Its humanitarian message had a strong appeal for audiences who understood and felt poverty and injustice. Its happy ending, however naive, expressed the hope that springs eternal in people who find the present weary. It had the vitality to experiment and to become natural in performance, and, finally, it had the strength to live on the product of its own evolution. (34)

This valedictory bespeaks all the ingredients in Fitzball's choice of dramatic forms. Far from being hackneyed, the melodrama, in the hands of an artist like Fitzball, may rise to theatrical nobility. That purpose of noble art will be the controlling image that will define Fitzball, in all of his spectacle, merriment, and grotesquerie.

Chapter I
The Life and Times of Edward Fitzball

In order to assess the writer, knowing something about Fitzball's life is important in putting his work and ideas into their proper perspective. He has been deigned thusly: "This gentleman's works stand in the same relation to dramatic literature of the country as that in which the Chamber of Horrors', at Madame Tussaud's, may be said to stand with reference to the rest of the collection" (a' Beckett 4). Trewin has conceded that Fitzball may be simply seen as "...an amiable routine dramatist now amongst the nineteenth-century writers of the most forgotten...a lurid writer of the spectacular: demons, fairies, ghosts, blue-red flames (Bengal lights)." (*Pomping Folk* 109-10) However, these demure condescensions seem myopic in retrospect, inasmuch as Fitzball appears neither routine nor forgettable. Moreover, his dramatic versatility was greatly helped by an inclination towards theatrical experimentation. To be sure, Fitzball was not an opaque writer, or melodrama an oblique genre. Both the art and the artist were direct and clear in their goals and values. Being victimized by mulish critics, Fitzball suffered needlessly. This is not to say that the dramatist always yielded commendable products. However, it must be added that Fitzball's objectives and dramaturgic system were often overlooked by judges too quick to condemn. Perhaps this glance at his life and at the playhouses, in which he so conscientiously labored, will shed light upon one of the theatre's most forgotten, yet most creative, artists.

Early Life
Edward Fitzball was born at Burwell, near Mildenhall, Cambridgeshire, England, in 1793, the second son of Robert Ball, a farmer, who died in 1803. Edward was the grandson of a prominent physician on his father's side and would adopt the maiden surname of his mother, which was Fitz, in his later plays. Educated in New Market, at the Albertus Parr's School Academy, Edward soon became an apprentice to the printing house in Norwich, from 1809-1812, when his mother sold the family farm for some 12,000 pounds. It was as a printer that Edward first entertained the idea of writing professionally, as a poet. In 1814 he wed and lived happily until his wife, Adelaide, died in

1850. He took the *nom de guerre* (pen-name) of Fitzball because another writer was called Ball (Patrick 783). After marrying he began a short-lived poetry journal, but its failure only encouraged his dedication towards a literary career (Stephen 638). Emulating the poet Robert Blomfield, Fitzball began to dramatize his narrative poetry in 1829, the date of the implementation of his new surname.

In 1819, however, Fitzball wrote his first melodrama, *Edda*, and submitted it, for consideration as part of the season's bill, to Tom Dibdin, manager of the Surrey Theatre in London. Appreciating the style in *Edda*, Dibdin encouraged Fitzball to write by convincing a London socialite, a Mrs. Opie, to be Fitzball's patron. Fitzball presented his first, producible work at the Theatre Royal, Norwich, in 1820. *The Innkeeper of Abbeville,* or the *Ostler and the Robber,* was later transferred by the sly manager to the Surrey in 1821 (Adams 520). Critically, Fitzball was at his most prominent between 1817-1837. The succor given him by Dibdin caused Fitzball to concentrate on the drama after his Surrey premier; nonetheless, he maintained a virtuoso interest in writing other types of literature, too. From the outset, Fitzball began toying with the sensational triad in developing a characteristic theatre of the macabre. In an 1821 comment in his *The Revenge of Taran*, Fitzball alluded to this concept while seeming to scorn the supernatural elements in horror; ironically, the supernatural would become a fixture in his later plays of the fantastic and grotesque. He wrote, "The design of the story is to prove that a tale of real horror may be produced by normal means, without resorting to superhuman agents as in *The Vampire* (by Planche) and Frankenstein (by Milner)" (*Taran* 1). Nevertheless, a surfeit of "superhuman agents" did arise in his theatre of the macabre to frighten the wits out of the numerous audiences who came from all walks-of-life for such enjoyment. It is noteworthy that these lurid qualities underscored much of the versatility shown by Fitzball in his other literary outlets, such as the novel, poem, burletta, and opera (as its librettist) ("Fitzball" 289). The macabre, an inchoate factor in his early works, would soon become Fitzball's artistic trademark, in tandem with his most popular plays.

Fitzball's Career

Fitzball began his association with the Surrey as a hack, or house-dramatist, a profession much in vogue at the time. The manager was one Watkin Burroughs, who revived *The Innkeeper of Abbeville* in 1826. The rhetorical question arises: Would a mercenary theatre manager revive a routine drama by a routine playwright? The most practical answer—not in the least rhetorical—is no. The Olympic Theatre again revived the work in 1830. Fitzball stayed at the Surrey as its "play doctor" until 1834. The *Theatrical Inquisitor* reviewed *Edda; or, The Hermit of Warkworth* in 1820 by stating that the play had "...nerve, power, and energy" (46). Fitzball's plays were never enervate. No less than the great Robert Louis Stevenson, himself a novelist drawn to melodramatic strands, pointed to Fitzball's uniqueness:

The stage is its generic name; but it is an old, insular, homebread staginess; not French, domestically British; not today, but smacking of O. Smith, Fitzball, and the great age of melodrama. (221-2)

While at the Surrey, where he was most comfortable, Fitzball wrote some thirty plays. Always, however, the writer would be engaged by other institutions while in the service of another. Fitzball was never an exclusive hack; he was itinerant, to say the least. The following list shows the many theatres and the numerous plays, in parentheses, relative to Fitzball's career. Such indicate a busy professional life of one who worked ceaselessly: The Coburg (four), the Olympic (five), the Adelphi (twelve), the Hull (one), the Edinburg (one), the Alexandria (one), the St. James (three), the Haymarket (one), the Astley (ten), the Princess (one), the Marylebone (six), the Grecian (one), the Garrick (one), the Royal Pavilion (one), the Lyceum (three), the City of London (one), the Vauxhall (five), the Victoria (four), the Drury Lane (twenty), Sadler's Wells (three), and the Covent Garden (twenty four). Fitzball scripted more plays at London's two patent-playhouses, the Covent Garden and Drury Lane, than at any other house. In addition to writing for formal houses, Fitzball staged dramas for private social affairs. Fitzball never ignored any opportunity to showcase his talents, regardless of the type of theatre involved, or the circumstances surrounding him. His most notable periods were those spent at the Surrey (1820-24), the Adelphi (1823-35), and at the Drury Lane (1833-51). At the Covent Garden and Drury Lane, Fitzball augmented his stay by acting as a "play doctor" for other scripts to be performed. It seems that managers were always willing to exploit Fitzball's many talents, to which Fitzball had no objection.

With an obvious proclivity towards his economic security, Fitzball, while not denying his artistic self, wrote dramas that would bring in the masses. His 20-year span at the Drury Lane suggested that his plays were most commercial; Fitzball knew that the theatre rewarded a dramatist for being useful, not for being only *artistic*. His frenzied "blue-fire" horrors seemed to reveal an alter-ego in Fitzball, who, as a person, was somewhat meek and solitary. In comparing the dramatic personality of his plays with that of the playwright, a paradox occurs. His monsters and dark plots belied a sensitive being, whose true self was most assured in his ruminations over his wife's death. Here, a poignancy in Fitzball is uncovered from a statement he made in his autobiography, *Thirty-five Years in a Dramatic Author's Life:*

But there is a sweet and beautiful hope of the paradise in my heart, the hope of the promise of God, that we shall meet again shortly in an endearing happiness: "Where the wicked cease from troubling—where the weary are at rest."(1: 249)

Yet, Fitzball was not a morose man. He was a theatrical factotum who loved his work, although he was critical of it. Always the poet and musician, he injected his distinct brand of merriment into the twelve librettoes he wrote, with songs such as "My Pretty Jane" and "Let Me Like a Soldier Fall." The latter was scored by Vincent Wallace and became famous as a memorable tune.

Mainly writing for the minor playhouses of London, Fitzball was in a position to meet many of the important literati of the day. Neither ignored, nor merely tolerated, Fitzball's literary miscellany was given its share of reactions by these men-of-letters. Through his association with Alfred Bunn, Fitzball met the musical entrepreneur Michael Balfe, who, according to his official biographer, C.L. Kenney, was much taken with "The Terrible Fitzball," a sobriquet given him by critics because of his raucous Blood-and-Thunder dramas. After seeing Fitzball's operetta, *The Siege of Rochelle,* on October 29, 1835, Balfe remarked that the production had a "...stringing together of some very charming melodies and one or two pieces of remarkable merit" (110). With critics never neutral about a Fitzball play, the dramatist seemed unconcerned with any disapprovals, as long as the public approval was there. As a populist Fitzball put great emphasis on public acceptance of his art. Balfe endorsed Fitzball's poetic tendencies thusly: "At any rate he was a poet in feeling, and had some acquaintance with grammar, as well as some regard for the logical sequence of ideas" (Kenney 109). If Balfe did not gush over Fitzball's talent—which Fitzball was wont to do over other people's achievements—he did respect the curious playwright. And it was a hallmark with Fitzball never to reject esteem, possibly because he received it so rarely from the "social critics."

Quite aware that his career was a critically checkered one at best, Fitzball deemed himself an astutely practical man of the theatre. A funny character indeed, as if he had popped out of one of his own plays, Fitzball was known to appear about anywhere. Doubtlessly, part of "good old Fitz's" charm lay in his imperviousness to abject criticism. He persevered by sheer evasion and whimsy—with talent thrown in—his elfin appearance hiding his true intellect and perception. Arguably, Fitzball survived scurrilous attacks on some of his plays by the outward demonstrations of bravura and caprice, in himself and in his works. It was as if the man and dramatist merged into the Romanesque world of Blood-and-Thunder on stage. Celebrities were often astonished at his actions. The great tragedian Charles Macready was once beset by Fitzball to star in a play by him. The Surrey's manager, David Osbaldiston, who had acted the title role in *Jonathan Bradford* and had appeared in other Fitzballian fare, recommended the actor to Fitzball, who at once implored the actor to appear in a drama. After meeting the impetuous playwright, Macready scorned that he "was introduced to Mr. Fitzball, the Victor Hugo, as he terms himself, of England—the 'Victor No-Go' in Mr. Keeley's nomenclature" (Pollack 384). Fitzball probably ignored such as an insult, as he characteristically did others; his life, filled with such comical incidents, would make for a good play. The theatre journal *Figaro in London* gave an account which typified the hilarious circumstances in which Fitzball, a human chameleon, socially and artistically, would often find himself.

Poor old Fitzball was peeping out of a private box during the performance of *Walter Tyrrel* with his chin supported by the iron spikes that are placed between the boxes and the gallery. He made a thundering row with a bludgeon on the floor of the box, thinking no one saw him, but we saw him." (180)

An odd mixture of thinker and clown, Fitzball was paradoxical at best. Nevertheless, Fitzball was, for the most part, thought creative, even if eccentrically creative even for the theatre. If indeed critiqued, his plays always struck some type of emotional response from the reviewers, many of whom found themselves confounded by Fitzball's circus-like effervescence. Of *Paul Clifford,* one review had the following to exclaim:

Fitzball's operatic drama of *Paul Clifford* was the concluding feature, at the Covent Garden Theatre, on June 3, 1837, and it was performed in a manner anything but creditable to actor or to manager. The audience were much amused in the second act by the execution of a leap on horseback. (Rice 54)

Whether they were praising or condemning, the critics were forced to concede that Fitzball's characteristic brand of dramatic hullabaloo was amusing and thrilling for audiences. The working classes, for whom Fitzball created his outlandish plays, enjoyed the simple gaiety, emotionalism, and spiritedness offered by him (Wilson 60). And the public was Fitzball's metier, not the press. If, as Shelley once wrote, "poetry should reflect the best and happiest qualities in man," so Fitzballian fare was melodrama at its happiest and best. As a theorist, Fitzball felt that the drama should be emotionally uplifting. His artistic "potboilers" never evaded that dictate. For him art was entertainment, simply and finally.

Because he had spent so much of his career with minor houses, Fitzball felt naturally wary about writing for the prestigious Covent Garden in 1828 (Stephen 638). Nonetheless, both the Covent Garden and Drury Lane Theatres had to succumb to the public's growing taste for extravagant melodramas. And these houses were able to accommodate the large, physical demands of the genre through their stages. Richard Cumberland duly noted the peculiarities of those two playhouses in an 1806 comment that endorsed the stages as being "more suited to spectacles and melodramas" (Roose-Evans 75). The conundrum still remains: Did a certain type of drama demand a certain type of stage in the nineteenth-century, or vice-versa? To be sure, the theatrical exhibitionism of melodrama had much to do with the accommodations of the stage itself; however, the appetite for grand spectacles was very much part-and-parcel with the contemporary view of the theatre. Melodrama, particularly the grand style, was the mode of the day. James Roose-Evans suggests that this grandiose style of theatricalism commanded a comparable style in staging. Of course, all of this was most suitable for Fitzballian theatrics. In fact, it would be awkward to assess Fitzball's drama and his era without reference to the social and artistic ramifications that commanded the type of theatres in which his plays were performed. Fitzball's rapport with these playhouses is integral with his vocation. Both the writer and the theatre are interlocked in a final analysis of the man as artist and craftsman. Therefore, references to certain dramas will only be made in relation to remarks concerning specific playhouses under discussion. A more pronounced analysis of Fitzball's plays will be made in Chapter IV. Comments Roose-Evans:

Since the stages of Covent Garden and Drury Lane have been so enlarged in their dimensions to be henceforward theatres for spectators rather than play houses for hearers, it is hardly wondered at if their managers and directors encourage those representations to which their structure is best adapted. The spendour of the scenes now in a great degree supersedes the labours of the poet...even the most distant spectator can enjoy a shilling's worth of show. (75)

22 The Terrible Fitzball

The *entertainment value* of the playhouse was very much connected with the *entertainment value* inherent in the grand manner of Fitzballian drama. Such value had its roots in the philosophy of Horace, whose great work *Ars Poetica,* written around 10 B.C., specified that the goal of drama should be entertainment and education. The seventeenth- and eighteenth-century critics and practitioners of drama had been influenced by this approach, and melodrama was a more recent example. It may be deduced that Fitzball, with his colleagues, knew that England's turbulent society needed qualities from theatre and so appeased it with a distinctive breed of play. Melodrama simply was a product of its time, an artwork that consoled the social anxieties suffered by a people going through the various complex upheavals in life. Life was enigmatic enough, so a simpler, yet magnificently displayed, kind of theatre was established to meet the demands of that emerging psychology. Future comments on the realistic counterparts to the sensational triad, and Fitzball's interest in the uncanny, will address this issue of art transforming life. John Pick proposes this equipotent impression of society and theatre:

The new industrial towns and cities contained new potential audiences with the enforced leisure time that industrial shift system gave, some spare money for recreation and, increasingly, the rudiments of education." (21)

A similar correlation may be drawn between the popularity of films in the American Depression of the 1930s: people were poor, yet they afforded themselves the luxury of attending the cinema for escape and leisure. The same was true of London in the 1800s: amidst urban poverty was recreation—not known in the early farming culture.

Industrialization gave folk the time to attend the theatre. Because Fitzball spent so much time in the theatre, as his work, his interest, and his passion, it would be well to distinguish exactly what kinds of playhouses attracted his style of dramas. The line of demarcation between the legitimate and minor theatre is not so formidable as it may appear. The adjective *minor* did not mean *inferior*. On the contrary, this simply reflected governmental status and no more. A patent theatre merely meant one officially sanctioned to perform plays by the British government, and, although the subject is lengthy in defining, a word on the patent theatres will absolve any notion that Fitzball was forced to present his works in substandard grindhouses, even though some of them, admittedly, were in sections near the London slums. Practically speaking, Fitzball hacked his way through so many minors because there were only two patent houses: the Covent

Garden and the Drury Lane. Again, politics and society were to be factors in the very theatrical plants themselves.

A patent theatre was one duly licensed by the government to present legitimate drama under the auspices of the Letters, or Charters, or Patents. Historically, Charles II had given such permission to Thomas Killigrew and Sir William Davenant in 1662 for the establishment of two acting troupes, "The King's Servants" and "The Duke of York's Servants." The companies would perform in Killigrew's Drury Lane and Davenant's Covent Garden Theatres; the latter had been called earlier Lincoln's Inns Fields. For some two centuries this monopoly was in effect, yet the Lord Chamberlains's office had the authority to license other facilities as patent houses if necessary. The Theatre Act of 1737 dictated—and this is of importance to Fitzballian drama—that "legitimate drama" would be played only at the two patent houses. Therefore, much of the drama outside of these houses was, in effect, *illegitimate* theatre. Naturally, the disobedience regarding this piece of politico-artistic nonsense was keen: plays were being done everywhere and the inspectors of the law were eased to permit the infraction. In 1843 the law was properly reevaluated. With all other laws pertaining to the theatre rescinded, the Theatre Act of 1843, consolidating all the laws on dramatic activity, stated that a drama had to be submitted to the Lord Chamberlains's Office for permission to be staged. Nonetheless, all manner of drama could, thenceforth, have a chance at being performed. The terms legitimate and illegitimate drama became aesthetically blurred (Hartnoll 248). In retrospect, however, by "legitimate drama" it was meant a play in five acts, which "had little or no singing, dancing, and spectacle, and depended primarily upon acting" (Hartnoll 285). It is obvious that Fitzball would have encountered considerable difficulty in being produced through this definition of legitimate drama. It is also plausible to speculate that the public's new taste for the exhilarating properties of melodrama may have been instrumental in fostering a political change that the 1843 law reflected. In short the old forms of drama were being replaced by melodrama and the new renegade genre has not relaxed its grip yet. Trewin points out that the Victorian love for melodrama carried over into Edwardian times: "All of this drama was melodrama and the Edwardians were devoted to it" (*Edwardian Theatre* 168). Melodrama was becoming the new theatre, and Fitzball's type of aesthetic was to find much favor.

Since Fitzball wrecked his brand of theatrical madness on some 24 playhouses, ranging from the Coburg to the Covent Garden, it would aid our understanding of the artist and of the man to inspect a sampling of these various theatres. Therefrom, it may be possible to gauge Fitzball's reason for writing such plays for some of these theatres and their attending audiences. With one theatre dubbed "The Blood Tub," it is little wonder that Fitzball heaped horrors upon its patrons. Also, the houses selected will serve as artistic laboratories where Fitzball's talents came into full play, to the amazement of his censures.

Stephen Wischhusen acknowledges that:

During the heyday of gothic drama, that is between the years 1792-1825, there were in London only these theatres to perform legitimate drama—Drury Lane, Covent Garden, and, in the summer months when the other two were closed, the Haymarket. (115)

He goes on to mention that horror plays were staged, with fame, at the Lyceum, Coburg, and the Surrey Theatres (115). Called by Fitzball "London's superior theatre," the Coburg was renamed the Old Vic in 1833. Built by Rudolph Cabanel on September 14, 1816, the house engaged some of London's best actors and even induced fine thespians from the provinces to come there as well (Mander and Mitchenson 2623). Its premier play was the spectacular melodrama *Trial by Battle; or, Heaven Defend the Right* by William Barrymore. Based upon an actual murder trial several weeks before the play opened, the drama would be suceeded by the same type of inspiration in *Jonathan Bradford*. This precedent would not be the only one concerning Fitzball's association with the infamous Coburg.

Seating some 948 people, the Coburg's audiences were consistently rambunctious. One might think that melodrama's innate volatility was adjutant to the explosive nature in its patrons. Called "The Blood Tub," the Coburg presented some of the most horrific plays in London, thereby echoing the Grand Guignol tradition of France and England. Edmund Kean, among many others, ranted his kind of "evil acting" bombast to the thrills of the audience. However, it is interesting to note, the Coburg was not a grindhouse. Rather, despite its offerings, it was most opulent, marked by its famous "looking glass curtain," which had to be replaced due to the heaviness imposed by it on the ceiling (Mander and Mitchenson 263). Fitzball wrote his first version of *Thalaba the Destroyer* for the regal house on August 13, 1822. Based upon Robert Southey's "Roderick, or the Last of the Goths," Fitzball interpreted its lore as a "...fine strain of morality that runs through the whole...of guilt, suffering, and repentance" (*Thalaba* 1). Such an ethical slant would seem to belie Fitzball's being merely an opportunistic hack and no more. Of the writer's apparent artistry and thought, the critic, known by the sobriquet "DG," wrote that the play "...is the work of the ingenious Mr. Fitzball" (*Thalaba* 1). The Coburg was well equipped to present theatrical modes of gothic and mystical eastern fantasy. Plays having an aura of *The Arabian Nights* in their execution were most popular at the time. Licensed to produce burlettas (rhythmic dramas accompanied by an orchestra), the house lost its minor status in 1843, as a result of the law being revamped. Where economics in theatre was concerned, the British government was forced to renege on its preposterous ruling about what was a patent house and what was legitimate drama.

The Coburg's real essence stemmed from its display of Grand Guignol horror. Using actual crimes as the bases for many of its bloodcurdling penny-dreadful sagas, this *cause celebre* brought the theatre its greatest amount of notoriety (Mander 264). Located in London's Lambeth Parish and surrounded by a shantytown—much in the same way that theatres are surrounded by Forty-Second Street in New York—the Coburg attracted a kind of audience who might be found as characters *in* a Fitzballian play. Most of the theatre's dramas pandered to the psychological aesthetics of the audiences. In other words, the plays given there were of the simplest and most gruesome type. Many of the plays were adaptations of more austere works. Fitzball was a master of that skill, to be sure. As an example of the fare given at the Coburg, it was common that the lurid scenes from Shakespeare were made even more ghastly to suit the pleasure of the patrons. The "play doctor" was kept busy at the Coburg to the extent that "The Blood Tub" was no empty slang expression. As Rahill has remarked:

That was the sort of thing they wanted at the Coburg—exciting combats, harrowing horrors, and buckets of blood—and that is what they got...after 1833 it touched new depths of spine chilling melodrama. "Blood" or "murder" was usually to be found in the titles so that it came to be known as "The Bleedin' Vic." (140)

Renamed the Royal Victoria in 1833, its ironic new title did nothing to cheat the patrons from what they had come to expect in "The Blood Tub." It was there that H.M. Milner's Frankenstein Monster stalked in 1823, an example of the macabre activity so welcomed by the populace. However, the Coburg maintained melodrama's Horatian edict by offering plays that were not only entertaining but educational as well. The Coburg's forte, the crime play, even within its storybook milieu, did yield a genuine concern for a real social problem: crime. The Coburg merely publicized criminous behavior through theatricalization, with the endless moral commenting that crime was unsavory and destructive. That the public would understand the message the theatre could only hope. As far as the production of the plays was concerned, an attempt at historical realism set the tone. Rahill states, "They [the plays] were vividly realistic projections in settings of contemporary reality—murder localized and authenticated" (140). Among the famous murders dramatized at the Coburg were those based upon the infamous Polstead case and cannibalism of Sweeny Todd. It seems appropriate here, because of the dramatization of factual events, to mention melodrama's historicizing of facts for public attention. Moreover, because Fitzball so often used history as either a base or theme for a play, it would be well to understand melodrama's general attitude towards history-on-the-stage. Fitzball's *Joan of Arc* and *Jonathan Bradford,* when analyzed, will hearken back to this dramatic procedure. Also, the melodramatizing of history is pertinent to the dramaturgic flavor of the times since history was so often called upon as an impetus in drama. Of course, all genres take license with history as a foundation—and much of history itself is an interpretation of some occurrence—but melodrama did take a peculiar poetic license in the enactment of historical events for entertainment. Because melodrama did use history as a basis for many plays, a word about what it means to be theatrically accurate in historical representation seems necessary. George McCalmon and Christian Moe's *Creating Historical Drama* makes the useful point about how drama should handle history when applicable. The position should be remembered concerning Fitzball because he not only adapted history, but he regulated other plays and other literary genres to suit his purposes.

Historical dramatic writing, however, begins with a fabric either of facts or of legendary happenings currently accepted as the same. The fabric is then embroidered upon by the imagination and invention. The warp and woof of historical drama are factual events in the life of an actual person or group of persons, a town, a nation, a social institution, a religious movement, or even humanity at large. But the dramatization must use material which can stir an emotional response in the audience—thus making such material dramatic as George Pierce Baker once pointed out—and which can be adapted for the special requirements of the theatre. Because drama by its very nature must be dramatic and adaptable to the stage, the writer usually has to select, arrange, and modify the data of personalities and events. (4)

The verb *modify* is essential to Fitzballian dramaturgy, especially in his dealing with facts, as in *Jonathan Bradford,* where in he transformed an historical crime into a theatrical event. Regardless of his adapted source, Fitzball saw his first duty as that of an impresario of thrills and enjoyment, out of which would issue the constant, melodramatic moralizing. It is interesting that of the four plays done by Fitzball at the Coburg, all have some link to history, such as *William the Conqueror; or, The Days of the Curfew Bell* (1824), for example. The Coburg's interest to Fitzball was in the reputation that the house produced plays identifiable with sensationalism.

Another theatre enjoyed by Fitzball was the Adelphi. Built by John Scott, and opened as the Sans Pereil on November 27, 1806, it sat 1500 and espoused the "Adelphi drama," which became a byword for the transformation of legitimate drama into stark melodramas to circumvent the licensing law. For example, *Othello* was changed into a burletta. Mander informs us, "*Othello* had a low pianoforte accompaniment, the musician striking a chord once in five minutes, but always so as to be totally inaudible" (5). We now take for granted the adaptations of one type of entertainment into another—drama translated into opera is a classic example—but such was a novelty in the 1800s, especially on a large scale. In 1825 Fitzball adapted James Fenimore Cooper's novel *The Pilot* for the theatre. Cooper was a favorite source for Fitzball, and this play proved to be so popular that it was revived at the Covent Garden. Originally, the drama ran for 200 nights, with the wonderful actor T.P. Cooke enacting the tar (sailor) role of Long Tom Coffin. Of his performance, it was noted that he overdid nothing and that there was "no bad by-play, blabbing of the landlubber; not too much pulling of the trousers; no ostentatious display of pigtail; one chuck of tobacco in the cheek without any perceptible chew" (Baker 85). It may be deduced, then, that acting was presented in a realistic style, at least for the times. The Delsartian method certainly cannot be construed as realistic from a modern vantage point, but, considering the innate bombast of melodrama, the acting style was in keeping with what was acceptable during Fitzball's era. Later, an explanation will be given about melodramatic acting as a special type of response to the demands of the genre. Although more will be written about Fitzball's plays in a later chapter, excerpts from some of them will be given relevant to the theatres in which they were performed.

To demonstrate Fitzball's abandoned impulses, he substituted a British setting for that of Corper's original, American setting. Nationalism was the justifying dictate here (*Spectator* 345). Maurice Disher concludes that Cooke, on call as a contract player at the Adelphi, had persuaded Fitzball to write a nautical play for him; however, the dramatist felt such a transaction would prove cumbersome. Nevertheless, the adaptation became one of Fitzball's worthier efforts and a seminal example of the numancia drama (94). The Adelphi was the arena for one of Fitzball's most typical works, a play ushering in the sensational triad in all of its awful glory. The play was the grim *The Black*

Vulture, which opened on October 4, 1830. Archetypical of the theatre of the macabre, at its Blood-and-Thunder best, this chilling cauldron of horror and monsters was effectively stirred by the appearance of the marvelous actor 0. Smith. As the evil creature, Smith, an expert in this kind of part, was reviewed as "...grim, horrible if you will, but it was picturesque and imaginative and therefore not revolting" (Baker 77). This evidence helps us reject the notion that Fitzballian drama was only exploitation and no more. Never disgusting in his use of the macabre, Fitzball injected his usual charm to make the drama imaginative, a staged nightmare of festive delight. In fact, this talent was Fitzball's strength: taking horror and manipulating it in such a way as to make all of it a frightfully enchanting fable. Therein, Fitzball's relation to a fairytale world was apparent: his dramatic worlds were actually fantasy worlds, and his monsters, those of nightmares. His horror was as much projected towards the mind, as it was towards the stage. In this regard, he was not purely an exploiter of the macabre; rather, he was a magician casting a shivering spell over his audience.

By 1821 the Adelphi had become London's most popular playhouse. Fitzball left it in 1835 but returned infrequently, upon request, to draft new plays. Frederick Yates was the theatre's manager. However, the *Spectator* lamented the passing of the old Fitzball brand of drama: "We miss the striking scenic effects, powerful acting, and the rich drollery that made the theatre so popular during Yates' management" (946). Fitzball's height of popularity at the house was during Yates tenure as manager.

Now comes a look at the theatre as responsible as any for the promulgation of Fitzballian fare, the Surrey. Within its "Surreyesque drama," Fitzball dispatched some of his most notable works. As Universal Studios, for the purpose of comparison with the Surrey, was Hollywood's horror mecca, so the Surrey Theatre was London's acme for Grand Guignol terror. Opening in 1782, at a cost of some 15,000 pounds, the amphitheatre was the product of Charles Dibdin and Charles Hughes, who also acted as its managers. As an equestrian theatre, one specializing in dramas about galloping steeds as part of the action, the Surrey was once termed the Royal Circus, as a challenge to London's best regarded equestrian theatre, the Astley, where Fitzball would later work. One of Fitzball's most lauded plays was *Marmion; or, The Battle of Flodden*, an adaptation of Sir Walter Scott's dramatic poem. Premiering on June 12, 1848, the play was still another appeasement for the Scott frenzy then sweeping England. Fitzball's fame as an adaptor was enviable because of his ability to theatricalize any material. He had converted *Peveril of the Peak* on

June 2, 1823, just 30 days after Scott had penned the novel. His dramatization of Scott's *The Fortunes of Nigel*, on June 25, 1822, was called "creditable" (White 167). Fitzball had accepted his lot as a hack with his characteristic ease. Nevertheless, his involvement with the Surrey proved to be a mixed blessing. He would write in his autobiography:

The unlooked-for effect of my melodramas on the public, induced the then managers of the Surrey, to give me an engagement of six, if not eight pounds per week, by which I bound myself to write for them on any subject they might propose, never dreaming of such a subject they might suggest. (2: 402)

During his stay at the Surrey, Fitzball the songster wrote, as part of the operatic *Siege of Rochelle*, "Sweet Burn Side" in 1858. There was an occurrence, however, that undermined this mixed blessing. Fitzball was approached about dramatizing a real murder on stage. To be known as *The Murder of Wear*, the play was to be done realistically, even down to the genuine murder weapon. For some reason of conscience, Fitzball balked at this exploitative device. Seeing the authentic weapon on stage obviously attacked the playwright's sense of passion about what should be included and excluded in a drama, which, for Fitzball, was not "a slice of life." Fitzball mused about his first intercourse with the Surrey, which evoked a anxious relationship: The very first melodrama I had acted, I simply left at the stage door; it found its way to the manager, and a fortnight later I was in full sail, (2: 361). Eccentric, but not callous or banal, Fitzball possessed a theory of what good theatre was and never spurned it (2: 403).

Of all the minor theatres, the Surrey had the most eruptive audience. Often the activities in the seats were more animated than those on the stage. No play was sacrosanct, no dramatist too revered to escape possible dishonor by patrons. Rahill laments that not even Shakespeare was spared the jeers from the unsightly "common folk" in the auditorium: "*Macbeth* was performed amidst the most hideous medley of fights, foul language, catcalls, shrieks, yells, oaths, blasphemy, obscenity, apples, oranges...cans of beer" (143). It may be supposed that the last three items were used for weaponry against the actors on stage, the patrons' sophisticated means of overtly disliking a particular piece of drama. Yet, in all of this chaos, Fitzball learned his vocation superbly, never forgetting that a hack was a special kind of beast in the theatre's lair. But he also never forgot the difference between good drama and ersatz pabulum. He asserted acutely: "I detest and always shall pieces of gingerbread; I never wrote them except per order" (*Drama* 99). Regrettably, many of his critics missed this deft veracity. All the while though, Fitzball was making drama accessible to the masses, even if sometimes the masses proved themselves unreceptive. Fitzball's calling was still an honorable one in making the theatre democratic and understandable, on behalf of the working man, in the working man's theatre, the Surrey.

Having burned twice, once in 1799 and again in 1805, the Surrey, when restored, fell under the managership of Robert Elliston. *Jonathan Bradford* was one of the house's eminent successes. By 1848, however, the fine, old structure had deteriorated into simple roughhouse revelry, a haunt for derelicts and gangsters. It sauntered through this travail, unhelped by manager George Conquest's valiant attempts at reconstruction, until it was razed in 1901, sadly bringing to an end one of England's most known playhouses. Fitzball had been a hallmark in its 40 years of vital melodramas (Wischhusen 17).

Fitzball's bid for social legitimacy—he already had artistic regard—came form his association with the two patent houses, the Drury Lane and Covent Garden. With melodrama quickly becoming the theatre's main attraction, most of the playhouses in London were extolling the genre to the delight of travellers coming to see plays. Signaled the *Athenaeum,* "The Drury Lane catered exclusively to holiday transients" (262). The Drury Lane and the Covent Garden Theatres were prepared to meet the specific demands of grandiose melodrama, which meant, of course, meeting the demands of Fitzballian fare. Built in 1663, burned in 1672, rebuilt by Sir Christopher Wren in 1674, and again modified in 1764, the Drury Lane was a magnificent structure seating 3,060 persons (Sobel 261). To give an indication of the mammoth quality of the house, a visitor to the theatre in 1810 noticed the following dimensions: the theatre's hall was supported by "fine Doric columns, and illuminated by two large brass lamps;" the boxseats held some 2400 persons; the pit accommodated 850 people; the galleries seated 1300 viewers; the stage was about 33 feet wide; and the proscenium was 19 and one-half feet tall, with "the whole constructed so as to render the circular appearance of the theatre nearly complete" (Nagler 449-50). This information may offer an indication of the size of a patent theatre commensurate with the area needed for one of Fitzball's extravaganzas, such as *The Seige of Rochelle*, *Joan of Arc*, and *The Queen of the Thames*, all of which demanded large sets. Fitzball's association with the Drury Lane was a rewarding one.

Having written two versions of *Uncle Tom's Cabin* for the Olympic and Grecian Theatres in September and October, 1852, Fitzball capitalized on the famous American novel a third time in penning a version for the Drury Lane on

December 27, 1852. This latest play was more fitting to Stowe's novel than had been its predecessors; this was a laurel for Fitzball, who was usually not especially faithful to any primary source. Almost daily, Fitzball would concoct theatrical schemes he deemed necessary to enthrall his patrons anew with the "Tom" craze. He was matter-of-fact about his dramaturgic meanderings therein: "it did not require a remarkable ability, as it was only to reflect scenes and put them together" (2: 261). Inferentially, the play was probably a series of tableaus, since the tableau was very much a part of the melodramatic production scheme. The Drury Lane was important for Fitzball's career in two ways: 1) it helped to break Fitzball into a socially-structured theatre of prestige and 2) it was a theatre in which Fitzball executed his social thesis playwriting. In fact, his last play there, *Christmas Eve*; or, *Duel in the Snow*, presented on March 12, 1860, was very much socially minded. The drama exposed the personal imbroglios that would emanate from a marriage based upon cupidity and infidelity. Unfortunately, Fitzball was no Chekhov or Ibsen in championing such crucial issues. Fitzball was a melodramatist, and he fell into the trappings of the genre. In this respect, he was much like the American dramatist Clyde Fitch, whose dramaturgic denouements would usually proscribe a social thesis conclusion. This is one of the reasons that Fitch barely missed being considered a social writer and, thusly, became known as a melodramatist, but quite unlike the Blood-and-Thunder type, that included Fitzball. Nonetheless, the Drury Lane experience showed another side to Fitzball's talent, which certainly the Surrey and Coburg did not demonstrate. *Nitocris*; or, *The Ethiop's Revenge*, a play attacking slavery and racism, was presented by Fitzball in 1855, but failed to impress the critics, who, for the most part, had typed him as an unwavering Blood-and-Thunder dramatist. Disturbed that his artistic versatility was thematically quelled, Fitzball wrote, "...it was too vast, too antique, and too learned for appreciation" (2: 304). The more robust *Christmas Eve* fared better.

If Fitzball had been pained by the reaction to his early social play, he felt comfort in the critical acceptance of his last work, a determinedly melodramatic foray. In the climactic duel, Fitzball calls upon his expertise in the Scott notion of romanticism: the finale is something out of Dumas' novel. The Captain and Sir Charles duel. The Captain, who has falsely charged Charles with matricide, is slain. However, also mortally wounded, Charles swoons into the arms of loving Emily, his friend, just as the bell tower rings midnight on the snowy Christmas Eve. This rousing *tableau vivant* of the characters emotionally frozen before the audience, the eerie striking of the watching clock, and the dramatic sense of pity were all that were needed for the critics to cheer, as much as critics in the nineteenth-century could cheer in print:

a dying pierrot...suspended by a number of masqueraders, his fellow-duellist, in the disguise of a New Zealand chieftan, looking on. Mr. Fitzball adopts this as the closing scene of his drama, and the rest is occupied with incidents calculated to account for such a catastrophe. (*Illustrated London News* 251)

In his autobiography, Fitzball attributed the lachrymose overture in the scene to his inspiration for it: a French painting of a duel he had noticed. Lest it be thought that simply no criticism was favorable towards Fitzball's sense of social commentary, *The Miller of Derwent Water*, performed at the Olympic Theatre on May 2, 1852, met the *Athenaeum's* praise that Fitzball had penned a worthwhile thematic idea:

The tragic action illustrates the monopolizing forces of capital! A rich man, to whom a poor man rescues the sale of his hereditary mill, erects one in opposition and by underselling ruins and latter. However fortune, runs away with the miller's daughter and marries her. The drama was successful. (570)

As would be expected, nineteenth-century appreciation of newly aroused, social issues, written to be seen as such, cannot be compared to our contemporary sense. With even the European realists at odds with what to display on the stage, and now with much of that power dated through age, Fitzball may be critically admired for even considering material away from his typical flash. He took the space of the Drury Lane and used it for grand spectacle and for grand themes, though undergirded by the omnipotence of melodrama. His predisposition towards monsters and outrageous excitement did not invalidate his experimentation with other plots or themes. It is viable to conclude that the melodrama, if not in Fitzball's hands particularly, did contribute to the maturation of the social thesis play in the hands of others. At the Drury Lane, Fitzball manipulated the melodramatic technique in offering yet another inspection into the theatre's possible aesthetics.

The next theatre which brought Fitzball prestige was the second patent house, the Covent Garden, where, for an interrupted duration of 25 years, Fitzball would write some 24 dramas. His first play was a quickly paced murder mystery, *Paul Clifford*, which opened on October 28, 1835; his final work was a doctoring of Oliver Goldsmith's *She Stoops to Conquer* in 1864. Built by its manager, John Rich, in 1732, the theatre had a seating capacity of 1,879 when it burned in 1808. The rebuilt structure seated 3,000 and was managed by John

Philip Kemble until his retirement in 1817. Then, his brother, Charles, assumed the managership of the theatre, which was worth in excess of some 150,000 pounds, and produced some of the finest and most realistic versions of Shakespeare ever seen: his 1823 rendition of *King John* became legendary. Thus, the theatre had a rich heritage when Alfred Bunn, for whom Fitzball worked, took over in 1833. Shortly thereafter, however, David Osbaldiston, who became a Fitzballian actor, gained control of the theatre and instilled in it operas, as a fixture, until, as seemingly usual, yet another fire claimed the playhouse. It reopened six months later (Wischhusen 13).

Fitzball was hired as a hack and wrote plays of all manner, ranging from good adaptations of Hugo, as in *Ouasimodo,* to zany burlesques, such as seen in his merry parody of Eastern exotica known as *Zazazizozu.* Fitzball often complained about this type of tour-de-force: "I hate everything that tends to turn the profession and the drama into ridicule" (2: 401). Since the rage for melodrama was intense, Fitzball was responsible for transposing a type of Surreyesque drama to the hollowed halls of the Covent Garden. To the regal stage that had once known the brilliance of *King John*, Fitzball now was forced to subject it to the galloping horses of *Paul Clifford.* While the play's action scenes were lauded, the more intellectual aspects of the play's mystery were overlooked by the audience, typical of the new breed that desired stark physical activity over "high dramatic thought." Fitzball knew well that his Blood-and-Thunder melodramas were his stock-in-trade and bemoaned that the more serious, artistic melodrama had not about it the drawing power of the former's appeal. Commercialism outweighed art, of course, so Fitzball, with resignation about the donneé from which his plays came, both theatrically and mentally, confessed,

The new sort of audience was not to be attracted, however, it might be pleased, by this sort of elegant production, for although they laughed heartily...they would have forsaken us, but for the coach and horses of "Paul Clifford." (2: 34)

As much a prisoner of his time, as he was a product of it, Fitzball always approached his art in an ambivalently analytical way. Knowing that his popularity had profited the Covent Garden, under Osbaldiston's parsimonious management, (2,000 pounds) Fitzball's vocation haunted him: "...with my nod of mortar, the drudge the stopgap of many a high sounding failure, when salaries could not else have been paid" (1: 104).

As the replacement of H.M. Milner, the hacker of *Frankenstein* fame,

Fitzball shunned the fact that, more so than the Drury Lane, the Covent Garden was being transformed into a surreyesque theatre, "a great minor theatre for Surreyesque drama" (1: 23). The Covent Garden made a fitting courtroom for Fitzball, wherein his stamina was tested by both positive and negative reviews of his plays. For instance, the 1836 drama, *Mutual Expense*; or, *A Female Travelling Companion*, was adjoured thusly by the *Times:* "a portion of the dialogue reaching our ears...was unquestionably as miserable, bald, disjointed chat as ever we heard" (3). But, the positive review of *Walter Tyrell* caused Fitzball to ruminate about the matrix of playwiting. In realizing Fitzball to be the strange creature he was, the ignoble critique given him must sound amusing, particularly in that "Old Fitz" began his mutterings after an encouraging review, not that unflattering reviews affected him greatly. His paradoxical ways never ebbed, nor ever died.

At the fall of the curtain, everyone expressed his gratification, and all coming round me, paid me the highest respect and commendation. That was the proudest, most triumphant moment of my dramatic career. A man does not have to be a Greek scholar...to become a dramatist, or to be a great judge. The real taste of wine is in a quality of nature, as much as the real knowing of a good painting is a mental one. There is no account for such things. (2: 223)

This panegyric—and one can only imagine the pace uttered by Fitzball—gives much insight to Fitzball's dramaturgic soul. The *Spectator* thus touted the play: "The author...instead of writing such brief practical dialogue as the spectacles in general require, produced a sort of hybrid between the ordinary Astley's piece and the drama of high art" (1055). "High art" in Fitzballian criticism was as rare as water in the Sudan, but the remark, terse though it was, did show that Fitzball could appeal to his judges every so often, and that he was a master of merging entertainment with art, the Horatian edict. Nevertheless, while making the Covent Garden wealthy through his plays, Fitzball felt the creeping cancer of obsolescence, foisted upon him by people who thought Blood-and-Thunder poor theatre. While writing the lyrics for Peake and Redwell's musical, *The Bottle Imp*, Fitzball became increasingly uneasy about his fare because the so-called intelligensia, often out to prove its cultural taste, even if hypocritically, was growing critical of Blood-and-Thunder as viable theatre. The classics and Shakespeare, even if bowdlerized, were returning to favor. Osbaldiston was succeeded by Charles Macready in 1838. With his ally gone, Fitzball found himself freelancing more and more as a contract dramatist for other theatres while still employed at the Covent Garden. In the late 1840s he resigned from the theatre which had given him so much of his fame. He would write for other playhouses for the remainder of his lifetime, and some of them bear witnessing, inasmuch as he left a particular contribution in each.

Heartily welcomed at the Astley Theatre, Fitzball was clearly in his element when he wrote *Marmion; or The Battle of Flodden Field*, which was presented on June 12, 1848. The dramatization of Scott's poem met with reassuring reviews, such as this one from the *Illustrated London News*: "The subject is well chosen, affording great capabilities for scenic display and pageantry, all of which have been seized upon and made the most of it" (392). Fitzball was obviously amused by the jovial happenings at the Astley when he wrote about his tasks there: "The playwright has neither the assistance of high music, nor high poetry, and has, moreover, to shape his histrionic abilities to the footsteps of horses" (2:140). Rahill makes the following discernment about the theatre of "horse sagas": "The Astley Theatre specialized in spectacular equestrian theatre and achieved its greatest glory as the Royal Amphitheatre, so named for it after the fire of 1803" (131). By either name, the playhouse was a popular diversion, and Fitzball scored a triumph there with *White Maiden of California*, which had numerous horses therein—naturally.

At the Royal Pavilion Theatre, Fitzball distinguished himself by again exploiting an American phenomenon, the Indian play. With Major Richard Rogers' *Ponteach* (1766), George Washington Parke Custis' *Pocahontas* (1830), and John Augustus Stone's *Metamora* (1828) as American inspirations, Fitzball eagerly wrote a fine "Noble Savage" play, *Oconesto; or, The Mohawk Chief* on September 3, 1838. Reviewing the spectacle, *Actors by Midnight* wrote: "...the play had hairbreadth escapes, midnight murders, cataracts, savages, tomahawks, and scalping knives. Nothing could better suit the taste and retain the good humour of patrons of this establishment" (5). And nothing could have pleased Fitzball more than the riveting zeal of this harrowing play, filled with raging Indians and chilling adventure, all the ingredients that institutionalized high adventure, as an international pastime, in all manner of fictional art. Within this dramatic mold, and in others too, Fitzball was in his oyster. He had no need to satisfy the realistic qualms of a certain population here; he could let his fancy run the gamut in a world where our fears—our "tomahawks"—became deliciously and terrifyingly real—in the theatre and in our minds.

Fitzball's free-wheeling dramas were more than wanted by the Sadler Wells Theatre. With an almost limitless reservoir of plot ideas, several of them lifted from other sources, of course, "The Terrible Fitzball" used this theatre as a feeding place for the crowds hungry for his brand of escapism. His first rendition of *Joan of Arc* played at the Sadler Wells on August 12, 1822, but it was for the aquatic drama (numancia), introduced there by Charles Dibdin, which became the playhouse's insignia. Fitzball's numancia was *Nerestan, King of Persia*, which was one among many sea adventures he wrote. Rahill remarks, "Fully twenty percent of the text for the typical aquatic melodrama was taken up with stage directions and descriptions of the dumb show" (134). Actorish pantomime dominated the arena, which was filled with a constructed sea, on which the main action took place, simply because the area was so large and distanced from the viewers. With battles, sea monsters, and rugged heroics, the element of morality was, of course, the theme. Accentuating all of these were the special effects, not unlike some from the Middle Ages: models of ships, demons (the "Hell-Mouth"), and pyrotechnics. The intention of the numancia was to present the most elaborate of adventure for the throngs who attended the theatre. With Fitzball writing, this goal was always accomplished, whenever he could have full sway, and whenever audiences were attentive to his panache.

Fitzball's Later Years

In 1842 Fitzball was engaged by the Surrey to write *Ombra; or The Spirit of the Reclining Stone*. The failure of this play, with the audiences of the infamous Surreyesque drama, probably caused Fitzball to reassess his style. One entity he had never scorned was the audience, which he held dear. Sallying between the Covent Garden and the Surrey and whatever other theatre wanted his services, Fitzball probably came to the conclusion that his theatrical antics could never be taken for granted regarding patrons. To be a good melodramatist, and Fitzball was a master one—yet, even a master errs occasionally—the writer must reflect upon his lot and his direction. In a volume of prose and poetry called *The Black Robber*, Fitzball pondered his status: "No illuminated caverns; no bleeding spectres, appearing at the awful hour of midnight, with blue burning lamps, rush through my castles to terrify the sensitive inhabitants of the earth" (199-200). Nevertheless, the fact remained that, for good or bad, Fitzball was thought the best of the Blood-and-Thunder artists, but his sensitivity for internal conviction and questioning helped to establish his thorough professionalism and integrity. In Fitzball the Terrible and in Fitzball the Philosophical, there was a marvelous disparity between commerce and art, colored by a sense of sadness and yearning. Yet, to his credit, Fitzball rarely misdiagnosed his audiences, who almost always lunged into a theatre where a play of his was being performed.

The remaining years of his life saw Fitzball writing for a myriad of houses. As with those sketched above, each of these samplings demonstrate, unequivocally, that the old master, for the most part, was still up to the test of writing. Fitzball provided three successes for the Marylebone Theatre: *Hans von Stein; or, The Robber Knight* (August 11, 1851); *Vin Willoughby; or, The Mutiny of Isis* (August 25, 1851); and *The Greek Slave; or The Spectra Gambler* (November 20, 1851). His *Children of the Castle* (November 23, 1857), a gothic mystery, prompted Fitzball to conclude, "No audience ever appreciated language as they did—received by acclamations" (2: 347). For the St. James Theatre, he scripted a comedy, again revealing his knack for the jolly and the light. *The Widow's Wedding* (1859) was a successful change from the more heavy-handed works associated with the dramatist. He was unsuccessful with the Haymarket's production of *Bertha; or, The Gnome of Hartzberg* in 1855. The *Magic Pearl*, a play reminiscent of the frothy and high fantasy of his early days, was Fitzball's last play. It played at the Alexandria.

By 1873, however, the dramatic elf's "twinkling eye" was dimming, both in body and in spirit. *The Magic Pearl* had not been wholly successful with the critics although the public had enjoyed the piece. Having outlived his authorial peers, and away from his married daughter, this innovator of "red-blue fire" sensationalism found himself retired and alone. Regarded as the finest portrayer of "stage deviltry" ever, and as a key framer of the sensational triad, which had brought chills and money to the London theatres, "The Terrible Fitzball" died of consumption on his modest estate in Chatham, England, on October 27, 1873, forgotten by the theatrical institution he had worked so indefatigably to popularize (Stephen 638). In passing, his sobriquet, "The Terrible Fitzball," ascribed to him by the trade papers (and encouraged by him) because of Fitzball's spectacular feeling for "Bengal fire" as a theatrical effect, is recalled in his auobiography:

There is a hint of this (smoke)
The more noise, the more smoke, the more coloured lights the more commotion, the greater the panacea for universal ills. There is a hint of this in the words of the Terrible Fitzball when he vindicates Bengal Fire, "of which I have been accused of being the inventor," the much-reviled blue fire. With evangelical warmth he (Fitzball) preaches, "The merits of this fine scientific chemical preparation...are not simply applied to effects on the stage, but are used in greatest emergencies...Blue-fire is a discovery well qualified in the pages of humanity." (2: 103)

Fitzball's Ideology

For the most part, this biographical brief has been gleaned from Fitzball's two-volume autobiography, and the smatterings from other references, with the subject's personal revelations its most revealing aspect. Although little travelled from the London theatres, and socially withdrawn, Fitzball considered himself "the most practiced author on the boards," taking pride in his commercialism, if not always in his vocation (2: 386). A cross between the robustness of a P.T. Barnum and the contemplation of a Samuel Coleridge, Fitzball craved a national theatre that would help in disseminating both a commercial and respected drama for theatregoers, thereby aiding the creative spirit of regarded dramatists, in not forcing them into being mundane hacks. Nevertheless, Fitzball was quick to add that the hack kept the commercial theatre solvent and popular. His reflections indicated a genuine *Graustarkian* (a highly romantic, literary feeling) attitude along with the frustration of a career often fraught with disappointment. Because of this enigma, a personal and artistic paradox, sallying between sensationalism, on the one hand, and pensiveness, on the other, Fitzball's *Weltsmerz* seemed more prone to the ambivalent criticisms of the reviewers than if his style had been more orthodox. Simply put, oftentimes the critics simply did not know what to make of this dramatist who, at one time, would fill the stage with horror and, at another, with loveliness. Fitzball's inconsistencies made him prey to criticism and misunderstanding. One such example of Fitzball's uneven uniformity may be found in this remark of his: *"Macbeth, Othello,* and *Richard III* would act without language" (2: 217). Regarding himself as a throwback to the Elizabethan poets, and a constant user of inflated, albeit poetic, dialogue, such an attitude seems strange, particularly since Fitzball loved Shakespearean prose and poetry and used pantomime only intermittently, as in his numancia. His plays were always *concours d' elegance,* or "shows of plays," and a disregard of language would have been inimical to his style. But such was his contradiction and a possible reason for critical misappraisal.

For Fitzball there was little moderation in writing or in socialization, when he did attend affairs. On one occasion, to the embarrassment of his hosts, he addressed the famous architect Frederick Gaye as "...the modern Hercules of modern architecture" (2: 441). Fitzball remarked that he could not understand why those involved seemed to be put off by his appellative extremity during the party. Most of the time, Fitzball appeared socially bewildered. Afterwards, he merely hopped around the other guests in his usual, frisky manner, a manner probably well known to the others in attendance. Fitzball was given to outbursts, quite unlike his usual personality, at anytime, thereby furthering consternation about him. It was as if Fitzball possessed a double-sided personality. The more extroverted self emanated from his outrageous plays—and sometimes from his merry frolics in public—while the more introverted self came to light in his theoretical musings about theatre and about his life. To be sure, neither one was boring.

Because he harbored a desire to produce classical plays, Fitzball's mawkish and lurid works often possessed a classical ambiance about them. While it is true the classic melodrama was covered with such traits as poetic language, sometimes pseudo-poetry would be more appropriate; emotional and alarming personas; and the consistent moral judgment at the conclusion of the play, Fitzball's works, particularly his more cogent and structured ones, demonstrate that he was no poetaster. In fact, his *Antigone* and *Agamemnon* have in them some fine poetry in the closet drama tradition of Seneca. It is not hyperbolic to suggest that they would play well as theatre, inasmuch as they were neither ineptly nor desultorily written. If he had stayed with tragedy—*Edwin, Heir of Cressingham* shows that he had the skill—perhaps he would have attained heights as a "romantic tragedian," but melodrama was the mode of the day and Fitzball succumbed. This 1817 drama, even with its melodramatic tints, is void of the typical Fitzballian furor. But, it was that *furor* which made him famous and commercial, and typed as well. His thoughts about drama-as-theatre divulge much about the theorist's aesthetics:

When we read works of greatest purity, the parables for instance, we do not, in the theatre of our mind's eye, personify and dress the different characters spoken by the Apostles...How many thousands are there who owe their entire knowledge of the history of England to Shakespeare and to the stage? Had Shakespeare been locked up in the library...he would have been about as popular as Spenser's "Farie Queen." (2: 409)

With its simplicity and frenzy, melodrama, in the hands of Fitzball, welcomed the people into the theatre because it had a style and scope understandable to all, much in the way that Shakespeare, and all writers who have had that rare ability of so doing, was able to discern. As a populist-of-entertainment, it was fitting that Fitzball would labor in the minor houses, where the masses, unruly as they might have been, would gather after their toil. It is equally fitting that his experience with the patent houses would prove happy. All people enjoyed the excitement and the happiness which his show of plays gave to them because it, if for only a short while, purged them of emotional and mental weariness in ways inconceivable to those unconcerned with escapist art. His artistic peccadilloes notwithstanding, Fitzball was able to focus in on what formulas made theatre attractive to all concerned and much of his ideology had to do with eruptive displays of the macabre, still an eminent source of entertainment.

The minors had shown that way to the favor of the masses, prospering from their great spectacles and armed conflict, sieges, sea battles, and the life to more orthodox melodramas overworked with threads of bloody realism from Dr. Cripen burying in his cellar the remains of the wife he has murdered, or Jack the Ripper, stalking his prey down mean Whitchapel alleys. (Rahill 145)

As has been noted, Fitzball was more than an outlandish horror dramatist. Yet, his legacy seems to survive, if anonymously. Conjecturally, the 1975 British cult film *The Rocky Horror Picture Show,* directed by Jim Sherman, has elements in it (i.e. outrageous combinations of the sensational triad, narrative absurdities, and a melodramtic flair of music and drama) that may remind one of Fitzball's grotesque burlettas. Such camp entertainment insinuates that Fitzballian drama may have been a cinematic precursor and that film might have been his calling if he were alive today. Film certainly would have afforded him the wherewithal for his "blue-red fire" effects. Moreover, it may be said that popular culture is Fitzballian theatre, that whatever is common to man is common in Fitzballian theory and practice, and that whatever is seen as nightmarish in man's soul can be wonderfully converted by Fitzball into something cathartic and pleasing. Never obscene or vile, Fitzball paid obeisance to what was good and worthwhile in man through his moralizing of virtue overcoming vice in dramas decidedly romantic and unreal. But this was his strength in finding the common denominator in man's eternal conflict with his world and with himself: the inability to effect a certain nobility in vanquishing his deepest fears. For all of this, Fitzball emerges as a ringmaster in his circus of pop-culture theatrics. The need for such diversion is at the heart of human culture, as M. Thomas Inge recounts:

In truth there has always been a popular culture. Something is popular, after all, it succeeds in reaching and pleasing as many people as possible. And, popular culture attempts precisely that, no more, no less. At its simplest popular culture is the culture of mass appeal. A creation is popular when it is created to respond to the experiences and values of the majority when it is produced in such a way that the majority of the people have easy access to it, and when it can be understood and interpreted by the majority without the aid of special knowledge or experience. Every human society at every stage of human history has had artist and craftsmen who have produced such materials. Artisans have always sought to fashion objects and ideas which appealed to a select few and to fashion others which delighted audiences as wide as could be imagined. (443)

Using Inge's comments as an appropriate theme behind Fitzball's orientation as artist and as ideologue, it becomes obvious that Fitzball was a populist who fashioned a drama to be accepted with delight and purpose. John Ruskin once wrote, "Of human work none but what is bad can be perfect in its own bad way" (Medved x). In his "own bad way," Fitzball experimented with and yielded a kind of sensationalism of refreshing perfection. And "refreshing perfection," within any goal, has always been the ambition of art, even at its most bizarre and painful. In his own peculiar way, "The Terrible Fitzball" nurtured that sort of refreshment to those willing to see.

Chapter II
A Socio-Psychological Foundation
for the Sensational Triad

As has been noted, melodrama took its inspiration, often in lurid and emotional strides, from any place where human frailty and desperation ran amok. It exposed man's consequences in domestic, adventuresome, and fantastic circumstances. Melodrama, whenever showing realistic disturbances, was quick to take its impetus from authentic travails: crime, divorce, and antagonism. Its necessary *conflict* was, in many respects, torn from a *National Enquirer* brand of alarm, which remains to this day one of the genre's enduring, and infamous, qualities. And the genre's power was tantamount to the dramatist's deployment of these fears in whatever manner he deemed proper. These fears were the ingredients of the sensational triad in Fitzball's Blood-and-Thunder melodrama: horror-terror, crime, and madness. His theatre of the macabre, which illustrated the triad so pungently, was very much an imitation of these forbidding elements in life.

There is in Fitzball's sensational triad a feeling of transposed reality. Understanding that melodrama often clutched onto realistic events or attitudes for its source material, it is not overly hypothetical to suggest that Fitzball, in his capacity as a user of melodrama, recapitulated some of the more tumultuous aspects of his environment for inspiration. His masterpiece, *Jonathan Bradford*, was based upon a factual murder. And it was common for many a dramatist to theatricalize instances based upon an experience. Playwrights continue to adapt their experiences onto the stage still. Therefore, it is conceivable that Fitzball, aware of the anxious transformations in his society, may have acted upon them in a literary way, giving full sway to imaginative embellishments of those entities that represented blatant difficulties and dread. This is not to suggest that Fitzball was a social scientist who conducted empirical experiments about what was horrible, criminal, or insane in his times. Rather, it is my contention that Fitzball, even if unconsciously, sensed the pangs of his society and thrust those images onto the stage in metaphorical symbols. The power of theatre has always been in its ability to transcend the ordinary by changing the ordinary into universal symbols. Hence, for Fitzball, a monstrous apparition may have come to symbolize that which was evil and destructive in human life; a villain, that which was craven and tyrannical; a hero, that which was noble and steadfast. Consequently, this chapter will inspect the implications and ramifications of the sensational triad as found in society and in art, with attention paid to how Fitzball controlled the triad as a theatrical and dramatic instrument. Therefrom, the viewer and critic could translate the triad into a social complex.

Horror-Terror as Triadic Imagery

Victorian England was the Empire at its most prestigious. The Industrial Revolution was the basis for England's political and social prosperity. The Romantic Movement was aimed at attacking the capitalistic ills visited upon the poor because of industrialization. Romanticism's spiritual and escapist nuances were directed towards equality and respect for all of mankind and were in opposition to any mode of oppression. Abiding by the romantic tradition, melodrama offered hope through its moralizing and uncomplicated happiness. The laborer needed such respite, as Martin Day notices:

Moreover, the reformed spirit of the 1830s continued under Victoria. The Poor Law Bill of 1838 extended benefits to the Irish, and the Tithe Law of the same year reduced the money sums paid by the landowners to the Church of England. The Municipal Act (1840) further extended voting privileges. But reform had not kept up with the discontent of the workers. Britain's enormous productivity had been achieved by frightful exploitation of the laboring classes, who were usually condemned to dire poverty, filthy conditions of work and living, debility, and painfully short lifespans. (*English Literature: 1837-Present* 4)

With decay surrounding them, the poor of London barely knew anything else. It is a sociological position that one's environment usually dictates one's intellectual and emotional relation to the rest of mankind. It is a curious fact, then, that denizens from London's slums frequented theatres which provided the most horrendous forms of entertainment. The Coburg, known as "The Blood Tub," and its crowding by the poor, indicates what type of entertainment appeared the most popular. Other, more sophisticated theatrical forms were ignored. This neglect may have been based upon the nescience, or apathy, of the viewers but, for whatever reason, the working class clamored for excitement in theatre, and excitement of the most brutal kind. Theatre economics demanded solvency, so what the audiences demanded is what they received. The melodrama appealed to this motivation by providing plays of the most ghastly and flagitious kind. The essence of the artistic use of horror and terror often comes from the artist's environment. In this section, horror and terror will be analyzed as both artistic imagery and social-psychological nuances from which a dramatist, like Fitzball, might draw for symbolic reasons. For theatrical purposes, Stephen Wischhusen acknowledges the gothic play as a type quite favored. Its innate horror was one of Fitzball's best designs.

The word "gothic" in its literary sense conjures up a world of ruined castles and awesome landscapes, inhabited by ghouls, demons, and phantoms, culled not only from the lower forms of human life, but also in surprisingly large numbers from the landed gentry, to live a life of necromancy and magic, only to have their machinations thwarted at innumerable eleventh hours by the might or the righteousness. That this work now witnessed by man on cinema screens and television, evolved and flourished nearly two hundred years ago may appear strange, but as an entertainment form, gothic drama reigned supreme over the English stage during the latter part of the eighteenth century and early part of the nineteenth century. Its appeal, like its celluloid successor today, was to the masses—the middle and lower middle classes who went to the theatres; those whose entertainment read almost the selfsame thing in novel form as rapidly as the books appeared on the circulating libraries' shelves. (9)

The entertainment horrors were indulged in as a refuge from the exasperation of meeting real horrors (i.e. poverty, toil, crime, humiliation) daily. For Fitzball, it is obvious that a distinctive concept of the *grotesque* played an important part in the development of his sensational triad. It is also obvious that Fitzballian sensationalism had its roots in the *tragedy of blood*, which was popularized by the Roman playwright Seneca and the English Jacobeans. Perhaps Fitzball's alteration in style was his sense of humor. His theatre of the macabre was not the tragic and anxious world in either Senecan drama or, for instance, in John Webster and Cyril Tourneur tragedy. In those instances hope and victory were displaced by damnation and defeat. The Jacobeans used melodramatic techniques in producing tragedy, not in formulating melodrama. The downfall of the protagonist was crucial to both Senecan and Jacobean tragedy, whereas in Fitzballian melodrama, the fall was averted by a usual "Deus-ex-Machina" intervention of some sort. Nonetheless, Fitzball did evoke the grotesque and the tragedy of blood syndromes in his morbid exercises, which were colored by a Grand Guignol atmosphere and aesthetic.

In approaching the concept of horror, as a triadic element, we must define the *grotesque*.

Grotesque is a term applied to a decorative art in sculpture, painting, and architecture, characterized by fantastic representations of human and animal forms often combined into formal distortions of the natural to the point of comic absurdity, ridiculous ugliness, or ludicrous caricature.... *By* extension, grotesque is applied to anything having the qualities of the grotesque art: bizarre, incongruous, ugly, unnatural, fantastic, abnormal. (Holman 245)

This definition suits Fitzball's milieu in characterizing his villains; monsters, of course; and his weird and shadowy plots. In The *Devil's Elixir,* for example, the tone of horror is exacerbated due to the monstrous appearance and diabolical devices of Gortzburg, the demon. In defining *horror.* as an artistic atmosphere and as a practical mechanism, the grotesque must be acknowledged and understood. In Fitzballiana drama, horror, like everything else, was dramatically overstated. Fitzball's confession about language implied his predisposition toward hyperbole: "...stage language should always be, like the scenery, a little over-colored" (1: 119). But the grotesque, whether in life or in art, is more than ugliness. It is really absurdism running amok, without logic or equilibrium, in a chaotic and maddening way. Fitzball used the ramifications of *grotesquerie* to make his plays distinctively strange and quite idiosyncratic. In defining the *tragedy of blood,* as part of the composition of horror, it is easy to see how the definition fits into the brutal, violent, and frightful dimensions of the macabre melodrama. Fitzball's lurid plays certainly had their share of blood and intensity to warrant such an alliance.

The Tragedy of Blood is an intensified form of the Revenge Tragedy popular on the Elizbethan stage. It works out the theme of revenge and retribution (borrowed from Seneca) through murder, assassination, mutilation, and carnage. The horrors which in the Latin Senecan plays had been merely described were placed upon the stage to satisfy the craving for the morbid excitement displayed by an Elizbethan audience brought up on bear-baiting, spectacles, and public executions. (Holman 533)

A parallel exists between Fitzball's dramatic and social milieu and its counterpart in the sixteenth- and seventeenth-centuries. With the exceptions of bear baiting and public executions, the populace of these two eras were oddly alike in taste and in modes of entertainment: the tragedy of blood for the Elizabethans and Jacobeans, the melodrama for the Victorians. It may also be remembered that melodrama was conceived during one of the most embattled and bloody periods in history, the French Revolution, whose Reign of Terror used public executions to a ravaging degree of tremendous proportion. Therefore, the use of horror in entertainment, *prima facie,* has an almost primordial capability in transcendence from one time to another. And it appears that the insalubrious fixation on real horror says much about man's culture and his fascination with the dreadful. *A fortiori,* Fitzballian horror seemed to be fulfilling the license evoked by the Jacobeans, for his dramas were surfeits of such chills, even if they had songs and a virtuous conclusion as dramatic necessity.

Relying upon a largess of horror and terror, coupled with adventuresome plots, Fitzball's plays seemed to have as much involvement with a Senecan stylistic, as it did it with that of the Jacobeans, in appealing to the frenzied tastes of a Grand Guignol audience. In essence, Fitzball's Blood-and-Thunder received its impetus from the "Blood" of the Jacobeans and the "Thunder" of Seneca; he simply took the macabre licenses of his predecessors and transformed them into a grotesquerie-of-entertainment for his particular time. Since Senecan, Jacobean, and Blood-and-Thunder melodrama were so interconnected, at least in Fitzballian terms, Senecan drama should be addressed in completing the concept of the theatre of the macabre:

...the employment of sensational themes (usually in antiquity involving Greek mythology) involving much use of "blood" and "lust" material connected with unnatural crimes...and often rhetorical style marked by hyperbolic expressions, detailed descriptions, exaggerated comparisons, aphorisms, epigrams, and the sharp line-forline dialogue known as stichomythia; and lack of careful character delineation and much use of introspection and soliloquy. (Holman 484)

As may be discerned, many of the elements found in this definition of Senecan stylistics may be transposed to that of classic melodrama: the inflated language; use of soliloquy; "hyperbolic expressions"; and stichomythia, which plays a memorable part in many of Fitzball's interaction between characters. In fact, one of Fitzball's excellent traits was a good ear for quickly paced dialogue, a good example being in *The Flying Dutchman,* which will be detailed later. Fitzball adapted the exorbitant horrors of the Jacobean theatre (1603-25), and the rhetorical flair of Senecan tragedy, to the bombastic and adventuresome style of Blood-and-Thunder, to yield a piquant type of hybrid, theatrical entertainment. For Fitzball, the theatrical definition of horror and terror seemed based upon transforming *decorum* and *verisimilitude* into entities shocking and nightmarish. Knowing the psychological propensities of his audiences, Fitzball was able to take advantage of that *Zeitgeist* in leading them to accept the fantastic as real. If one were surrounded by social and psychological dread, by *monsters* in one's own struggling existence, then, psychologically, a fictionalized horror may be more readily accepted as a symbol of whatever fear one might have. With justification, Fitzball was probably aware of this kind of empathy when he wrote *Jonathan Bradford.* He took the horror of an actual murder and theatricalized it on the stage, in front of people who faced crime constantly in London's underbelly. Not only did these people empathize with the terror of crime, they cathartically enjoyed, possibly, seeing crime, for once, rendered helpless on the theatre stage.

Fitzball's unsophisticated audience may not have read about supernatural apparitions in *Hamlet* or *Macbeth,* but they were well aware of the natural powers of murderers and the like: the dread on stage was a pleasing escape from the dread on the streets. And that was all Fitzball's dramatic license needed. Dale Cleaver has defined art in this way: "an object or event created or selected for its capacity to express and stimulate experience within a discipline" (2). Ralph Harper notes, in *The World of the Thriller,* that *literary fear* strikes a raw nerve in man's mode of existing. His thoughts could just as easily have been those of Fitzball's in this regard in describing the dreadful.

The "fears and terrors of the night" may be unreal imaginings, but they are no less really felt in the present, and therefore they give their character to the present. We may grieve over the past and dread the future, but the grief and the dread are felt now, not then or later. In our own feelings we live in the present and in no other time. (103)

Peripatetically, literature of the fantastic, which always involves horror and terror as atmosphere, and as some form of physical representation, warrants a consideration because Fitzball's works have much of what is fantastic in them. The haunting romantic components in melodrama were very much interlaced with that which was unknown and eerie. In fact, the whole notion of gothicism was wrapped up in haunted castles, ghostly figures, and the dark qualities of the imagination.

In his "Preface" to *Seven Masterpieces of Gothic Horror,* Robert 0. Spector intimates Coleridge's edict that the reader (and the viewer) of artistic horror (here, literary horror) must suspend his disbelief and "disregard superficial absurdities and participate in the process of 'recreation' by relating the fiction to his own emotional, imaginative, and subconscious life." (2) Moreover, Spector suggests that man has a deepseated fascination with the macabre and that he "...has turned a Freudian and surrealistic eye upon a type of literature that once provided an outlet for those same repressions more than a century and a half ago" (11). With his brand of sensationalism projecting the viewer into a drama world, Fitzball created a surrealistic and primitively emotional environment that had as much to do with psychology as it had with drama. Michael Booth further gives credence to this dream world psychology affected by fantasy literature, in which melodrama has no small place. It is because of this dream world that the writer may do what he will within its context: the dream world has no boundary. When the dream world in fantasy is contemplated, then melodrama becomes acceptable as part of that matrix, a matrix of popular escapism, adventure, and rewards.

Essentially, melodrama is a dream world inhabited by dream people and dream justice, offering audiences the fulfillment and satisfaction found only in dreams. An idealization and simplification of the world of reality...melodrama is therefore a dramatization of this second world, an allegory of human experience dramatically ordered a world of absolutes where virtue and vice coexist in pure whiteness and blackness...a world of justice where after immense struggle and torment good triumphs over and punishes evil, and virtue receives tangible material rewards...it is this romantic and escapist appeal that goes a long way to explain the enduring popularity of melodrama. (*English Melodrama* 14)

Given Booth's reason for melodrama's appeal, the crucial aesthetic of that dream world is that the use of horror and terror cannot be discerned as realistic, but only as fantastic. For example, the enjoyment and chills of seeing *Dracula* on stage holds no relationship to the painful psychosis of vampirism. Horror in art is always a distortion of horror in reality, and it is one's mindset which makes the distinction. What makes "the things that go bump in the night" artistically challenging is that they are intrinsic to the thriller, the nomenclature for all literature which deals with suspense, crime, and high adventure. In the world of the thriller, the presence of chaotic dread, upsetting any semblance of order, causes the necessary tone of mystery to overwhelm everything else. Ralph Harper makes some judgments that have significance for the darkened and qualmish posture of the melodrama of the macabre.

In the language of Karl Jaspers' existentialist philosophy it is the literature of boundary situations. Man is always in situation, but only occasionally for most men is life reduced to total questionability by any particular situation. The plots of thrillers, unlike the novels of manners, ideas, romantic love, travel adventures, are principally designed to illustrate such critical situations. (*Thriller* 51)

In tandem, Fitzball temporized the claustrophobia of social fear with the confining fears in his thriller yarns. Like that of the thriller, Fitzball's *theatre noir* compounded its shadowy existence with flagitious manifestations in mood and in plot. The source of terror must be foiled if order is to return. Such is the necessary valediction in any mode of the thriller, melodrama included. Harper asserts that the author must provoke the reader into taking the macabre seriously for effect:

> It is when evil or the threat of evil undermines our confidence in the natural or social order, and the reader is shaken up, that the thriller gets off to a good start. Whenever a writer fails to persuade his readers to take evil seriously, he cannot expect the readers to care whether justice is done. The "shocker" is the mass media's imagination of the absurd, making credible the chaos which the champions of justice and gentleness will successfully control. (*Thriller* 9-10)

Empathy lies in the viewer's ability to transpose the conflict on the stage to the pangs in his own life. And with those pangs comes a desire for justice and reward. Empathy, especially for horror and terror on stage, is made quite dominant anytime fear on the stage has a basis in reality. For instance, whenever a "Jack the Ripper" is seen as a dramatic figure, the audience may be moved to greater degrees of fear because there do exist such psychopaths in reality. Fitzball used the truth behind *Jonathan Bradford* in a similar way. Even at its wildest, fantastic literature always presumes some basis in fact. In melodrama, then, horror has its source in an external and internal force. In melodrama the villain expedites that force. Tragedy, on the other hand, uses conflict in a most different way. Its concept of horror is internal.

> In tragedy, therefore, "no villain need be"; in Meredith's fine phrase man is "betrayed by what is false within." In melodrama man remains undivided, free from the agony of choosing between conflicting imperatives and desires. He greets every situation with an unswerving, single impulse which absorbs his whole personality. (Smith 7)

Whenever the hero slays the monster or villain in melodrama, the play ends. When Oedipus blinds himself, the dire range of his personal horror takes on philosophical dimensions. Oedipus' villain, conflict, is within himself, not in the sphinx or in his bleeding eye sockets. In tragedy, melodrama's horror is atmospheric and tonal; in melodrama the tone and mood are changed by the presence of some foreboding villain, human or supernatural. In Fitzball's case, his most mordantly macabre dramas were those set within a gothic framework, in a haunted and lurid *mise-en-scene*. The foundation for his theatre of the macabre always comes from a psychological and physical convergence. Eric S. Rabkin illuminates the basis for the fantastic in art thusly:

The fantastic is a quality of astonishment that we feel when the ground rules of a narrative would are suddenly made to turn about 180 degrees...all playing on or against our whole experience as people and readers...satirizing man's world or clarifying the inner workings of man's soul. (41)

Is it possible, then, that the eerie has more of a foundation in human affairs than in only artistic diversion? Within a social and psychological context, the answer is positive, especially whenever the trials and problems of man are inspected.

The French theatre promoter Prevost once remarked that the commercial theatre was at the mercy of producing what audiences wanted, and what they wanted was "...the marvelous fairytale spectacle, crime play, and supernatural" (Rahill 20). That aesthetic has changed little since the eighteenth century when Prevost lived. That which is fantastic, macabre, unreal, and lurid remains art's most lucrative and popular guise. Writes Harper:

Terror...is the acknowledgement of a specific dread (horror), which acknowledges the nameless. It is as intense as horror and like horror it cannot be sustained for long; unlike horror, however, it is pure anxiety, unnerved with loathing. Terror is uncontrolled fear which momentarily at least drives out all other awareness of reality. Its demands are insistent, rising in crescendo, until nerves can stand no more. Just as horror dulls the sense, so terror heightens them. (*Darkness* 49)

Contemporaneously, the plethora of "horror cinemas" in urban areas served the same cultural capacities as did the many Grand Guignol theatres of nineteenth-century France and England. Each showcased danger, crises, tension, and bloodcurdling chills to the delight of the patron. Each showcased realms of horror and terror for profit. For Fitzball the real crisis is always in proportion to the threat offered by the villain: this determines the validity of terror and the type of horror. Fitzball distinguishes clearly between what is made dreadful and what is not made so. H.P. Lovecraft, whose literature still frightens hosts of readers long after his death, put the macabre into a precise context and aesthetic mold years ago. His thoughts imply much that is in Fitzballian sensationalism.

The oldest and strongest emotion of mankind is fear and the oldest and strongest kind of fear is fear of the unknown. These facts few psychologists will dispute, and their admitted truth must establish for all time the genuineness and dignity of the weirdly horrible tales as a literary form...the weird tale has survived, developed, and attained remarkable heights of perfection; founded as it is on a profound and elementary principle, whose appeal, if not always universal, must necessarily be poignant and permanent to minds of the requisite sensitiveness. The appeal of the spectrally macabre demands from the reader a certain degree of imagination and a capacity for detachment form everyday life.... The true weird tale has something more than secret murder, bloody bones, or the sheeted form clanking chains according to the rules. (12)

Fitzballian horror appealed to "the detached, dreamy, and fairytalelike" emotional response in his yearning audiences. As in the weird tale of Lovecraft, the horror melodrama has a unity of design, meaning that all its dramaturgic segments fit together, regardless of any apparent preposterousness at first glance. As in the short story, the drama maintains its initial mood and tone throughout the plot. Lovecraft knew that "the weird tale" must retain its initial mood for effect. The following excerpt from Lovecraft acknowledges the heritage man has, in an almost primeval way, concerning the artistic macabre, that haunts his very soul.

There is here involved psychological pattern or tradition as real and as deeply grounded in the mental experience as any other pattern or tradition of mankind; coeval with the religious feeling and closely related to many aspects of it, and too much a part of our innermost biological heritage to lose keen potency over a very important, though not numerically great, minority of our species... A certain atmosphere of breathless and unexplainable dread of outer, unknown forces must be present; and there must be a hint, expressed with a seriousness and portentousness becoming its subject, of that most terrible conception of the human brain—a malign and particular suspension or defeat of those fixed laws of Nature which are our only safeguard against the assaults of chaos and the demons of unplumbed space.(13-5)

In Fitzballian fare surely "the phenomenon of dreaming" takes over the viewer's psyche. Lovecraft hints at the Fitzballian mystique whenever he underscores the sensation of dread, which a spectator would greet in a journey into Fitzball's *danse macabre*. For Fitzball, dramaturgically, it was very important to initiate a certain mood and tone at the beginning of a play and sustain it throughout the various acts.

In assessing the people's need for entertainment, Michael Booth notes that the British literacy rate was incorrigibly low, that housing was squalid, that the political situation was turbulent. Therefore, the Victorian tastes welcomed the thriving blast of theatrical sensationalism (15-6). In Fitzball the gothic sense was carried to its full terror by the antagonist being supernatural. Charles Edward Whitmore, in his classic text *The Supernatural in Tragedy,* uses *terror* to mean more than *shock*. He sees it as a subtle, "more spiritual dread" which "the unseen world may provoke." For Whitmore, terror, when at its highest point of undertaking, falls, then, into a kind of awe and astonishment. Moreover, he states, "...the fear of ghosts is the fear of being touched by ghosts. The supernatural terror may accordingly be defined as the dread of some potentially malevolent power, of incalculable capacity to work evil..." (5-6) .

It is our dread of physical and spiritual involvement with the supernatural that makes that entity so gruesome and, ironically, attractive. Fitzball obviously understood the difference in dramatic technique in handling human and inhuman sources of dread, inasmuch as he perfected both in a combination of abominable tones: "...gruesome physical realities, such as scenes of murder and of sadism, with terror...in the presence of ghostly things" (Penzoldt 9). Appropriately enough, all of this is part of the sensational triad, and the melodramatic use of *sensational* and *sensationalism* is uniquely applied. More than the denotation of the adjective and noun, Maurice Disher points out that the *sensational* is fraught with connotations of the gruesome and the dreadful: "Henceforth, the word 'sensation' referred not to the operation of the senses, but to the violent emotional excitement of the literary fashion known as 'the romantic and the terrible' " (36). Thus, Fitzball's romantic heritage was coupled with his macabre sensationalism in yielding the sobriquet, "The Terrible Fitzball." All that this implied was the frenzied use of the triad in creating an artistic atmosphere of fearful delight.

More than only physical manifestations of dread, horror and terror, for Fitzball, were states of mind. The old bromide that the true masterful use of horror and terror lay in what the viewer did not see, but hence imagined, had much to do with Fitzball's sensationalism being set apart from any disgusting exploits of dread. Of the three aspects in the triad, horror-terror, crime, and madness, Fitzball appeared to cater to the first, as his comment on *Der Freischutz (Demon of the Wolf's Den)* suggested:

...one touch of thrilling, grand, and horrific chords had power to throw over the whole of my poor compound an air of reanimating...awful grandeur.... The incantation scene was really introduced in a style of surpassing splendour. owls flapping their wings—Serpents hissing in the air—shadows moving and every concomitant of terror and diabolism were summoned into requisition. (1)

When Fitzball deprecated this kind of wonderful dread in *The Black Robber,* that anthology (1819) predated *Demon of the Wolf's Den* by some five years. By 1824 Fitzball's soul searching appeared over and he was back at his old, dramatic tricks. This transduction of real fear into that on the stage, for a while at least, would issue respite in the viewer. Hence, the stage was/is a trammel for our fears.

Having its basis in the socio-psychological history of man's existence, Fitzball, consequently, did not whip up the fact of human fear. In 1651 Thomas Hobbes had written in *The Leviathan* that man found "nothing but grief in the company of his fellows" and that he was in the perpetual position of "continual fear and danger of violent death; and that the life of man was solitary, poor, nasty, brutish, and short" (42). Fitzball merely theatricalized in fancy what he sensed in truth, which is the point of all theatre. Les Daniels' conclusive *Fear: A History of Horror in the Mass Media* notes that the twins of luridness, horror and terror, are historical manifestations of a corporate psychology.

Innumerable essays have been written attempting to explain the fascination for terror tales; there are enough theories to fill a book, but none of them are completely convincing. The fact is that the muse of the macabre has inspired more variations in style and subject than many glib commentators have encountered. The myths and legends of ancient days are often full of horrors...all of the narratives that have survived from the distant past have some fantastic invention, only a few centuries old, and it developed almost simultaneously with the idea of fiction...part of the enthusiasm for the macabre may be attributed to ancestral memories of the days when demons were almost expected to put on an occasional appearance...the macabre is dependent in large measure on the way in which it violates decorum. (7-9)

This liberating factor in the artistry of the macabre may be the best argument for its usage. Fitzball's works were often called romances for such a reason: "... frequently used as a term to designate a kind of fiction that differs from the novel in being more freely the product of the author's imagination than the product of an effort to represent the actual world with verisimilitude" (Holman 459). Such a designation suited Fitzball's freewheeling style and plots without a doubt. But, of course, there were decorum and verisimilitude in Fitzball's plays, if one accepted the dramatist's sense of what was logical. To enjoy Fitzball, one had to "suspend his disbelief" totally.

For Fitzball horror and terror were as much a state-of-mind as they were a state-of-vision. Fitzball's stratagem was to set the audience up for the terrors to come through his fearful devices and contrivances. G.R. Thompson defines the terms associated with the gothic in a precise way. By route of his definitions, we may later see their justification in Fitzball's sensational aesthetic, in combination with the contributions of the grotesque and the tragedy of blood.

In literature the Gothic refers to the kind of work, usually fiction, that developed out of the sentimental romance into the Dark Romantic tale of terror. The word Romantic usually evokes an ideal world...symbolic of the aesthetic harmony of the cosmos. Adding the adjective Dark may evoke an image of the lonely, isolated self, pressing onward despite all obstacles which either indulging or struggling with internal evil, the very source and conflict of energy. But when the word Gothic is applied to literature, it merely evokes images of ghosts, demons, trapdoors, and castles. In America, Gothic fiction is frequently associated with the dime novel, in Britain perhaps more precisely called the "shilling shocker" or the "penny dreadful" ...for the mass audience. The Gothic romance seeks to create an atmosphere of dread by combining terror with horror and mystery. *Terror* suggests the frenzy of physical and mental fear of pain, dismemberment, and death. *Horror* suggests the perception of something incredibly evil or morally repellent. *Mystery* suggests something beyond this, the perception of a world that stretches away beyond the range of human intelligence—often morally incomprehensible—and thereby productive of a nameless apprehension that may be called religious dread in the face of the wholly other. (2-3)

This lengthy excerpt from Thompson validates Fitzball's systematic device of combining romanticism, darkness, gothicism, terror, horror, mystery, grotesquerie, and the tragedy of blood into a total methodology of disseminating his brand of sensationalism for the theatregoer. Horror and terror are the support system for crime and madness, inasmuch as both emerge from a frightening point-of-attack in the plot.

That the dreadful is eminent in tone and mood "...whether physical, psychological, or metaphysical; whether in body, mind, or spirit" (G.R. Thompson 3), melodramatic horror and terror are disassociated from tragic counterparts because the former physicalize dread in a persona, whereas the latter cultivate dread within a character's mind and soul. In Maxwell Anderson's *The Bad Seed,* Rhoda, the demon-child, displays both psychological and physical evil: the first in deceiving those about her; the second in murdering at will. She is a consummate monster, albeit a melodramatic one, because there is no soulful conflict in will. Macbeth, on the contrary, commits heinous crimes, but the effecting of those misdeeds is secondary to his emotional damnation. In melodrama stark physical aberration (monsters and the like) connote abnormalities of mind and body, as does any physical act of cruelty or evil. Fitzball wastes no time in exposing Gortzburg, the monster in *The Devil's Elixir,* as being evil in mind and body. Anderson does the same with Rhoda, except he presents her as a darling child, a monster all the more sinister. Shakespeare's Caliban, but for differing reasons, becomes as monstrous mentally, as he has always looked physically. All three characters merge villainy into an outward appearance. Even Rhoda begins to look the part of a villainess as the play progresses.

Terror, it seems, attempts to expand and awaken the soul while horror would destroy it. In terror "an awful sense of the sublime in which the sense of self is swallowed up in immensity is shown; whereas, horror rises up from within, with a great consciousness of dreadful evil" (G.R. Thompson 34). There can be no horror and terror without some kind of theological "fall from grace." Every villain demonstrates tremendous, almost diabolical, wickedness in melodrama; consequently, some spiritual dimension enters the circumstance. With the goal of melodrama being a resuscitation of virtue and goodness, then the philosophical reason behind the conflict must lie in a representation of immorality and Godlessness. More than just theatre, Fitzball's drama was one of compelling faith against a triad of evil. Philip Brophy, although discussing the use of horror in film, makes a statement that is identifiable with the horror aesthetic of Fitzball.

The horror film always changing as each new film sets a precedent of special effects, plots, realism, horror, suspense, humor, and subject matter... "Horrality" is thus a mode of textuality that is dictated by trends within both the genre and in realism. (13)

Fitzball's orientation to the macabre may seem dated. We are little afraid of rattling chains, Dickensian ghosts, and blue-fire, but the rationale for horror is still current. The type of horror may change, but the reason for horror, and its terror, will remain as long as man has reason for anxiety, discomfort, uncertainty, and fears of all kinds. The power of horror is directly linked to the reality of dread in the world: end the dread, which can never be, and the need and aesthetic for fanciful horror will end as escape and as therapy. In remembering Hobbes, Fitzball's morbid aesthetic seems safe from disappearance as reality and as art.

Crime as Triadic Imagery

The second part of the sensational triad is crime. Unlike horror and terror, crime, as a social and theatrical phenomenon, was more easily identifiable and artistically transferable to the stage. Real crime was an archetype to its staged counterpart. Again, in order to realize the relationship between theatre and its social inspiration, crime will be approached criminologically, socially, and, then, as a theatrical theme. Historically, crime may be determined as the onslaught of a society in anguish. And nineteenth-century London's industrialization caused as much suffering and crime for the many, as it caused pleasure and prosperity for the few. David Thompson makes a solid assertion about the ravages of the Industrial Revolution wrought upon those with whom crime was a daily display.

> The new industrialization with the consequent growth of sprawling towns, combines with the aftermath of the Napoleanic wars, produced the twin evils of crime and poverty in much more acute forms. The rapid growth of population and the equally rapid redistribution of population over the face of Britain, the changing type of population produced by town life, the importunate evils of crime and poverty, made this old machinery (local governmental) out of date and hopelessly inadequate, most acutely in the towns. (*England* 63)

In fathoming crime as an historical and social phenomenon, one might do well in recalling the social-protest plays of the 1960s. Stringently, theatre has often adapted real turmoils to its creativity. The Living Theatre, for example, emphasized the problems of people beset by woes of conscience and injustice: crimes of the will. Of course, melodrama's innate style and approach to art prohibited a documentarian tendency, or even a realistic, at least sociologically, address to crime of any kind. Fitzball's approach to crime was not as social commentary, since he was not a social-thesis dramatist, but, rather, his view of crime was a sin in need of eradication for the uplifting of virtue. In presenting the victory of hero over criminal (villain), Fitzball was illustrating a metaphorical "positive thinking" exercise for his weary and beleagured patrons, permitting them the gift of even-staged hope in combating their particular plights. His was a most romantic direction, but, even so, Fitzball's usage of crime as a motif, nonetheless, indicated his social awareness. For the poor, melodrama's dashing heroes were cathartic substitutes for themselves: figurative power over genuine helplessness, metaphorical victors over common defeatists, and encouraging hope over hapless resignation. In his own way, perhaps, Fitzball's outlandish and romantic dramas made crime and villains conquerable in the eyes of those made fearful and wretched by a life of desolation. Michael Booth echoes this presumption by extolling melodrama's effect on the poor, the class most victimized by violent, crazed, and horrible felonies. This truism remains an embarrassment to any culture defined as civilized and caring.

The reasons for the enormous popularity of melodrama in England and in America in the nineteenth-century are not hard to find. In both countries rapid industrial expansion created huge urban working classes living in conditions of the utmost drabness and squalor, who demanded entertainment as relief from the long working day. Their level of literacy and taste was low, and the environment of melodrama with combination of cheap sentiment, violent incident and scenic thrills, was just what they required. Furthermore, the times in which they lived were times of political and military excitement (with a) background of war and violence...More generally, the Victorian public thrived on sensationalism. Into this rushed the melodramatist, who knew what his audience liked and gave it to them. No matter how crudely presented, there was much material from contemporary life. Pathetic stories of domestic woe in city and country, violent stories of modern crime...were closer to the hearts than dreary dramas of events hundreds of years ago. (*Hiss the Villain* 15-6)

Melodrama, it should be noted now, was essentially a story-drama. By this, it is meant that melodrama was a narrative account and self-contained. We presume that the beginning, middle, and end of the drama were all there was to appreciate. In tragedy, of course, Aristotle dictated that it must have the same three sections and be complete; yet, the cosmic and/or philosophical slant of a tragedy gives the impression that its after-effects of the tragedy may be positive or negative: hence, the insinuation and implementation of sequels to continue the action. Aeschylus' surviving trilogy, *The Oresteia* (458 B.C.), is a case in point, as is Sophocles' sequel to *Oedipus Rex*, *Oedipus at Colonus* (401 B.C.). In melodrama, however, with the foiling of the villain, there was no need to pursue the good characters' activities further. It was taken for granted "that they would live happily ever after." In tragedy, however, that presumption could not be taken for granted because of the ramifications in the protagonist's tragic activities. Aeschylus had to follow-up on the tumultuous future of Orestes, after his murder of Clytemnestra and Aegisthus, and Sophocles felt compelled to follow Oedipus' last days, as the blind hero fights with his sons and curses their fate. Tragedy lionized the serious plot and grandiose characters, who were almost too large for one play. Melodrama, as a rule, ended the play with the end of the villain. There were exceptions, but in the nineteenth-century the rule held.

The narrative nature of melodrama was the force behind the genre's fame: the ordinary person could follow the story and understand the moral. For an audience largely uneducated, this was—and continues to be in modern melodrama—enough. The masses were induced into the theatre by proposals of amusement, the primary ingredient for commercialism in art. Familiar with London's seaminess, Fitzball's villains—the human ones—symbolized corruption, a contamination that Kellow Chesney attributes to the confederation of "the criminal class."

When respectable people spoke of the dangerous classes—phrase enjoining a good deal of currency—they were not talking about the labouring population as a whole, nor the growing industrial proletariat.... They meant certain classes of people whose very manner of living seemed a challenge to ordered society and the issues of laws, morality, and taboos holding it together. These "unprincipled," "ruffiantly," and "degraded" elements seemed ready to exploit any breakdown of established order. They roused a natural anxiety among a ruling class conscious to the strains to which rapid economic change was subjecting the whole organism. (38)

It would be up to the realists to dissect the brooding foundations for human behavior. Nonetheless, Fitzball, in his own Dickensian procedure, showed the dismay of criminal life and deeds. In agreement with Hugo's pronouncement of theatrical beauty juxtaposed with ugliness, Fitzball's theatre of the macabre did, in fact, portray criminals as the rogues they were. For Fitzball, all human villainy was the result of a crime of one sort or another, and he did not prettify his miscreants as "Francois Villion" types. They were felons brimming over with atrocities; only the secondary villain was shown as a comic ne'er-do-well. The main rogue was malignant and gave the play its premise of evil battling good, physically and philosophically. Garishly, the staged criminal aped the same sordidness of London's underworld:

The thieves, cheats, bullies, beggars, touts, and tarts...all belonged, more or less, to the dangerous classes. London society had made itself dependent on a large community of men and women who were estranged from it and hostile to its canons; the semi-barbarous tribes who formed...the marches of the underworld (Chesney 39).

This listing of criminous types is indigenous to many of Fitzball's rascals. The sensational triad is synonymous with villainy, *definiens*. The heroes in Fitzball's rousing adventure plays, *The Red Rover* and *Robin Hood,* were a pirate and revolutionary, but their *crimes* were commendable. The true villain's acts merely reflected his mental aberrations.

Like his counterpart in reality, the stage criminal preyed upon his victim's vulnerability and misfortune. The criminal, both fanciful and real, was seen by Frederick Engels as (what else?) a social revolutionary against bourgeois values.

Those members of the 'surplus population' who—goaded by their misery—summed up enough courage to revolt openly again society become thieves and murderers. They wage open warfare against the middle class who have for so long waged secret warfare against them. (Chesney 91)

It is highly unlikely that a double-dyed melodramatic villain ever possessed the noble social conscience of an Engels radical. However, Engels was correct in characterizing the criminal as one opposed to the status quo and the bourgeoisie. Degraded socially and mentally by his "betters," the criminal struck out ruthlessly. This was certainly a type in Fitzballian fare. *Jonathan Bradford's* Macraisy, as we shall see, despises the upper and middle classes and, consequently, fights against them. Therefore, social polarization is a tenable cause for real and dramatic villainy: anarchy against the establishment. London's "undrained, unpoliced, ungoverned, and unschooled urban jungles, where lawlessness flourished as naturally as disease' was the festering locale for the criminal (Chesney 91). Melodrama was a workingman's theatre; so many of its characters issued from that sort of environ as well, unless the melodrama were exotically or fantastically oriented. In any case, it was crucial that the audience be able to identify with the plot in some satisfactory way. One reason that the classics failed with the lower classes, unless they were melodramatized by play doctors, was because they were alien to a public empathy. Economically, noble art still suffers unless it panders to the public. Fitzball knew this truism; therefore, his bread-and-butter plays were directed towards a public wanting recreation, not tedious art.

Chesney's list of the categories of villains, interestingly enough, has those types found prominently theatricalized:

The types of criminals were murderers, whores, beggars [at night] turned thief, arsonists, and the like. Mostly, however, murder, theft, gangsterism, characterized the abnormality of the street villain. A *trasseno* was an extremely wicked criminal. (377-84)

Fitzball's villains were assuredly *trassenos,* albeit some of them did confess their sins before dying—an old melodramatic and Roman Catholic tradition. Chesney goes on to provide slang expressions for these blackguards, who differed in techniques, depending upon either a city or country criminal preference. These terms, for instance as they might apply to the crime drama, were *kidsman,* or organizer; *monkry,* or general rogue; and *flash house,* or the abode for thugs. Fitzball's villains were too exacting, too well-drawn, to be happenstance. The playwright was careful in depicting his villains in such a way as to suspect that he was familiar with London's underworld—if only indirectly through many of his patrons, who came from those dark surroundings. Remember that the Coburg was set almost in the middle of a slum where crime would be flagrant.

Crime as a Social Issue
J.J. Tobias reiterates a general cause for the upsurge in London crime:

An industrial revolution entails profound social as well as economic changes, and the first industrial revolution found society unprepared for the problems that emerged during the upheaval. There was a lair of leisure and building up of tension." (*Crime* and *Society* 37)

Such dereliction must have spawned a macabre environment of its own, with crime a factor in demographically populated areas, although the rural locale was not immune to its hideous attack. It is as if London were a "Naked City" with its million stories to tell on the theatre's stage. From 1751 to 1851, England and Wales' population teemed with 18,000,000 souls. In 1750 London had 676,000 people; in 1820 she had 1,274,000. The population increased by ten per-cent every decade (*Crime and Society* 35-6). Tobias laments, "In the last half of the eighteenth-century and in the first half of the nineteenth-century, the society was in violent transition" (*Crime and Society* 37). With this tremendous increase of impoverished persons, huddled closely together, and hapless, to say the least, it is no wonder that crime exploded, particularly in the wake of a strong demarcation between rich and poor. The social parallels between that time, which ushered in crime and melodrama, and our own, which is seeing violent crime rising and melodramatic entertainment overpowering all other genres, are inescapable and disturbing.

Again, melodrama was and is a child of revolt, both socially and artistically. As a factor, there is always the breeding of violence in the sensational triad, and the criminous part of the triad gauges violence more notably than do the other segments. As was mentioned earlier, Victorian London was sorely partitioned socially, but spicy skulduggery among the upper classes and harrowing brutality among the lower seemed to equalize the factions. The theatre, of course, was quick to interpret these imbroglios, with writers, such as Shaw and Pinero, to come as censurers about sophisticated misdeeds. The classic Blood-and-Thunder writers were satisfied in writing about ordinary, everyday crimes, with which their audiences could identify.

Lest anyone misinterpret the ubiquity of crime in London as not that meaningful a social issue, the transportation of some 160,000 convicts from London to other cities for incarceration should impugn that position. London was fraught with crime, and the dramatist was quick to comment upon the fact (*Crime and Society* 37). Of the crime play itself, Disher discloses:

> In essence the crime drama was a social thesis play. Its themes of oppression, lust, and general insalubrious largess exploited these vices in the hopes of alembic reversals in society. The crime play was a temperance play in reality. The crime melodrama may be more a part of social rather than dramatic history. (142)

More than dramaturgic contrivances and histrionic rantings, the crime melodrama, simply put, exposed a social ill, dramatized it, and left that problem's reprimand to those authoritative enough to combat it. Unfortunately, the play's advice fell upon people unable, or unwilling, to effect a lessening of crime. Through the Horatian dictum, the crime play desired that its theme be inspected socially, by way of entertainment; therefore, social concerns were oftentimes central to the play. The theatricalization of this social phenomenon is interesting in its own right. Rahill points out that staged crime still was subject to the melodramatic flair.

> In adapting actual crimes for the stage, melodramatists were not meticulous in their regard for documentary fact. They whitewashed culprits, gave unjustly condemned unfortunates the benefit of reprieves denied them in real life, distorted motives, invented villains, suppressed material facts, and solved mysteries. Throughout the nineteenth century into the twentieth century, the sordid and sensational details of criminal prosecutions came to the aid of the faltering intervention of melodramatists. (14-5)

Rehill's consolidation of the crime play's composition omitted the fact that, characteristically, the main villain was drawn as a transgressor with seemingly unlimited abilities. Of course, the staged crime was subjective and, therefore, took dramatic license whenever suitable. Nonetheless, the horror and terror associated with a given crime were cultivated for the sake of the expectant patrons. In the midst of London's population expansion, 100 per-cent in 231 years, came the onslaught of crime, and the theatre could not avoid dramatizing the phenomenon because staged crime and violence had always attracted public attention (Pike 407). Luke Owen Pike said that murder—the main fodder for Fitzballian crime plays—was infamously rampant: "The greatest of all crimes of violence is homicide. When that diminishes, there is no doubt that all the allied offenses will diminish with it" (408). From 1860 to

1873, to give an idea of the persuasiveness of crime as potential dramatic material, there were 973 murders reported, and, from 1862 to 1873, there were 414 charges of manslaughter (Pike 472). Reflectively, Fitzball's sensationalism became immersed with murders, so that the parallel between actual homicide and staged killings bears witnessing: types of crime popular in the streets became types of crime popular on the stage. To indicate that the criminal faction was of extreme importance to that same life which the drama was supposed to mirror, there were, in 1805, 4,605 criminals in London; in 1854 there were some 29,359 (Pike 475). Since crime was an engrossing theme in transpontine theatre, a definition seems needed, so that the criminal-villain may be categorized as a certain character. Gwynn Nettler says, "As defined *by* law, a crime is an intentional violation of the criminal law, committed without defense or excuse and penalized by the state" (33).

Artistically, crime, for the melodramatists, was a hybrid formed from sin and a specific felony, and, because the thrust of melodrama was directed towards some type of spiritual regeneration and victory in virtue, most of Fitzball's miscreants were "sinful criminals," created to carry on the eternal battle, as much in spirit as in action, in evil against righteousness. In *Jonathan Bradford,* particularly, the murder has this effect. The viewer is appalled by the natural brutality of a stabbing, but, moreover, the murderer's subsequent anguish convinces the viewer that crime is inimical to all things civilized. To good effect, the dictum of Horace is applied.

It is an interesting phenomenon to see the link between the criminal, the impoverished, the environment, and the playhouse itself. Without a doubt, then, as now, impoverished neighborhoods were obvious breeding grounds for crime, and the given playhouse in such a location tended to reflect its environment. Cicely Hamilton presents a cogent argument for this theatrical and social confluence.

The rapid growth of London over the water may have filled the pits and the galleries of the surrey-side theatres, but it did not fill their more expensive seats—on the contrary, it probably helped keep them empty. The tastes of the playgoers domiciled in a rough and not overly respectable neighborhood were not always akin to the tastes of the playgoers domiciled in Mayfair and Bloomsbury.... In the contrast between the two sections of the audience, the tastes and wishes of the gallery were bound in the end to prevail; the gallery was there at all times—a constant, dependable factor. (149-50)

Hamilton confirms that the theatre was, in a way, a social depository for brigands who, otherwise, would be in the streets, effecting crime of their own.

Ironically, some of the audiences, to whom the crime melodrama played, were far more felonious than were the criminals on stage. In this case, surely art not only reflected, but, in some instances, copied the lives of its patrons. That many of the villains in these melodramas existed in squalid surroundings, and, thereby, had at least an environmental relationship to the audience, may be a reason for the genre's popularity. This social foundation of life in theatre intimated an impetus for transferring *criminal life* into *criminal drama*. The general background supporting this duality between these entities, criminal life and theatre, demands at least a peripheral understanding. There were/are always rationales for criminality in both life and theatre. Certainly, Fitzball gave reasons for his villains' misconduct.

W.C. Reckless, the noted criminologist, in *Criminology: A Book of Readings,* has given poverty and haplessness as primary reasons for crime's perpetuation among the lower, working classes (23). In the nineteenth-century, as now, the main difference between white and blue collar crime resided in conniving on the one hand and violence on the other. In life, as in drama, the malefactor was driven by cupidity. The criminal took advantage of a tumultuous and unbalanced society wrought by industrialization. A socialist may have seen the criminal as a crusader against covetous, burgeois institutions and uninhibited by any social moral ethic. The dramatic miscreant lived by a law unto himself and considered norms as weak and assailable. Fitzball's Macraisy is an archetype of criminal justifications. London provided a hinterland for felons, and melodrama inspected that strange and prostituted lifestyle. Tobias remarks,

Another writer went so far as to speak of the hatred of the poor for the rich and their detestation of the existing laws and institutions. Others felt that industrialisation, large-scale organization, and the factory system were demoralizing the nation. (*Crime* and *Society* 183-4)

Beyond the lust for money, genuine and fictive criminals are bigoted against the bourgeoisie. Without a loathing for man's norms and mores, the villain could not exist.

As a complement to crime's place in society, it is interesting to note that the police (in drama, the hero) were an integrated factor. In fact constables roamed playhouses in search of ruffians and malefactors. All the dramatists, including Fitzball, were privy to newspaper scandal sheets for inspiration. Real crimes, coupled with imagination, were transformed into compelling excitement. Certainly this was true in *Jonathan Bradford* and all other tabloid-induced plays. Crime was profit for London's commercial houses, and the villains were duplicates of rogues in police annals. Because of its liberalism, gaiety, and social setting, the theatre was vulnerable in becoming a *flash house* for masquerading thugs. Since the theatre was open to all types of people, many of whom shared the same predatory vocation in life as that seen on the stage, it was no surprise to suspect that miscreants were in the seats and wherever they could find a suitable place for pickpocketing and the like. In fact, Edmund Kean once remarked that the Surrey's audiences were made up of ignoramuses, the like of which he had never seen. This gives an idea of the composition of the audience seeing sensationalism on stage. In America the Astor Street Theatre Riot in 1849, in which some 200 participants were killed, confirms the point that the theatre could be a dangerous place (Garff 86). The theatre, crime, and the police had much in common. Order fought chaos in life and on the stage. Crime stimulated art, or so it seemed.

Criminologically, the brigand would travel distances from his home, usually ending up in the seedy sections of London in either prostitution, theft, murder, or any number of sundry felonies. Oftentimes, highwaymen would *case* an inn for their victims, as in *Jonathan Bradford*. The ubiquity of crime was so strident that *Blackwood's Magazine* did indeed in 1818 write that "one strong feature of the times is the prevalence of atrocious crime" (*Crime and Society* 141). No matter how one saw the situation, London was a ripe city for criminal execution and crime theatricalization. For a melodramatist to avoid this truism was tantamount to being blind. In *Crime and Police in England,* J.J. Tobias responds:

Another method of supplementing official pay was reserved for the men of a division of the Metropolitan (London) police. They were engaged on special duty at night at the theatres within their division the men were paid by the proprietors of the theatre a gratuity, equivalent to the pay of their police rank. Cavanaugh (the police narrator) first went on duty at the Drury Lane in 1856. A great deal was expected of him; the police had to open the doors, and make themselves generally useful. The most difficult task was that of the constable in charge of the gallery crowd. He had to try to keep order in queue outside of the theatre door, until the signal was given for the galleryites to be allowed in ...all semblance then of a queue lost out as everybody tore upstairs as fast as he could in order to get the best seats on the front benches. The poor constable had to prevent the fights which all too often would break out as people quarelled over a favored position...the constable had to maintain a constant watch to stop the occupants of the gallery from throwing orange peel, nut shells, and other surplus items into the stalls below. The inspector would patrol through the foyer to insure that theater-goers were safe from pickpockets (dippers), drunks, and beggars. (107-8)

Tobias' relation about the policeman's "bouncer-like" role in controlling the crowds at the theatre would parallel the control of a contemporary event of mass entertainment. The situation could be akin to a modern rock concert, where anything could become volatile: "The economic and social stresses of the Industrial Revolution favored the growth of a criminal class in London and, to a lesser extent, in other large towns" (*Police* 181). From this social volcano, nineteenth-century criminologists and—dramatists by implication—would offer narcotics, poverty, joblessness, madness, and the like as causalities for crime, many of which were oftentimes framed by the theologian as influenced by Original Sin. A flood of temperance plays attacked this moral blight, in much the same way as twentieth-century temperance tracts and plays would criticize liquor during Prohibition. The crime play would serve as a caveat for those unpolluted by proposing reasons for the antagonist's "fall from grace," even if that reason were implausible. Criminological perspectives tended to be cool and objectively scientific although, as we shall see, some of them were clouded by ideas now seen as dated and infeasible. Writes Tobias:

...there is one voice that cannot be directly heard—the criminals themselves cannot speak to us...he (the criminologist) can never see through the eyes of the criminals themselves. (*19th Century Crime* 10)

Tobias' allusion to the rationale for a crime—that which may be seen only through the eyes and mind of the criminal himself—is an intriguing entrance into the causes of crime, at least concerning the nineteenth-century, in which modern criminology was being born. Of course, in the crime play, the villain's actions are explained within the context of the plot. De Quiros has noted that the nineteenth-century was so laden with crime that only one in every four criminals was brought to justice (16). Such a statistic of lawlessness was apt to catch the eye of the playwright, who had, since the Greeks, been a voice on the state of current social affairs. This is not to say that all dramatists went out to write about criminals. It is to say that the melodramatist fed upon such human sensationalism and disgorged it to a waiting public. This was the era of "penny-dreadfuls," pulp magazines, and the Grand Guignol, all of which romanticized the eternal battles between good and evil, often with culprits seen as dashing rogues. To writers such as Fitzball, the deluge of crime was too strong and too obvious to escape theatricalization. Fitzball not only based some plots upon reality, he often drew his criminals to fit current criminological ideas about what the average ruffian would look like.

Havelock Ellis' classic *The Criminal* (1890) indeed investigated the felon as a peculiar type of individual, whose physiognomy would portend the degree of crime he would commit. To relate one's physical appearance to one's deeds is scientifically risible today, but we must remember that criminology was in its infancy in the 1800s. In short, Ellis contended, with a foundation in phrenology, that ugliness in body would often connect to ugliness in deed; therefore, the villain, and this route continued into early films and plays of the twentieth century, would appear haggard and loathsome, his nefarious acts an extension of the physical dread he carried. This attitude has remnants even in contemporary aesthetics: the villain is still seen as a dark and menacing figure. As a side note, to accentuate the villainy of the brigand, the "heavy" would always kick a dog in many a silent film. Hugo's romantic flank of the beautiful and ugly is immediately bought to mind. Not only then would the melodramatists pit morality against sin; he would also stage a sardonic visage against a noble one. It must be remembered that the audiences of the time were, by-and-large, unsophisticated; therefore, they had to have these polarizations emphasized. We still look for modifications of these traits in the villain and hero today: the "twirling of the mustache," the penetrating eyes, and the swarthy-shifty demeanor challenging the noble chin, the fair complexion, and the heroic posture. The great filmologist William K. Everson, in his *The Bad Guys: Pictorial History of the Movie Villain*, presents a psychological portrait of the rogue, which is as appropriate to the stage villain, as it is to the film brigand. It proves why the criminal is important and intriguing.

Psychologists assure us that crime and violence on the screen is healthy, because it purges us of those repressed tendencies. Whether it does is something for the doctors to argue over, but the inescapable fact remains that crime on film (and on stage) is fun, for us the audience. In a world increasingly rampant with restrictions and laws and codes, it's good to see authority being deflated, laws ignored, and stifling order turned into exhilarating chaos. And it's comforting too to be reminded—as the last reels (or denouement) invariably do—that the lawbreaker must pay the piper, and that despite excesses, most laws are quite endurable. (XI)

To the theatregoer, the criminal served a dual role: a rogue against the establishment and a blight to be eradicated for the good of all. It was in this latter guise that Fitzball colored most of his brigands. In seeing the villain vanquished, the patrons were able to raise their cathartic emotions to a rousing pitch. Concerning crime, there were those felonies of the *city* and of the *country*, but Fitzball oftentimes merged them in making his heavies particularly heinous. Gabriel Tarde, the noted nineteenth-century criminologist, differentiated between urban and rural crime. In urban crime there was "a slow substitution of greedy, crafty, and voluptuous violence for vindictive and brutal violence found in the country" (Mannheir 297). Based upon Tarde's classification, the urban miscreant would effect burglary, fraud, and swindling (the "dapper city slicker"), while the rural scoundrel would murder and vandalize. Each one had about him an air of hauteur, which the stage would accentuate, of course. As a sidenote, the excellent villains in the *James Bond* films are indicative of Tarde's theory. Usually, the fiends were unredeemable, and Fitzball made use of both types vis-a-vis Tarde's presumptions.

The influential criminologist Caesar Lombroso initiated the psychological causality of crime by theorizing that a felon may be socially maladjusted. He divided the categories into the following sets: occasional misbehavior, insanity, immorality, of natural inclination (the "Bad Seed" syndrome) (De Quiros 11). Modern criminology has extended Lombroso's basic discoveries, yet much of what he wrote remains fundamentally valid. The romantic villains contain his conclusions. when Fitzball's villains were described—the human ones, of course—Lombroso's theories were justified. To fathom crime, and its dramatic reflections, the criminal was analyzed as to *where he was, what he was,* and *how he became villainous.* Therefore, the criminal part of the triad was as much sociological and psychological, as it was artistic. Intertwined in all of this, socially and dramatically, were the social and sub-cultural structures begetting felonious behavior. Elevating a particular environment and psychology, the criminal exposes the underlying basis that made him evil (Nettler 69). With the rigorous afflictions brought about by the Industrial Revolution, it would not be difficult to argue that the criminal—insanity notwithstanding—was a product of such turmoil. The third part of the triad, madness, will address the sensationalism of an abnormal mind, about which environment could do little to redress.

In summation to this second segment of the triad, it would be well to inspect a random sampling of what theorists said concerning this aberration. Fitzball combined all three parts of the triad to make his villains artistically memorable. In this there is a sense of agreement from early philosophers who felt that physical and mental blemishes converged to make a criminal. Homer is known to have referred to the physical peculiarities of Thersites in naming him a criminal, as Ellis recounts: "...ugly and deformed, with harsh and scanty hair, and a pointed head...."Other references to this phenomenon are noted in the philosopher Socrates being counted as physically criminous, with the sage promising to alter his appearance. And Aristotle, Galen, and Polemon theorized about the correlations between physical and mental abnormalities: simply, if one were physically ugly, he would be likely to commit heinous acts (Ellis 263). As preposterous as these notions now appear, it is enlightening to know that the melodramatist had cultural and scholastic precedents in his characterful formulas.

Before scorning these early beliefs, it must be remembered that the melodrama was playing, as Castelvetro once remarked about theatre, for the ignorant masses. And, since melodrama brought forth an uncomplicated moral, its world had to be black-and-white in appeal. Aesthetically, the villain still has certain physical traits that are ingrained in the characterization, if not so obvious now, and the hero still maintains his share of certain virtues for the moral combat to come. Those melodramatic traits have, in essence, changed little. In John Webster's *The Duchess of Malfi* (1612), all of the flagitious afflictions stem from the decaying and perverted society about the characters themselves. So contaminated become these personae that crime rises as a natural inclination to satisfy desires and ambitions. The Industrial Revolution's waste of humanity, which has overtones of contemporary outrages against mankind, gave crime the necessary fodder in which to grow. Lombroso, Tarde, and Fitzball, as chroniclers of their times, commented on what crime was and how it was spread. For Fitzball, crime was central to the triad. And if crime compiled horror and terror in tone and atmosphere, it was madness, the last element of the triad, that maneuvered crime.

Madness as Dramatic Image

If crime produces horror and terror, either directly or by inference, what weaves the web for crime to exist and cause such anxiety? It is the third and most transparent of the triadic components: madness. In melodrama a psychosis and/or neurosis finds its manifestation in the villain. It is a foregone conclusion that the *atrocious crimes* whether real or staged, were works of lunatics, or, in the nomenclature of melodrama, *madmen*. To speak of madness was to speak of villains. This truism was appropriate to Fitzball, whose twisted and destructive villains remain the playwright's best characters. There were, of course, degrees of madness. Not all madmen were bloodlusting murderers. Some were Machiavellian—although political science now deduces that this trait is not wholly egregious—and some were barbaric. Then, of course, there was the buffoon, who is plainly simpleminded and of no real threat. It was the aura of menace which characterized the best sort of staged madness. Exercising his particular dementia, the villain would thrust the most ruthless and selfish manner of evil upon the hero. This was true of both human and supernatural beings, although the villain from-beyond-the-earth would hardly be analyzed as mad, since his actions were not subject to the rules of psychology. Nonetheless, all villains had madness in their actions, a madness perceived as such by the audience and by the characters in the play. Operating through their own set of standards, the madman's desires—and there is always lust in the villain's goals—were improvident and lacking circumspection. Really, then, it *was* the villain's assault against life's mores and norms which psychologically defined him. And it was his violent methods that made him more than an ordinary iconoclast. It was madness which made conflict, and from conflict came virtue, the opponent of madness.

Unlike classic tragedy, where madness is foisted upon mortals by the gods, the melodramatic madman has no cosmic interpretation. His lust for power, money, and carnality are very human, and it is through that humanness that his terrible deeds are all the more hideous. The hallmark of classic melodrama resides in this battle between righteousness and madness, and a madness that is not subtle, but almost uncontrollably violent and exceedingly dangerous. It is danger that brings about the necessary conflict. The mad villain has become the prototype for the melodrama of today. Ralph Harper points to the *James Bond* villains as throwbacks to earlier concepts of madness in outlook:

There are two kinds of villains in the Bondiad (James Bond novels which highlight villains): the independents like Dr. No and Drax, who are megalomaniacs, and the organization villains like Le Chiffre and Blofeld, who are sadists. Seen by a "cardboard booby" they are as bogeymen to a little child, a Mardi Gras *grotesque*. (*Thriller* 31-2)

As with the other parts of the triad, the intention here is to define a term. In the subsequent analysis of Fitzball's dramaturgy all of the parts in the triad will become apparent, inasmuch as all of them have a dramatic connotation beyond their usual denotation.

The extent to which madness operates is in conjunction with what the fiend does to the hero and the heroine, and the only reason to label a figure as being mad is insofar as his actions imperil the hero and heroine. He is also the main interest in the melodrama. Whether the madman is completely psychopathic or partly schizoid, but with some redeeming qualities, the madman is a criminal, *ipso facto*, and a social pariah of deviant and criminal proportions. His misdeeds have social and political implications, as Vernon Fox attests:

> Crime is defined in the law as behavior sufficiently deviant to damage society and to merit, therefore, legal action and the intervention of society into the lives of citizens who so deviate. It is a sociopolitical event. (28)

In Fitzballian fare, the hero symbolizes the normalcy thus assaulted by the madness in murder, theft, organized crime, white-collar offenses, political deceit, and professionally plotted crimes (Fox 17). Characters in melodrama represent either good or evil; therefore, whenever the villain attacks the hero, he is, in a sense, attacking society. As in the lurid plays of Fitzball, wherein the villain is human, the street scoundrel, criminologically, is the most virulent blackguard, the kind identifiable with the theater-goer.

The acme of both real and staged madness results in violence, especially when the culprit is dangerous. And violence was/is one of classic melodrama's keener attractions. Fitzball's plays are imbued with riotous ferocity. And, to be truthful, there is in man's soul a perverse allurement to dangerous outbursts. One may see this by the extreme popularity of melodramatic entertainment through the years. The sensational triad is built upon this potentiality to yield an almost sybaritic form of vehemence. The Grand Guignol remains dominant in modern culture due to its emphasis on the lurid, the grotesque and the violent. Mankind has always been surrounded by nuances of violence; therefore, it seems natural that art's reflection should entail those nuances. With madness as the core behind human and theatrical disturbance, Theodore and Renee Millon offer a cogent definition of madness, a term of intrinsic complexity on stage and off:

> The locator of a working definition of insanity would do better to jump off of a cliff rather than hope to pin down a psychologist for help! The circumlocution involved therein would astonish even the most esoteric phenomenologist! For my purpose, the insane displays adaptive inflexibility in relating to others, or in achieving his ends. He selfishly relies on a monolithic personality. Secondly, his dealings with his environment foster vicious circles, whereby he is constantly beset by confrontations through his outlandish desires and actions. (6)

If one quality defines the dramatic madman, it is "outlandish desires" that are ruthlessly pursued at any cost. The madman must also show aggression, or, in the words of Arnold Buss, "the response that delivers noxious stimuli to another organism" (1). Never far from beastly activities, the madman of melodrama aggressively telegraphs his severe personality disorders beyond mere meanness and contumacy. With the advent of Freudian psychology and criminological sociology in the nineteenth-century, the villain was inspected as more than a thug. The consummate brigand, therefore, might possess a compulsive, schizophrenic personality; antisocial reactions; and sadistic tendencies (Coville, Costello, and Rouke 120-7). In fact, with the influence of psychology, a whole new methodology of literary criticism, psychological criticism, was created regarding all literary genres. Though generally neglected, the melodramatic character may now, within this artistic range, be subject to such an analysis. This is to say that the melodramatist has more to say to mankind than the superficial nature of his work would indicate. Certainly, in modern melodramas, such as Patrick Hamilton's *Angel Street*, Frederick Knott's *Wait Until Dark*, Edward Chodorov's *Kind Lady*, and Martin Vale's *The Two Mrs, Carrolls*, the villains are more than extraordinarily iniquitous: they are depraved. The chilling and enthralling aspect of madness in melodrama is the startling occurrence of it. This is the artistic ploy of madness. Never really dormant, if one is keen enough to sense it—and that is the excitement in watching madness take shape on the stage—madness always asserts itself in either a physical or mental trapping. As John Fraser skillfully cites, violence in all art portends or mirrors that *Hydish* nature in all of us *Jekylls*.

Violence, in this view of things, demonstrates the "real nature of man, his fundamental disorderliness and will to destruction, his hatred of constraints, his resentment of ideas and ideals and all other artificial constructions. Hence, the artist who deals honestly with violence...holds up a mirror in which he can contemplate the essential filthiness, nastiness, and beastliness of mankind. The truest artists from this point of view are ones like Celine, Zola, Burroughs, Selby, Sade, and Genet, or Shakespeare. And behind these hover not only some of the Existentialist feelings about the meaningless of absurdity of existence, but...the violence and indifference to nature. To involve oneself in violence, is to compel one into thought about oneself and man and society, sometimes very painful and diconcerting thought. (109-10)

Madness in melodrama, certain of its outrageous and predictable flair, does have an Existential quality about it. The madman has thrown social responsibility and gregarious concern to the wind, in seeing the world as absurd and exploitable. Without this realization, the villain may neither embody the roots of madness, nor extend the macabre mood of the play. This *Schadenfreude* is the key to violence. If it seems that the sensational triad revolves around the villain, that is a correct assumption. Michael Booth acknowledges the grim power of the villain, that is in a dedicated alliance with the gloominess of macabre drama. Fitzball almost defines his plays by the actions of the mad villain.

> The moving force of melodrama, however, is not the hero, as a rule a passive creature, but the villain. The villain thinks, chooses, initiates action, alters his plans, makes new ones. The hero is merely the punching bag of the villain's brain, the pawn of his chessboard. The villain is a remarkably purposeful man: revenge on the hero, the acquisition of his money and property, and the possession of the heroine are his objectives, and with relentless singlemindedness he pursues them. (*English Melodrama* 18)

In short, the villain defines the caliginous nature of the macabre drama and does so until he is dispatched. Soulless, the villain has no idea of his insanity and, therefore, uses any means for his diabolical end. In Augustin Daly's *Under the Gaslight,* the evil Byke ties Snorky to the railroad track. The whole intention of this act is to ready the audience for the cliff-hanging rescue, the culmination of the morality play. Without cosmic dimensions, madness in melodrama is there to provide a ruthless blackguard and an obstruction to goodness. In these capacities lay moral judgments and reactions. As the harbinger of the triad, the villain becomes an heretical metaphor to the symbols of goodness and, therefore, completes the moral spirit of the melodrama. In the previous constituents of the triad, horror-terror and crime, a connection was theorized between each trait and society. Horror had an aesthetic bond with the type of florid and ghastly plays wanted by the populace. Crime had its link with the notorious lifestyles and squalid circumstances suffered by the laboring class. In each case, then, the public's shadow was cast onto the stage, in either a figurative or "dramatically licensed" way. But what of madness? Was there more to this phenomenon than merely a dramaturgic scheme? Or, was its pathology in some way presented vicariously on the stage? Of course, the realists and the naturalists would treat such issues in the accepted social-thesis manner to come. However, it is accurate to say that insanity was an acute problem in the nineteenth-century, in a time where the medical and lay concepts of this predicament were confused and baffling, to save the least. Oftentimes, insanity was treated as criminality. Thus, the dramatist had a social prescription for the mad criminal.

In *Discipline and Punishment,* Michel Foucault, in describing the structure of nineteenth-century English prisons, states the following about the human contents of the typical cells in the building: "All that is needed, then, is to place a supervisor in a central tower and to shut up in each cell a madman, a patient, a condemned man, a worker or a schoolboy" (200). The madman was just another sort of felon in the light of day, or a scourged embarrassment hidden in the dark of the family attic. And, although the following quotation concerns nineteenth-century America, its poignancy and application have much in common with England's attitude towards insanity. Otto Bettman inveighs correctly about a social issue that still haunts mankind and gives the artist matter for comment.

Doctors of the period remarked on the high incidence of insanity in America. In his article, "Despotism in Lunatic Asylums," Dr. D.B. Eaton noted that insanity "had become more frequent and more fatal"—at a ratio of increase far exceeding that of the population. And the causes of this increase, according to Dr. George Beard's classic treatise American Nervousness, the country's rapid growth, the displacement of people by moving West, and the overcrowding of cities. (150)

The parallels between conditions in America and in England concerning mental abnormality and its causes (overcrowded cities, disorientation, displacement, and poverty) are unsettling and substantial. Moreover, staged madness may have had its impetus by way of the asylum. The actor Edwin Forrest once went to an asylum to study insanity for his role in *King Lear*. Fitzball was a keen observer of mankind in all of his conditions, so it may be reckoned that he had observed the mad in their habitat of the streets or hospital. In any event, as with horror and crime, madness-on-stage had its share of human reflection. And, as with horror and crime, madness was given full reign on the melodramatic stage in the person of the villain, a characterization of true art by Fitzball.

The Triad's Conclusion

With the sensational triad now explained, as both social and artistic modes, the upcoming criticism of Fitzball's plays will demonstrate this playwright's efficacious use of the triad. The historical place of crime in Fitzball's London; the eternal interest in horror and terror as artistic devices of human consciousness; and the psychological interpretation of what madness may indicate in human terms become obvious tools in Fitzball's dramatic response to these traits in society. Combine the sensational triad with Fitzball's "blue-red fire" and there emerges a dramatic grotesquerie of exceptional appurtenance. Through his unity of design, Fitzball weaves a unique world abnormally enchanting. It is a dream-world where virtue ends evil and escapism foils reality. Fitzball's macabre theatre is fanciful and the sensational triad vulnerable to the hero's quest, quite unlike the triad's forbidding power in reality. The sensational triad is compelling because it is the circumstance upon which so many of Fitzball's plays are built. It is compelling because in the narrative tradition—as old as story telling and as new as film—man's imaginative inclination towards the uncanny is unending, as Drake Douglas well surmises in his book *Horror*. In Fitzball the unusual is made usual.

Why, then, this fascination for a world that no longer exists, this desire to be frightened by creatures whom we know lived only in the imagination of man? Why, in the latter portion of the ultra-scientific twentieth century, does civilized man still cling, like the most superstitious peasant and ignorant savage, to his tales of vampirism, lycathropy and monster-making. Why has horror not gone the way of other outmoded fashions? Perhaps the answer—without involving ourselves in pathological and psychological meanderings—lies in the mind of man itself, springing from mankind's hereditary fear of the dark. Why, then, do we permit ourselves to revel in literature and films that play on this ancient fear, that help us to people the darkness with the strange and the terrifying creatures that, in our early years, caused us to lie trembling in our beds with blankets pulled over our ears? Perhaps we are striking out at our own childhood subconsciously proving to ourselves that we know those early fears to be groundless and can now turn to them for a source of amusement. Perhaps Georges Lefebre had part of the answer when he wrote of another time: "Melancholy and tears, despair and horror...reflection of ancient ruins...shook the boredom of ordered life." (10-11)

Chapter III
Fitzball's Dramaturgy: Aristotle's Elements

Because all theatrical forms are indebted, in one way or another, to the dramatic theories of Aristotle in *The Poetics*, the thrust of this chapter will be twofold in showing: 1) that Fitzball's dramaturgy indeed used Aristotle's six elements in necessary, albeit esoteric, ways to give the classic melodrama a theatrical integrity of its own, and 2) that the management of these elements in the melodrama was instrumental in giving this form its historic reputation. In short, Fitzballian melodrama will serve as a model in addressing these points, points that, hopefully, will serve as an illumination as to the melodrama's purpose and uniqueness in theatrical art.

Two exemplary plays by Fitzball will be analyzed. *The Devil's Elixir* will be critiqued according to Aristotelean foundations, and *Jonathan Bradford* will be investigated as standard Fitzballian dramaturgy in Chapter Four. Other works will be referred to, when warranted, for further examples of how sensationalism was exploited dramatically and theatrically. While popular with patrons, Fitzball's plays were often panned by critics unaware of the auteur artistry in his methodology. This chapter will hopefully correct those early misapprehensions. An inspection of Fitzball's macabre miscellany will demonstrate that the writer had worthy intentions and a stable artistry for much of what was casually termed "blue-fire" and Blood-and-Thunder. Ironically, the fare produced by Fitzball now may be criticized as a presage for today's macabre sensationalism, which takes dramatic form in the soap opera and horror film, entertainment's most lucrative, theatrical presentations. By these analyses, Fitzball's aesthetics and obligations for his era will become apparent, too. His vocation as a hack yielded some wonderful, escapist *trash,* as well as some expertly crafted dramas. And, since *theatrical tash* is a slang term for any theatricality that whisks the viewer into a fantasy world through its simple and exciting premises, then Fitzball should be commended for indeed helping man quit his troubles for at least a while. Art has always served that social service since its inception. Such exploitative fun is always the product of the dramatist who is knowledgeable in human psychology, a student of man's fancy and titillations. Also, the interspersion of the sensational triad within man's psychological matrix gives added interest to the direction of Fitzball's blend of horror, escape, and humanity.

Aristotle and Fitzball

In applying Aristotelean criticism to *The Devil's Elixir,* one must begin with the understanding that literary principles do not always underscore all of drama. Paul Young makes this distinction obvious:

The difference between the play which is literature and the play which is not literature, which is in fact only a form of journalism, is that one is internal and the other is external. It is to be felt more easily than it is to be defined. And the play succeeds because of its possession of qualities not in themselves literary, because it has the intangible but essential something which makes a story interesting to the multitude when it is set forth on action on the stage. (43-4)

To be sure, this "intangible something or feeling" was ingrained in *The Devil's Elixir.* First performed at the Theatre Royal, Covent Garden, on April 20, 1829, the play quickly became an impassioned prototype of Fitzballian sensationalism and brought Blood-and-Thunder to new heights of Grand Guignol exultation. Wimsatt and Brooks say that the aestheticism of nineteenth-century art encompassed "the exotic and the bizarre; the morbid and the ugly; and the gilded and the artificial" (487). In keeping with this current sense of aesthetic dogma, the *play* struck all the right timbres: righteousness and profanity, beauty and ugliness, satisfaction and lust. And all of these traits were gothically set amidst horror, terror, crime, and madness. The play emerged not only as good escapism, but also as a pungent morality play in the Faustian tradition.

Beginning with the two-act play's title—and most of the classic melodramas were either two or three acts in length—*The Devil's Elixir; or, The Shadowless Man: A Musical Romance,* one may presume that the Coleridgean "suspension of disbelief" is a mandatory prerequisite. With Fitzball, this mandate is always necessary. The first act has five scenes; the second, four. The noun *Elixir* and the adjective *Shadowless* portend images of the strange and the eerie at once. In fact, *Elixir,* not *drink,* or *draught,* has about it the eldritch sensation of the Jekyll and Hyde concoction. And *Shadowlessness* presages that disconcerting image of the vampire, who casts no reflection, or, at the very least, that of a ghostly visitor from beyond this earth. From the outset, Fitzball has intentionally created an initial atmosphere of horror and terror by the work's very title. And for nineteenth-century melodramatists, the title was a crucial preview of the plot to come. According to some of the lengths, the title and subtitle almost bespoke the entire play. In the best storytelling manner, Fitzball's titular theme would define persistently the tone of the plot. As a romance, one understood that the play would be fanciful and that its music would be an integral, emotional factor.

The setting is typically gothic and the conflict almost medieval in its clash of good against evil: the adversary is from hell itself and the protagonist is a cleric. The Faustian syndrome is thereby established in a battle that is symbolically archetypal. Fitzball's hero, Francesco, and the villain, Gortzburg, have about them a Jacobean aura and manner of design. It could be said of Fitzball what was said of Webster: "We feel that the author had a certain depth of tone and intricacy of design in view, combining sensational effect and sententious pregnancy of diction in works of laboured art" (Symonds 15). Redolent of Webster's *The Duchess of Malfi* and Tourneur's *The Atheist's Tragedy* in its presentation of evil incarnate, while lacking tragic dimensions, the play intones a Marlovian theme: damnation resulting from lust and the loss of soul. As an example of the type of drama emulated by Fitzball, Webster's 1613 tragedy deals with a Duchess marrying a commoner and the hatred that union causes in her brothers, Ferdinand and the Cardinal. Consequently, she is tormented because of her marriage to Antonio, the commoner, by Bosola, her brothers' henchman. Bosola, the demonically ridden protagonist of this tragedy of blood, murders the Duchess, her children, Antonio, and the Cardinal. Ferdinand kills Bosola and then goes insane. Before dying, Bosola utters the blank verse-type of poetic diction so enjoyed by Fitzball:

0, I am gone! We are only like dead walls or vaulted graves,/ That, ruined, yield no echo. Fare you well!/ 0, this gloomy world!/ In what a shadow, or deep pit of darkness/ Doth womanish and fearful mankind live. (Symonds 217)

Fitzball's tragically induced melodramas aspired to the heights of theme and poetry illustrated by Webster's masterpiece. Within such a popular thematic, one with which all people might identify in mentally lusting for utopian pleasures, Fitzball struck the type of melodrama that would never lack audience appeal (Marx 182). But such was the goal of all melodrama: commercial success. Thus, by its exaggerated polarizations between good and evil, which William Van O'Conner noted as theatrically valid in a Renaissance, or Renaissance-like, play, Fitzball was able to weave a drama of dynamic attraction (O'Conner 70). Using theological, as well as theatrical, means, Fitzball drew a villain of hellish proportions, a throwback to the demon-monster of the liturgical and Renaissance era. It must be always remembered, however, that Fitzball fancied himself a throwback, an anachronism, if you will, to Elizabethan prosody. Thus, there was a justifiable, intellectual rationale for this kind of work, aside from thrills.

Horror and terror, both physical and atmospheric, set the play's tone, but Fitzball's phantasmagoria differed from his Renaissance counterparts above in that it revolved around melodrama's dream-world, not around the ghoulish gore attributed to Webster and Tourneur (O'Conner 85). Fitzball's horror mingled relaxation with shock. His terror had chilling delight. And his heroes always arose victorious. His world was dark, true, but it also had sunlight, the ray of hope. In Webster and Tourneur, there was neither hope nor smile through the enveloping terrors of that pervasive dark. Fitzball's treatment of the Faustian theme was sincere, yet melodramatically exotic. However, it was this unholy alliance, this inspection into a controversial subject, albeit a popular one—a monk's involvement with evil—that raised the play above so much "penny-dreadful" material. As in all worthwhile melodramas indulging in the supernatural, the uncanny served as more than mere fear. Gortzburg became more than a hobgoblin; his physical and mental hideousness was a metaphor for any craven desire that degenerated after it was obtained. More than this, Gortzburg was the latent alter-ego of Fransesco. He was, in fact, the doppelgänger which, as in the case of the Frankenstein monster, caused much grief to befall his ally-in-crime, Francesco.

There is sometimes an unwarranted smugness about the role of the supernatural in drama, a patronizing attitude that such a component precludes seriousness. Of course, plays ranging from *Macbeth,* to *Death Takes a Holiday,* to *Outward Bound,* have made such notions vapid. Supporting grand theatricalism the romantic melodrama used the supernatural as a dynamic symbol of either good or evil, a spiritual manifestation of morality and carnality, in much the same way that the ancient Greeks used their supernatural entities. In many of his best plays, Fitzball consanguineously touted bygone eras and preternatural subjects, all constituents for romance. His exploitation of monsters was one of his most gifted attributes and a trademark of Blood-and-Thunder excitement. Gortzburg shared many of the qualities held by yet another Fitzballain devil, Vanderdecken, in *The Flying Dutchman; or, The Phantom Ship* (1827), which some critics have reckoned his best monster nautical play: "The most famous is Vanderdecken who arrives and vanishes in blue and red fire...The play also contains a spectacular ship scene, sinister spirits, and comic relief, necessary for melodrama" (*English Melodrama* 85). With this background material in mind, the analysis of *The Devil's Elixir* will suggest a more sympathetic and appreciable persuasion regarding Fitzball's style and his individuation of Aristotle's principles.

Fitzball was an able adapter, not only of other dramas, but of other types of literature. *The Devil's Elixir* was based upon Ernst Hoffman's *Peter Schlemile*. And *Schlemile* has come to mean a *simpleton* in the vernacular. Suggested as a project to Fitzball by the stenographer Stanfield, the play was originally rejected by the Drury Lane, until Fanny Kemble recommended that it be done for the Easter season. Because of the play's similarity to *The Bottle Imp*, then playing at the English Opera House, the management at the Drury Lane had thought the play repetitious. Fitzball received two hundred pounds for it and always considered the fee extraordinarily low (1: 178). The *Examiner* said of the extravaganza:

...the changes indeed work so beautifully at this house that old strangers as we are, we could scarcely believe but that it was some fairy vision. The clouds disparted and floated so noiselessly and etherially. (262)

The success of the play was due to Fitzball's concept of plot—the most important element for Aristotle of the six—in his overall dramatic system. To understand the distinction of the melodramatic idea of plot, Theodore Hatlen well explains it:

...the writers of melodrama were not men interested in the literary aspects of drama; they were men of the theatre...who knew all the tricks of the stage...skilled manipulators of characters and situations much like our present writers of "B" pictures and television plays whose approach to writing is grounded on the idea that anything is legitimate which works. The plot of melodramas relied heavily on story value. The audience did not come to probe character, to listen to bright parlor talk, or to consider perplexing social problems. They preferred those dramatic situations that showed characters against fearful odds. The art of playwrighting, therefore, became the art of devising scenes of excitement. Melodrama exaggerated climaxes and crises so that the structure of the play is a series of peaks of action, rather than a well-knit steady progression of logically related events. (91)

Plot

As is the case, any generality has exceptions. Not only was Fitzball no run-of-the-mill dramatic poseur, he was an artist of considerable theoretical and practical knowledge. He saw, as Hatlen correctly diagnoses, that the melodrama's power to tell a good story was of immense importance. Fitzball's plots, mainly by virtue of his being a hack, were tailored to meet the requirements of his audiences, which usually meant escapism. But the same truism could be aimed at Shakespeare—for no playwright thrived on an audience more than he—or at the majority of dramatists stretching back into the darkness of fifth-century Greece. Euripides used plot as only a background for the rapturous personage of Medea, for example. *Medea* is consumed by Medea's frantic and overpowering personality. Euripides' plot is no tidy chain-of-events; it is given meaning by a protagonist whose actions render the viewer engulfed (Harvey 171). It is for this very reason that in melodrama one remembers less of the plot and more the characters. The carefully wrought melodramatic plot is the stand on which the character speaks. This is why the same plot may be retold and rewritten in melodrama. Contrivance in melodrama is no malediction concerning plot. The plot simply fails if the characters are unattractive, uninteresting and understated.

To be sure, the *mimesis,* or *dramatic imitation of life,* pertinent to all renderings of reality, has not in Fitzballian terms the organic and scientific display theorized by Aristotle. Interpreting the sage's idea on plot, a melodramatist, more that any other stylist, uses his imagination to produce a journey into whatever bizarre, uncanny, and absurd notion he wishes to occur. The logic is that of *Alice* in *Wonderland* respective to Fitzball. And in worlds that cannot logically exist, Fitzball contrives them through stage wonders. A summary of the plot in *The Devil's Elixir* will indicate just how Fitzball created a plot for his own fantastic ends: a surrealistic combination of romanticism, medievalism, and humanism through philosophy and art.

Francesco, a monk, is besieged by the hellish demon, Gortzburg. The monster has recently been released from imprisonment, in the Land of Shadows, to wreck his revenge upon mankind by seducing one who is losing faith. That target is Francesco, whose piety is waning out of love and lust for the fair Lady Aurlia. When his fervor can no longer be restrained—in true Faustian accountability—Francesco agrees to succumb to Gortzburg's tantalizing offer of being transformed into the handsome, virile Count Hermogen by way of a magic drought, or elixir. Fitzball's curious twist in this "Jekyll and Hyde" circumstance is that there is another Hermongen, who is manly, who is Aurelia's lover, and who is—Francesco's brother. The bargain struck, which is Francesco's soul given to Gortzburg if Aurelia accepts his lothario nature, Francesco, as the impostor, imprisons the real Hermogen, and sets out to woo Aurelia. Luckily, however, Aurelia senses the difference in the masquerader and, penitent, Francesco is saved from damnation at the last minute, the usual cliffhanger in melodrama. Faith overpowering lust, Francesco and the released Hermogen are reconciled to each other and to Aurelia, and the thwarted Gortzburg is spectacularly thrust back into hell. Again himself, the cleric rediscovers his faith. Morality vanquishes carnality and evil fails in the presence of goodness, the persistent reward in melodrama.

At this point, a word about the Victorian infatuation with theatrical splendor should be stated. Sybil Rosenfeld sums up this historical fascination thusly:

Scenic illusion in this period was moving toward realism. Audiences wished to be transported to actual places and periods so that the scene designers' art was concentrated on reproducing a romantic aura of the world...through spectacular transformations the imaginations of the designers were given full play. (11)

Of curse, what Rosenfeld is alluding to, and which remains a staple of melodrama's attraction in any media, are special effects. Then, as in current fantasy, plot was secondary to belching fire, hopping hobgoblins in hell, and the wild invigoration on all levels. The play's frenzy spilled into the audience. For Fitzball the plot's unrealistic happenings were quite ordinary. Fitzball's horror-morality romance was executed before the illusion of physical sets denoting realism, but a realism based upon fancy and no more. Fitzball's magic, like that of P.T. Barnum, transformed realistic illusion into emotional reality. And commercially it worked. Beyond mere intellect, Fitzball coerced imagination.

At this juncture, mention should be made of 0. Smith, the delightfully protean actor who played Gortzburg. He had substituted the O, for his given name of *Richard,* after essaying the character "Obi" in a play. Excelling in powerful characterizations of the bizarre, Smith had played Frankenstein's monster, in Milner's classic version, and the creature Vanderdecken in Fitzball's acclaimed *The Flying Dutchman.* More will be written about Smith later. Theatrically, the plot in *The Devil's Elixir* comes forth as an expression of total theatre: a meeting of human conflict, through artistic denotation, with audience empathy as a singular goal. In short, the entire production combines all of the four pertinent ingredients necessary for theatre to exist: a script, an audience, a presentation, and a theatre space. Ordinarily, a drama sometimes lessens, aesthetically, one of these key functions, but this play covers each superbly. Fitzball was aware that some of his plays had failed to involve each aspect satisfactorily, as in the case of *Nitocris; or, The Ethiop's Revenge,* wherein the script was too "high brow." However, *The Devil's Elixir* was flawless, pristine, sensational theatre of the macabre. More than a potboiler, the play had a plot that was intriguing and iridescent. The *Theatrical Inquisitor* praised the work in this way:

> …the play might well be called a melo-drame; as the music does not seem to grow out of the action, but to be given at assist and accompany it. Act IV is vigorously drawn. (259)

As a side note about Fitzball's love for grandiosity, his tragedy *Edwin* possessed a plot filled with action and frenzy: ghosts, murder, and finely etched villains, one of whom leaps from a cliff in a dramatic suicide. Fitzball's plots, in his major works where he had the necessary time for contemplation, were important to him, even though his dynamic characters dominated attention. In *Edwin,* for instance, he composed the tragedy in Elizabethan blank verse, in an attempt to rejoin the heights of English tragedy, if only vicariously, and composed the song "The Robber's Glee."

The stage directions for *The Devil's Elixir* were written by observers of the play since Fitzball apparently little cared for such technicalities, but such an attitude was not uncommon. Most of his surviving works are the stage editions, or acting editions, which make this information all the more fascinating. It seems appropriate that a dramatist, who was professionally engaged to write for the theatre, should leave examples of practical scripts for posterity, inasmuch as the "working scripts" mirrored a concept of "the working man's theatre."

As noted earlier, Fitzball felt himself to be an anachronism. In his plot for *The Devil's Elixir,* he used a Chorus in the Greek tradition of commenting upon the dramatic action. As Gortzburg flies away—by the use of wires—the chorus chants, "Away, away, through earth and sky/ On demon's wings we fly! We fly! We fly!/ with fell intent,/ On mischief bent/ We fly, we fly we fly!" (Wischhusen 9). The hellish setting for the monster's departure is in no way fulsome, but is morbidly enchanting, eerie, and hauntingly romantic. This was the primacy of Fitzball's artistry. He used fright as theatrical grandeur, and his exploitation of that distinction was towards an epic sensation, not as a haphazard and tawdry shock effect. In any play of his, cheapness had no dramaturgic or theatrical place, and that was true of his potboilers as well. Fitzball's innate artistry prohibited such prostitution; therefore, his Grand Guignol association was one of integrity.

In concluding Fitzball's use of Aristotle's element, a contrast between his art and the ideation of Aristotlelean plot needs attention. For the sage, the plot (mythos) had to have a distinct beginning, middle, and end, all of which configured an internal completeness, with catharsis as tragedy's goal. Classic melodrama combined the episodic and climactic forms in plot. Summarily, the episodic plot "covers an extensive period of time, sometimes many years, and ranges over a number of locations...and episodic plays do not necessarily follow a close cause-and-effect development" (Edwin Wilson 154-5). The climactic form of plot demands that earlier events be explained, for dramatic information, for the audience's benefit. Classic Greek tragedy used this technique. This form also commands a brief time (temporal) span for the play's action. The dramatic construction is tight, with little accommodation for indulgent activities (Edwin Wilson 148-53). Fitzballian drama was a hybrid, inasmuch as it used qualities from both structures: this was the structural hallmark of melodrama's freewheeling attitude towards self-evaluation. We must remember that structural logic was the melodramatist's prerogative. Also, non sequiturs would often propel, *pro forma*, the action onward. It was a convention that melodrama devotees accepted as part of the genre's startling systematization. It was not uncommon for the villain, as in *Edwin*, to kill himself by suddenly jumping off of a cliff to end the conflict; however, such cockeyed action delighted the devotees, expectant of such alarms. Always the storyteller, Fitzball's pointed narratives may be summed up in a statement by Walt Whitman, concerning what romantic literature should deploy: "I seek less to display any theme or thought more to bring you in to the atmosphere of the theme or the thought—there to pursue your own flight" (Loban, Ryan, and Squire 489). Plot, for Fitzball, was a flight of romantic fancy that uplifted the spirit. Hatlen generalizes that this romantic ideology was germane to melodrama:

He [the melodramatist] is an adept storyteller and showman. He not only knows the potentialities of the stage, but also the audience for whom he writes. Logic does not interest him so long as his play gives the impression of credibility. (92)

Character

If plot were the element of authorial teasing, Aristotole's second element, *character,* was for the melodramatist one of dynamism, a *sic itur as astra* ("thus one goes to the stars"), a dramaturgic way for the playwright to find his greatest adulation. Under the aegis of characterization, melodrama scored some of its most memorable traits. It was the character, in the typical spectacle of the genre, that dominated the play, a kind of supererogation of all the elements into one. We have already noticed how Medea's passionate portrayal dominated the play in which she was featured, and Euripides, who stressed this mode of individual psychology in his characterizations, initiated this strong type of characterization that would become one of melodrama's most intriguing features. Kitto has described the following constituency to be found as usual in the tragic (Aristotelean) character:

> He must not be a saint, or his downfall would be revolting, nor a villain, whose downfall might be edifying but would not be tragic. He must therefore be intermediate, better rather than worse.... Medea, like all melodramatic protagonists, is never really different from what we see her to be. (Kitto 188-9)

From tragedy to melodrama, characterization was a presentational, rather than an internal, operation. Usually bombastic and captivating, classic melodrama extolled the virtue of glossy acting and resonate vocalization, spawned from of classical oratory. Oscar Brockett implies this bond between melodrama's histrionic relation to acting and the same idea in Greek acting in writing, "The Greeks seemed to have placed considerable emphasis upon the voice, for they judged actors above all by the beauty of vocal tone and ability to adapt manner of speaking to mood and character" (*History* 27). In fact the voice was one of melodrama's key factors regarding acting, and vocal training remained a prerequisite for acting well into the twentieth-century, when many a great actor's characterization on the stage was as much involved with the richness of the voice, as with the any other part of his character sketch.

Aristotle insinuated the modern concept of character through his definitions of *ethos,* or "the moral element in character," through which that certain "state of direction of the will" was exposed; and *dianoia,* the thought, or 'the intellectual element, which was implied in all rational conduct, through which alone ethos could find outward expression" (340).

Aristotle said that the best type of plot was that one which had surprises (reversals and recognition segments). Melodrama certainly qualified in that respect. However, concerning characterization, classic melodrama was straightforward: the villain and hero were early established, even if the hero, for instance, assumed a disguise until the play ended. But to set the Aristotelean comparison aright on character, and what we know as characterization, qualifications arise. Aristotle's second most esteemed element, *ethos,* had to do with the persona's ethical and moral makeup. It must be remembered that Aristotle's *Poetics* (335-322 B.C.) was dealing with tragedy and comedy, and the tragic hero's *hubris* (tragic flaw) was a result of ethical and moral plight. On the other hand, the more familiar *character* meant the physicalization of the persona's psychological disposition on stage. Hence, there were heroes, villains, comics, et al. In a way, then, melodrama took Aristotle's *ethos* and concretized it into a representative on stage. As seen by H. Coombes, literary art was always striving to inject into the viewer a certain feeling and/or empathy for the artwork and the characters involved in it. Melodrama placed the highest priority upon that directive.

When a good writer is expressing feeling he does it with the greatest possible precision. We see that this does not entail hair-splitting analysis or scientific lines, nor anything in the nature of lengthy exposition of inessentials. Rather it is a matter of finding exact and telling expression for an attitude which is the result of having felt the implications of a situation as fully, an inconclusive, as possible. As readers we both intensify and clarify our feelings when in contact with the worthwhile writer, who has both living feeling and a knowledge of his feelings. Instead of the vague, loose, and often muddled and other conventional feeling—expression of the inferior writer, he gives something individually and sharply felt. (95)

With some sharply-drawn personas, Fitzball issued excellent characterizations in *The Devil's Elixir,* such as a cunning and diabolical antagonist and a hero at war with his conscience. Francesco even managed to have a flaw, which may be called *pathetic,* rather than *tragic.* His fall was foiled, but Francesco's characterization had a certain depth akin to that of an "antihero." He was not the normal melodramatic hero by any means. Bernard Beckerman assesses character as "...the interpretation we attach to any individual's activity" (213). It is no overstatement to declare that character is the foundation upon which any drama rests. Without it, the plot goes nowhere. There simply can be no drama without conflict, and conflict comes from interaction among characters. Characterization spans the drama from its personas to its mood, and Aristotle's definition of tragedy seems inspired by the importance of characterization:

Tragedy, then, is an imitation of an action which is serious, complete, and has bulk, in speech that has been made attractive, using each of its species separately in the parts of the play; with persons performing the action rather than through narrative carrying to completion, through the course of events involving pity and fear, the purification of those painful or fatal acts which have quality. (Dukore 213)

Obviously, with the goal of drama (tragedy) being the catharsis of audience emotion (pity and fear), then the role of the drama's characters was preeminent. With persons performing various actions, Aristotle admonished that *ethos* must have indications of morality (goodness), propriety (honesty in depiction), and realism (empathy for the viewer), along with the personas being probable and comprehensible (Dukore 44). In other words, if the viewer could not, in some fashion, identify with the characters on stage, drama would fail in mirroring the human dilemma. Drama is a human art and, therefore, it must have the ability to attract and hold the attention of human beings. Fitzball was devoted to this principle, and his sensational triad symbolized the anxieties known to his patrons. As to character probability, what was staged as reality had to have some semblance to life. Melodrama, of course, took license with this proposition, as it did with many others, while adhering to a certain realistic theatricalism itself. The audience had never seen a demon in person, but it had seen devils on stained-glass windows; so, knowingly, Fitzball merely transferred icons from life to images on the stage. The probability factor remained inviolate. If the viewers were to be subjectively educated, the characters had to represent a philosophy or position in the dramatist. If not in the Ibsen tradition of the *raisonneur* (spokesman), Fitzball's plays always stressed morals. Even at its most lurid and unreal, *The Devil's Elixir,* through its contrasting characters, offered morality instead of lust, truth instead of deception. Above all, the characters demonstrated Fitzball's attitudes by being extraordinary symbols of social norms and derelictions. Edwin Wilson substantiates this attribute thusly: "...standing apart from ordinary people and being larger than life...they generally represent men and women at their worst or best, at some extreme of human behavior" (190). Fitzball was committed to enlarging this representation, as far as his theatricalism would permit.

S.H. Butcher has noted that Aristotle viewed characterization as presenting man the way he ought to be (12). Aristotle advocated that the hero should be "like" us because no pity or fear could be projected towards a character unlike us (Kitto 188). Though scientifically trained, Aristotle did not want the imitative process to be a slavish copying of nature. "A work of art reproduces its original, not as it is in itself, but as it appears to the senses" (Aristotle 127). If ever a genre depended upon an emotional, thus sensual, diagnoses of mankind, it was melodrama, whose portrayal of good and bad was based solely upon an emotional appeal: the hero was righteous, at least most of the time; the villain was a fiend, at least most of the time. By virtue of operating within a simple and clearly cut world, melodramatic characters were either good or evil. The melodramatic imagination, at least in Fitzball's tradition, had no interest in complex shades of gray: goodness had to triumph and villainy had to be dispelled. Commenting upon the concern for dramatic characterization, Robert Corrigan has written, "In a play, consequently, the agents do not perform for the sake of representing their individual dispositions; rather the display of moral character is included as incidents of the plot" (78). Opposite to an endless sea of interpretations of the great tragedies by each succeeding generation, melodrama's predictability in characterization remains pretty much standardized. For all purposes, the character of Gortzburg will forever be a villain, while Richard III, for instance, always evil as a Shakespearean character, is open to interpretation as an historical figure. It is ironic that melodrama, a genre open to great creative laxity, remains a rather conservative form in the theatre. Hatlen addresses this issue:

In the black-and-white world of melodrama, men are divided into sharply opposed classes represented by the unblemished hero and the unspeakable villain. The first premise of melodrama is that there are two distinct kinds of men; the first premise of tragedy is that all men are essentially the same. (93)

Because of the difference between melodramatic and tragic figures, the reader may be amused by the calamity foisted upon the hero—knowing that he will prevail—but disturbed by the tragic figure, by realizing that we all have the propensity to become an egotistical Macbeth or rejected Willy Loman. We may never fight a dragon over a fair maiden, but we may very well fight the *monsters* of political corruption and vocational duress. As a unique blend of believability and reverie, universal concepts and singular oddities, the characters in *The Devil's Elixir* command enigmatic inspection.

Because of the Faustian theme, the characters rise above blandness. Not banal in the least, Francesco becomes a desperate character, perhaps one with tragic essences, had Fitzball permitted the monk's hubris (pride) to ultimately destroy him. The characters maneuver in a world of contrasts (the spiritual and the carnal, the noble and the treacherous), but, as in all good melodramas, virtue emerges triumphant. Interestingly enough, the final conflict between Francesco and Gortzburg is as much spiritual as it is physical. Usually, the altercation between ordinary heroes and villains in the final act is one of physical degrees, with their diverse ethics subordinated. Francesco is one of Fitzball's most moving heroes because he is torn by the forbidden, thereby giving way to true empathy from anyone who has violated a sacred trust. But, it is the intriguing, malicious Gotzburg, as the play's most enjoyable character, who steals our attention. Gortzburg is the sensational triad personified. He is hellishly horrible, his presence exuding terror; his crime is of the most pernicious type, spiritual destruction; and his gleeful laughter is like that of a mad banshee. Ironically, it is Fracesco's mental instability over Aurelia that sets the action in motion; therefore, the triadic element of madness is really Francesco's since Gotzburg is immune to human rudiments. Penzoldt sees the monster character as a literary, creative gem:

> The ghost (or monster) is the most constant figure in supernatural fiction. It appears from the beginning of literature. As far as the ghost in English fiction is concerned, volumes would be necessary to deal with its importance in the Elizabethan drama and later in the Gothic novel. In appearance, too, the "modern ghost" shows greater variety than the Gothic spook...the ghost is restricted by rules of neither time nor place. (325)

The gauntlet between man and "ghost" has many overtones here, and Gortzburg's character is representative of the trend in English fiction for such monsters, who have the power of hell with which to do battle. In corrupting Francesco, there is the metaphor of corrupting spiritual goodness. Through Gortzburg the viewer realizes his own spiritual complexes that he must correct in order to foil his personal demons in life. Of course, the fascination with Gortzburg's character has to do with man's general fascination with the eerie and uncanny, supported by sin and evil. In Gortzburg, Fitzball is actually representing a symbol, a conglomeration of all of those fabulous, mythological horrors in nightmares and of fantastic art: the chimera, dragon, gorgon, ogre, hippogriff, vampire, ghost, zombie, et al. Above all, Gortzburg is the cleric's doppelgänger, a title rating him over mere monstrosity. It is our allurement towards monsters which makes this demon beguiling and provocative. C.J.S. Thompson, aware of this eternal captivation with the grotesque, makes the following observation:

> Monsters have always excited mixed feelings of awe, horror, and curiosity. The word "monster" comes from the Latin root meaning "to warn,"and suggests something terrible, to be interpreted as an omen...beyond the normal curse of nature. (1)

As with Richard's hunchback, Gortzburg's ugliness, criminologically, signifies an internal perversion of tremendous account.

The gaudy and bizarre costuming of Gortzburg requires notation, inasmuch as melodrama put much emphasis upon how a character was dressed. In fact, costuming was an extension of characterization. The demon wore red body wings and a half tunic, and was always appearing in concert with red-blue fire. When not speaking, the monster continually lurked behind a transparent gossamer-scrim, thus making his evil continually sensed. Such a special effect was common for supernatural beings.

A telling aspect in Fitzball's notion of characterization, which agrees with the *ethos* of Aristotle, is the moral fibre. If Aristotle looked at character as indeed the ethical and intellectual (dianoia) dimensions of a persona, it was the melodramatic characterization which extended emotionalism for all it was worth. Melodrama's structure of conflict was simply the battle between right and wrong. In the violent and unsure era that produced Fitzballain dramaturgy, and arenas such as the harrowing "Blood Tub," there arose a need for such simplicity. Therefore, Aristotle and Fitzball may not be so separated, philosophically, as one might speculate. Of course, Aristotle's total idea of what character should be was as much ontological as it was dramatic. What Fitzball and other melodramatists did was to take morality and physicalize it, simply and identifiably; the same was done with immorality and evil. If Fitzball's plot for *The Devil's Elixir* appears puerile, Francesco and Gortzburg are structurally engrossing. Mankind could empathize with the lust that so motivated the monk and the pain which came from compromising with evil. Although Fitzball's characters exist in a fantasy world, where demons may exist, they are not empty and inconsequential. By Fitzball's emphasis on morality and ethics, Francesco's struggle is a poignant one. As Robert Finch has said "A character must have will and purpose, for in the final struggle between the forces of good and evil, both melodramatic entities (the hero and villain) become distinct" (53).

Thought

Thought (dianoia) is the next Aristotelean element to be considered in *The Devil's Elixir,* and, frankly, it is the one element criticized as usually opaque in melodrama's composition. For classic melodrama, this reprobation signifies the genre's simplified theme of virtue triumphant over any adversity. Yet, this "Horatio Alger" scheme was melodrama's selling point and undercurrent. And, within that theme, the playwright was able to create sundry predicaments that would lead to its validity. For Aristotle, thought was "...the faculty of saying what is possible and pertinent to a given situation" (Dukore 37). F.L. Lucas has commented that thought is "the intellectual side of Tragedy...illuminating the poet's world like a tropical sun, first quickening, then scorching it to dust and disillusion" (125). Having to do with both of these capacities, melodramatic thought bears the Horatian dictum of entertaining and educating the masses simultaneously, thereby formulating a catharsis that is both emotionally and intellectually prudent. Oscar Brockett gives a confederate definition of this complex term when he writes,

Thought includes the themes, the arguments, the overall meaning, focus, or significance of action...the playwright cannot avoid expressing ideas through the events and characterizations of the play...implying some view of human behavior. (*Introduction* 40)

Wrote Aristotle, "*Dianoia* is the thought, the intellectual element through which alone *ethos* can find outward expression...Under *dianoia* are included the intellectual reflections of the speaker" (Aristotle 340-3). For Fitzball his artistic *Weltanschauung* was based upon the values of melodrama and of his middle-lower class audiences. "Romantic tragedy" was then justified by moralizing. By substituting unrestrained amelioration for disturbing uncertainty, Fitzball sustained a theme very much wanted and needed by a public, upon whose commerce the theartre depended. Melodrama countered tragedy's *Weltschmerz* with an empathic fairy-land attraction of the best vintage. Instead of being unnerved by tragedy's psychological revelations, the viewer was uplifted by melodrama's spiritual hope. Altshuler and Janaro saw melodramatic thought as socially functional in the 1800s.

For the changing audience of the nineteenth century, tragedy in the old sense was unthinkable. The audience demanded theatrical rewards for those who adhered to its most sacred values. There could be no such thing as a sympathetic middle-class figure with a real flaw. If he held values contrary to those of his audience, he became a villain whose destruction was just, because "it served him right." (235)

Ormerod Greenwood once chortled, "The playwright can either invent a plot or steal one" (9). With classic melodrama, the writers stole the values of the audience and wove them into commerically theatrical presentations. As long as these plots—and Carlo Gozzi once tallied the number possible at 37—met the exciting and felicific expectations of the laboring class-audience, the same theme and, oftentimes, the almost-identical plot could be hashed and rehashed continually. Hence, because of this constant theme, melodrama became tainted with many a hackneyed product, by inferior dramatists cashing in on the public's desire for frolicking escapism. It was the talented melodramatist who took the theme and inserted into it a captivating plot. In melodrama, the plot was built around the theme, and not vice versa. Robert Corrigan has written, "Any situation is potentially dramatic. The playwright chooses a situation in which he senses dramatic possibilities can be developed in interesting ways" (57). The adjective *interesting* thus becomes the important precedent between art and ersatz, particularly for a hack such as Fitzball who wrote almost constantly. Strictly put, the plot had to become as purposeful as the theme for true success. To be sure, audiences attending a Fitzball play knew what to expect by not *knowing what to expect*. Fitzball experimented with his plots, while keeping thought in tact. He failed whenever he neglected this *modus operandi*. With the critics, he always knew the odds were either against him or arbitrary, at best. Of course, the theatre of the macabre lent itself quite flexibly to trial-and-error testing, and Fitzball's operation of the sensational triad could take many forms.

Plot and theme were always subject to the conventions of melodrama. Corrigan defined the term thusly: "Conventions are mutual agreements about the meanings of actions, gestures, and words that let us interpret and understand the social behavior of others almost spontaneously" (66). As has been noted, melodrama offered great freedom in plot, but gave restrictions concerning theme. Greenwood has mentioned, "The most important tools of the playwright are his actors. The playwright's task is to give them something to bite on— something which kindles, challenges, and supports them" (155). This "something to bite on" in *The Devil's Elixir* is Francesco's conflict, in soul and in body, with Gortzburg. The angst of having a cleric so contaminated gives the play a crucial solemnity and slap at Victorian social and artistic propriety. The helter-skelter finale does not completely mask the Faustian motif by Fitzball, although the play's melodramatic *conventions* prohibit any Goethean comparison. But, then, Fitzball was writing for an explicit audience, who had no use for philosophical musings in the tragic sense.

Melodrama, because it does involve spectacular encounters with violence and pain, has been called "the drama of disaster." Of course, tragedy, with which melodrama is always compared, and duly so, since melodrama emanated from its more esteemed sibling, has a disaster of its own, but, unlike that of melodrama, tragedy's disaster is by far more psychological than physical. Robert Heilman comments on melodrama's nomenclature in defining disaster in philosophical and physical terms.

In disaster, what happens comes from without; in tragedy, from within. In disaster, we are victims; in tragedy, we make victims of others and ourselves. In disaster, our moral quality, though it may be revealed, is secondary to the action; in tragedy, it is primary, the very source of what happens. The two contrasting structures of experience we confuse in different ways; each mode of confusion is a ploy in some way representative to our time. In tragedy, we act; in the literature of disaster, we are acted upon. We court trouble if we call the literature of disaster tragedy, for when we do that, we implicitly equate all unhappiness with what is done to us, and in so doing we make it easy to lose awareness of what we do. In tragedy, we contemplate our own errors. In disaster, we mark the errors of others and the flaws of circumstance. In tragedy, we are without complicity in evil. (15-39)

Heilman's differentiation between the disaster ideology in tragedy and in melodrama is helpful in assessing the two forms' accentuation on calamity. In tragedy, the disaster is in the hero's soul as destruction; in melodrama, the disaster, usually the nefarious work of the villain, is averted virtuously. Immediately, one may see that foiling a physical danger is easier than doing the same with a plague in the soul. For Fitzball the thought of melodrama was established, in either original or adapted plays. Either way, the audience received the same message. Adapting—some might call it *pirating*—old plays into new ones was common in the nineteenth-century, and Fitzball found it a respite from having to think up, as it were, new plots daily. As long as the themes were covered, and as long as the audiences like them, theatre managers had no remorse, inasmuch as box office economics absolved the artistic soul. Booth addresses this:

Since adaptation and straight theft went about unpunished they were widely practiced. From the manager's point of view, it was much quicker and cheaper to pay an author a few pounds to translate and adapt a French piece than to get him to write something new. The melodramatist was therefore inclined to borrow a story rather than invent one. (*English* Melodrama 49)

As long as it was made understandable, the plot could come from anywhere, and did—certainly in the case of Fitzball who was as busy adapting, as he was inventing. Heilman sums up thought by comparing conflict with melodrama and, of course, with tragedy. Conflict in melodrama—and, hence, the theme—is external, but is internal in tragedy: "Tragedy is concerned with man's nature; melodrama with his habits, as if those habits were the whole. In melodrama, we accept the part for the whole" (79). Melodrama's use of figurative language (i.e. metonymy or synecdoche) is in keeping with the symbolism of the genre. The responsibility of melodrama is the predicable, happy ending, which is immune to the disaster around and about. Now, in that ending, someone may die but that death is justified, as in Aikin's *Uncle Tom's Cabin*, with Uncle Tom happily going to his heavenly reward. It is indeed fascinating to note that Aristotle felt that "the happy ending was inferior to the tragic ending, that it was a concession to the weakness of the audience" (Kitto

112).

As thought, melodrama may be recapitulated by Heilman thusly: "Most melodramas end with arbitrary scenes of poetic justice in which couples are paired off, and rewards and punishments are parceled out according to the actions of the characters in the play" (94). Therein, the theme was the unifying social and artistic core for melodrama's high and lasting appeal. Thought may not have been complex, but its simplicity was all that was required for a commercial and artist bonanza.

Diction (lexis) may be one of melodrama's most powerful ramifications and connections to Aristotle's ancient edicts. It is almost impossible to separate melodramatic acting from melodramatic writing. Actors were immortalized in the nineteenth-century because of the age's emphasis upon elocution, that rhetorical grandiloquence of charm and power. Wrote Otis Skinner on the importance of good dialogue:

Diction, then is the means of clothing our ideas, of sustaining our arguments and sympathies with our daily companions in vocal terms which drew no attention from the subject matter. In its perfect form it is the common currency of our conversational intercourse with our fellowmen and its due reflection in the pulpit, the platform, the forum and the theatre. (34)

If classic melodrama left any legacy, it was its indulgence in euphonic, rhetorical dialogue. Of course, such direction was common in the *belles letteres* of the day, and, consequently, the Golden Age of melodrama reflected that literary heritage. The use of "beautiful speech" on stage was also an attempt, at least on Fitzball's part, to rekindle the lore of antiquity, especially the poetic prose of Elizbethan times. George Kennedy comments that Aristotle saw rhetoric as a persuasive, oratorical tool: "As we have seen, Aristotle thought of rhetoric as an art of communication, parallel to dialectic, whereas he saw poetics as a productive art, like painting" (115). In his embellished imitation of life, at least life's combative forms, Fitzball looked at dialogue as a verbal painting, a verbal realization of the pictoralized *tableau vivant,* if you will.

Lucas scores Aristotle's reference to diction in six categories: 1) ordinary speech, 2) foreign words translated into the vernacular, 3) "metaphorical" language, 4) "ornamental" language used by poets, 5) nonce words, and 6) modified language for exact purposes (126). For the philosopher, language must be clearly stated and not be meanly (basely) used (Lucas 127). Aristotle stressed that metaphorical usage was a "gift" of natural genus and that it signified that the rhetor had an understanding for "likeliness": that is a consideration for correctly portraying in an artistic way that which he saw in life (Lucas 127). In brief, for Aristotle, language (diction) served the accurate purpose of verbalizing that which was novel and encouraging about life. Without it, thought and plot disappeared; hence, there could be no drama. Aristotle, of course, lived before the verbal experimentations of the absurdist. It cannot be argued that melodramatic diction did not extol virtuosity. It is also a fact that melodramatic characterization did not noticeably mature in the play: the genre's stereotyping prevented this. Lajos Egri has also objected to the fact that melodramatic diction had become so stereotyped that transitions and intonations were prohibited through the traditional interpretations as to how lines should be read (255).

Again, it must be recalled that the genre's formula and the audience to which it played did not encourage deep, philosophical transitions. The character's style of speaking and way of intoning—very much a part of the acting style of the day—completed the characterization.

In was because of the century's emphasis on elocution in every phase of public address, and theatre was no exception, that the voice became as a rich a commodity as anything in the actor's repertoire. It was not until this century that the beautification of the voice was de-emphasized for a stage career. One could tell the actor by his voice and be moved by it. This was especially noteworthy in an era of no stage amplification. Concerning Aristotle, Fitzball merged the dialectic (the rhetorical search for truth) with the productive aspect of a poetic. In other words, each melodrama had within its context a truth of being, and dialogue was a persuasive clarification to that encompassing truth. Cicero once claimed that rhetoric had three offices: to teach, to please, and to move (Lanaham 87). Fitzball's diction accomplished all three. If Aristotle would have had reservations with Fitzball, Cicero would have embraced him. Within this vein, and especially in Fitzballian *prosody,* the excellence of diction, its aesthetic goals and its cultivation in the Delsartian method of acting, James Golden has stipulated that the Victorian theatre agreed with the vogue that diction commanded in its union with acting. Golden's example from an elocution text gives an example of how emotion was translated from the stage to the audience; its concordat to diction will be made apparent in examples from *The Devil's Elixir.* We may only imagine how diction and acting merged to make melodrama the spellbinding pageantry it was.

When anything sublime, loft, or heavenly is expressed, the eye and the right hand may be very properly elevated; and when anything low, inferior, and grovelling is referred to, the eye and the hand may be directed downwards;…and when conscious virtue, or any heartfelt emotion, or tender sentiment occurs, we may as naturally clap the right hand on the breast exactly over the heart. (178)

If this treatise from John Walker's *Elements of Elocution* (1781) seems exacting for the body, dictums for the voice were as precise and heady. It is truthful to say that such theatrical demands are now dated. It is also truthful to say that melodrama was a very conscientious form: the fact that body and voice complemented each other elaborately. And, it is apparent to add, elocution suited the fantasy and ornate world portrayed. With the current style of theatrical realism in its sets, the oratorical manner of the actors created a type of contradiction in that realism. Wrote Aragon on the distinction between reality and the imagination, "Reality is the apparent absence of contradiction. The marvelous is the contradiction which appears in reality" (Martindale 87). With Fitzball, diction poignantly, even in its bombast, brought reality together with the marvelous—to make the theatre experience unforgettable. The following dictional samplings from *The Devil's Elixir* are rich in literary and aural gusto.

Always poetical, Fitzball's diction was as audibly pleasing as *any* passed on the Victorian stage. One example comes from the Chorus and Francesco who are both lamenting over a storm. The howling wind and crashing thunder portend evil afoot as Francesco, changed into his brother by Gortzburg's elixir, battles to jail Hermogen. The Chorus chants, almost in the Greek strophic manner. The drama of disaster springs forward in a tumultuous drive, immediately engrossing the audience with the macabre and the combative: "Oh, hour of woe! of, consternation! Thunder crashing/ Lightning flashing/ Oh, misery! oh, desolation!" Francesco wails, 'How my heart throbs, and by temples burn: demons seem to haunt me; the vivid lightning scorches me; save me, save me!" (Wischhusen 257). With the era's unique grammatical mechanics—a plethora of exclamation points, commas, and the quaint, poetic usage of anastrophe—there was a rhetorical chiasmus in the poetic dialogue. A consuetude of literary plenasm, Fitzball's diction had an esemplastic power that mitigated itself beyond the mundane. The poetic imagery was forceful and had a gestalt aura about it which blended that imagery into a haunting whole.

This mystery is made the more profound in the scene that has Aurelia giving the impostor (Francesco) a drink. With the evil Gortzburg behind a scrim, unseen by anyone save Fransesco, Aurelia innocently thinks the beverage will settle Hermogen (Francesco) down since he is nervous. The suspense is mordantly sprung as Aurelia comes to know that all is not as it seems: "But in thy wild imaginings, the horror that thou speak'st of lives: neither fiend nor flame is here. Drink, Hermogen, and heaven will bless this draught" (Wischhusen 27). Again, the grammatical idiosyncrasies set the tone of the genre's lavishness: the usage of syncope and other elisions, all for effect, gives the diction a poetic flair. Fitzball's strong sense of diction had the dual ability to be in the vernacular and in the figurative mold simultaneously, thereby allowing him the opportunity to play with language for emotional effect; within that scope, he was masterful.

Jackson Barry has observed,

Tragedy is an imitation of an action...as shown in some outward and physical way. Aristotle refers to the poet imitation what may happen, the universal, rather than what has happened, the particular—the province of historians. (158-60)

Fitzball used diction in no little way in creating "universal" figures, figures perceived by their very verbosity. For instance, this speech personifies the wickedness of Gortzburg by a stark imaging: "Ere the convent clock strike eight, at twilight, I promise Aurelia as a bride—if thou refuse her hand ere the hour, swear to become by slave forever" (Wischhusen 131). Fitzball's diction presupposed a *knack syndrome—the* classic term meaning a journeyman approach to art—respective to the theatre in which Fitzball found himself. Fundamentally, Fitzball's *knacks* rested upon a doctrine that would support his aesthetic, which took into viable consideration what his audience would understand and approve. If art—as it did often—emanated from this statute about "a people's drama," so much the better.

Corrigan, in criticizing Aristotlelean imitation, implies an allusion to diction: "Imitation is something derived from the imagination and was therefore a fiction which belonged to the realm of symbols and make-believe; and was something consciously made or crafted" (73). Carrying this symbolism into diction, which is a fundamental factor of classic melodrama, one of Francesco's soliloquies is as refined poetically as any to be offered. It smacks of Fitzball's Elizbethan-Jacobean learning, and indicates that an outer appearance does not necessarily indicate an inward essence. Moreover, the speech shows that Fitzball's characterizations were frequently not stereotypical. Francesco has been transformed into his brother, but his soul anguishes over the deception, rather than relishing it. The soul is still the cleric's and he cannot become, philosophically, a bogeyman as Gortzburg presumes. The elixir has changed the body, but the soul remains constant. There is a hint of tragedy in this soulful agony, within a prose that is one of Fitzball's loftiest examples of metre, cadence, and imagery.

How awful has solitude become to me: Francesco a prisoner. Too soon will my gaolers return, armed with monastic power, to extort confession from these guilty lips: ruin and shame await me. What's this struggling at my breast: Aurelia's picture. I'll not gaze on thee again; away, sweet sorceress! Who would not consign life's best enjoyments to hang one instant on the ripe delicious crimson of these honied lips. (Wischhusen 30)

"Honied lips" would be a ham actor's delight, but the soliloquy is an honest example of classic, melodramatic diction. This innate charm is part of the genre's appeal, and an integral evidence of Fitzball's dictional expertise. Nonetheless, with all of this wonderfully affected aplomb, by the 1880s realism was encroaching upon melodrama. The genre's peculiar pronunciations, syntactical oddities, and regal presentations of vocal interchange—particularly the stichomythia—were fast becoming obsolete in the wake of a socially-thematic vernacular (Grose 370) The "Grand Manner" was fading and, with it, vocal stylistics and verbal gymnastics. The idiom of melodramatic language was being replaced by the common tongue; yet, for all of its unrealistic bearings, Fitzball's diction was prototypical of a poetic diction, which made the theatre as intriguing audibly, as it was visually.

Music

The element of music was as germane to melodrama as was any element. The Aristotelean catharsis was, in fact, aided by music, and had been so since the Greek lyre accompanied the dramatics of the fifth century. In the *Poetics* the philosopher had noted catharsis as a "homeopathic purgation," which bespoke his medical training, in reference to Orestes' cure from madness, the last part of the sensational triad (Carlson 189). Theodore Shank has noted,

Artistic expression, then, involves making a perceptual form of something the artist knows of emotive life. He must make external and objective that which is internal and subjective. He must create an expressive form; it is an image of feeling, a world of art. (35)

Replete in this value judgment, melodrama's reliance upon its own definition, a drama with melody, does indeed create that "image of feeling." Barry sums up Aristotle's attenuated priority for music thusly:

The concept of music appears to have been primarily an accompaniment to the drama, dithyramb (ode to Dionysius) and other forms of poetry in dance, though Aristotle in the *Poetics* does give it a separate existence. (126)

It is ironic—and amusingly so—that the elements least esteemed by Aristotle would be melodrama's most accentuated: music and spectacle. The genre was topsy-turvy even from the start. However, melodramatists knew the cathartic appeal of music and, therein, indirectly aided Aristotle's purgative directive. Fitzball's use of the Chorus alludes to the basic place of music in the drama, and Michael Booth justly claims that music aided characterization as leitmotifs for a particular persona, either entering, leaving, or acting within the confines of a scene (*Hiss The Villain* 13). This was a singular value since the average audience for a melodrama was largely uneducated, a usual problem for the best of dramatists (Boulton 11). Pragmatically, the largess of music kept attention.

R.G. Collingwood has suggested that music indeed enhances man's artistic and practical vision of his world in an invigorating process. Music is, like drama, a communicative art. And the melodramatist, particularly a librettist such as Fitzball, realized this potential above any other arranger of the drama. Wrote Collingwood:

Music is one order of languages; speech is another...a tune is an imaginary thing, not a collection of noises. What we get out of it is something which we have to reconstruct in our own minds, and by our own efforts...sensual pleasure. (139-41)

For Fitzball music set the mood, tone, and, sometimes, the very pace of the drama; it was a seduction which, in tandem with the plot, overwhelmed the audience, cathartically. Music was, simply put, a confluence with all other factors in the play: it described the characters, it introduced the play's flavor, and it emotionally involved the spectators. Essentially, for Fitzball, music was the subtext of the diction.

"Music in melodrama," suggests Hatlen, "was an adjunct of production, rather than an organic part of the structure itself...a stronger source of emotional impact" (96). Empowering contemporary melodrama (film and television), as it did nineteenth-century plays by orchestration, music remains a prodigious contingent of psychological depth, in both the drama and in the audience. The modes of the "emotional impact" may change, but music's purpose stays viable. In *English Melodrama*, Booth traces the function of this least appreciated element by Aristotle by citing Thomas Holcroft's *A Tale of Mystery* (1802), England's first melodrama, as having dozens of musical cues, among them "music to express pain and disorder...threatening music...music of sudden joy." He reports that James Kenney's *The Blind Boy* had a score for virtually every emotion (37). Melodrama seemed to give musical accompaniment legitimacy and popularity, and this poignant marriage between arts developed keen transitions: "...music was often a stronger source of emotional impact than the performance of the actors and the drama itself" (Hatlen 96). It is little wonder that Fitzball, the poet-librettist-dramatist, with Elizbethan prosaic impulses, would enshrine his plays with a cumulative artistry underscored by music. *The Devil's Elixir's* protasis contains music as a zesty anticipation. Says Brockett of music's worth:

Music establishes or enhances mood and creates expectations; establishes the unreality of a play to show it is not real life; helps to define a character's personality through melody, rhythm, and tempo; creates the aura of an idea or theme in a play; lends variety to the play that diction may not do; and aesthetically pleases the viewers. (*Introduction* 47)

Brockett must have had Fitzballian drama in mind whenever he penned this definition, for, indeed, *The Devil's Elixir,* produced as "A Musical Romance," recalling the definition of a *romance,* used ballads, incidental and incremental tunes, and dreamy leitmotifs to create a hauntingly whimsical effect. Of Fitzball's extant works several scores remain, but most of the melodies are gone. Two gleanings of Fitzballian lyricism, which could border on the operatic since the songs lend themselves to a grand style of delivery, are worth examining. In keeping with his merger of music with word, Fitzball's songs actually sound much like his poetic prose. Eerily, the bouncing imps, who are the guards of Gortzburg's prison, the hellish Crystal Rock, chant the horrific opening song. One may well imagine Dore's romantic lithograph in the *Inferno* as these euminides musically set the tone for the macabre sensationalism to follow: "Blaze, blaze, then spectre light/ Boil, compound dark and fell;/ 'Tis the hour, 'tis the night, When the demon spirit/ Hurries to haunted dell." The stage directions of this acting version state that the imps are "blowing the fire with bellows, on which are magic characters" (Wischhusen 9). It is a conglomeration of Dantean and Shakespearean horror as these little savages sing in the tradition of the witches' rantings in *Macbeth.* They are drinking the devilish, narcotizing elixir, in an atmosphere right out of a Jacobean tragedy, whose horrid tone has a rapport in keeping with Fitzball's display: "The effect seems to be achieved largely through the iteration of broadly evocative words—devil, hell, blood, lightning, storm, whirlwind, fury, thunder, death..." (Hill and Williams 201). Fitzball's song magically leaves no confusion as to Gortzburg's heritage and character, spawned in the fiery recesses of hell. Musically, the dramatic tone is manifested, and the sensational triad aroused for further implementation.

By contrast to this grisly mood, Fitzball gives us one of his loveliest compositions as sung by the fair Aurelia, who is regretting and pining for her missing (imprisoned) Hermogen, now impersonated by Francesco, the purloiner. Reminiscent of Shelley's "The Skylark," her song is as soaring as the imps' song was gruesome. The composition has an aura of the Cavalier style and can easily stand alone as a poem: "I hear him yes, I hear him—gentle throbs my bosom swell,/ Ah, no, 'tis but the murmur of the streamlet in the dell. And by his side, I'd wander through the daisied meadows gay,/ While hamlet bells were ringing the month of May" (Wischhusen 21). With his iambic pentameter—not the Greek iambic trochaic—beat, Fitzball may be likened unto Sidney Lanier, whose book, *The Science of English Verse* (1880), studied the correlation between poetry and music, an alliance that made the American poet famous for his unique versification. Ronald Peacock has written that "musicalized diction" is rich in linguistic imagery and pleasure: "Such a texture, or image structure, borrows for the evocation of language the structure of music, achieving thereby a similar symbolic suggestiveness" (155). Attempting a Shakespearean rhythm, a Spenserian motif, and a Lovelacean mood, and injecting into this his uniquely haunting romanticism, Fitzball's *melos* is more than just music: it is a "musicalized diction."

As an accomplished librettist, Fitzball created tones of horror and of beauty side-by-side, as Hugo deemed necessary in romantic drama. These were a versatile coloratura, which exuded artistry in a grandly emotional picturesqueness and alacrity.

Spectacle

Aristotle's *opsis,* or spectacle, was melodrama's hallmark, the source of its enduring and influential charisma. Universally, spectacle in art touches the human spirit as does no other element. Man's history is a legacy of regal and savage spectacle, and his life, to avoid Thoreau's curse of "quiet desperation," has been in search for nuances of the spectacular in mind, spirit, emotion, and art. As melodrama's most coveted characterization, spectacle is central to the genre's fantasy and longevity, whether that spectacle is in a setting or in a character. And classic melodrama possessed it in abundance.

Aristotle defined the element as

...decoration—literally, the decoration of the sight [perhaps the stage setting]. It comprehends scenery, dresses—the whole visable appearance of the theatre. I do not know of any single English work that answers full the Greek word. (Clark 8)

Because drama is a stage story of human conflict, spectacle is the whole, theatrical effect that affects the narrative. Stephen Minot says, "The fact remains that live performances presented on a stage have certain assets not found in any other genre" (265). Spectacle is that "certain asset," stretching from scenes in hell to a musical extravaganza: it is an aesthetic amalgam of all theatricality and there is nothing in that experience untouched by it. Spectacle gives theatre, and gave melodrama, its epic quality, by which the viewers became aware that art was being presented to them, not life. Acknowledging spectacle's overwhelming license, Brockett implies the pageantry of spectacle in that it "...be appropriate, expressive of the play's values, distinctive, and practicable" (*Introduction* 48).

But spectacle is not synonymous with melodramtic bravura, as often thought. Simply, spectacle is the discerning and subjective theatricalization of what a given play is to represent. If the *play* is *Cat On A Hot Tin Roof,* the spectacle ambiance is realism in life; if *The Devil's Elixir,* it is fantasy incorporated. In short, by comparison to a person, spectacle is the individual style that a certain human indelibly has. The same is true of a play having a certain, theatrical aura of its own.

Early Broadway melodramas, such as Louisa Medina's *The Last Days of Pompeii* (1844), William Young's *Ben Hur* (1899), and Stanislaus Stange's *Ouo Vadis* (1900), were staged in historical realism, yet the staging and milieu of each reflected the grandiosity of nineteenth-century melodramatic dynamics: excitement, action, and elements of fantasy—all the traits that Fitzball provided and improved for the masses. Spectacle may be appreciated on three levels: escapism, moralism, and pageantry of sorts. Fitzball's blue-fire-Blood-and-Thunder qualified as an exemplification of these aesthetics. Wrote George Rowell in *The Victorian Theatre: 1792-1914:*

...the English playwright became a theatrical journeyman whose duty was to provide a platform on which actor, artist, machinist could display their skill. Spectacle supplied all the distractions which the new audience craved, without making any demands on them in return. It was, therefore, to the provision of spectacle that the ingenuity and resources of the theatre were now directed. (38)

If this entire effect sounds contemporary, it is because today's media entertainment is in the same artistic state-of-affairs as in the nineteenth-century.

Whenever there are massive, social upheavals—in the 1800s there was the Industrial Revolution; today, there is the death of the Machine Age and birth of the Computer-Retraining Age—the public turns to elaborate, spectacular entertainment fare. As a cultural populist, Fitzball propitiously realized that spectacle was the attraction of the bourgeois, as it had been during melodrama's inception: the era of chaos in The French Revolution. Curiously, revolutions, whether in vocation or in spirit—and these two are generally mixed—cause a bourgeois, not intellignesia, entertainment to arise.

For Fitzball spectacle bred emotionalism, and emotionalism bred catharsis, and catharsis bred profits for the theatre managers, whose value for the hack increased with each falling admission coin. Theatre and socio-political-economics are usual bedfellows. Fitzball transformed *drama* into a commonly accepted *play* through spectacle. The popular cinema directors transformed *film* into *movies* in precisely the same public-oriented way; thus, the comparison between Frizballian sensationalism and spectacle, and their cinematic counterparts in *B-films* and film-making, has foundation for being. Both art forms, though quite differing in execution, of course, share the same philosophy: entertainment for the masses. And the use of the spectacle was centrifugal to both art forms. Fitzball's romantic spectacle was, in essence, a revolt against pretentious art in the theatre, even though the dramatist aspired to creative and social heights. It was a revolt against a classical tradition, inured by the misguided Neo-classicists in understanding Aristotelean dictums; it was also a defense of romanticism. The uses of spectacle by Fitzball was a conspicuous ideation of classicism by a variegated artist. The importance of the two schools' dichotomies are approached by Curtis Page in this way.

There is, for instance, Stendhal's famous and often-quoted definition of Classic taste as liking that which our grandfathers liked, and of the Romantic taste as liking that which we really like ourselves. Deschanel has written on this confusion in the use of the word Classic as, on the other hand, that which is now accepted as good in Literaure, and, on the other hand, that which has certain definite characteristics as opposed to the Romantic; and of the Romantic as primarily that which revolts against the Classic standards, as well as having definite characteristics of its own. He shows very clearly that the writers now accepted as classics (in popular sense) were almost always rebels in their own times, and by their very originality of their talents imposed themselves upon the admiration of future times. That is to say, those whom we call Classics today are merely Romanticists who have arrived...the Classic appeals to the reason...The Romatic appeals to the imagination. The Classic temper seeks the calm, the Romantic for excitement. (206-7)

This seems always the case: genuis is overlooked and castigated in its own day by pundits, only to be renewed as praiseworthy by later generations. All revered today as memorable are rebels against the *status quo* in their time: only original thinkers and artists are the ones recalled by prosterity. For instance, Shakespeare was a populist for the peoples' theatre. Such a man was hardly one enslaved by someone else's rules, yet now he is a sacrosanct artist. The irony continues. It is this criticism of Fitzball, in retrospect, that may vindicate his artistry, inasmuch as he gleefully traded the calm of classicism for the excitement of romanticism. In writing about popular literature, Victor Neuburg suggests reasons for popular literature's appeal, which is indicative of the appeal in Fitzballian drama. Crossing class, or caste, popular literature, in whatever form, strikes a common denominator in mankind: pleasure for its own sake. Fitzball's popular literature performed this task theatrically and, hence, a type of folk drama was realized in artistic spectacle. Neuburg gives the basics for public attraction:

At its simplest, popular literature can be defined as what the unsophisticated reader has chosen for pleasure. Such a reader may, of course, come from any class in society, although the appeal of popular literature has been to the poor...also to children.... Central to my argument is the assumption that mass literacy is a powerful force in society. (12-3)

Neuburg's conclusion defines Fitzball's freewheeling, rococo spectacles. He appealed to adults and to children, especially through juvenile drama. A sampling of these plays solicit such reactions. *The Earthquake* (1829) gave the enthralled audiences the special effect of the earth moving and tumbling; *The Pilot* and *Nelson; or, The Life of a Sailor* issued momentous sea adventure and intrigue for the viewers in 1825 and 1827, respectively; *Thalaba. The Destroyer* (1823) wrenched out of the past breathtaking exotica; and *The Inchcape Bell* and *The Red Rover*, 1828 and 1829, respectively, offered terrific nautical and pirate adventures to thrill the explorer in every child and adult. Then, too, his theatre of the macabre gave out its unique brand of spectacular shudders. Earthly and unearthly, real and unreal, joyous and morbid, Fitzball knew popular drama's attraction because he knew "the common man" and his desire for enjoyment, at any cost. The Great American Depression of the 1930s illustrated the same maxim with Hollywood escapism. Though impoverished, millions spent their pennies for the fantasy of the silver screen. In Fitzball's society, they spent for the Golden Age of Melodrama. And spectacle was center stage.

Oscar Cargill warns that it is difficult to know exactly what the artist means in composing his masterpieces, that the affective fallacy may result: "Subconscious association of language and ideas produce effects of which it is fair to assume the author is not wholly aware. Quite apart from its creator, a work of art has a life of its own" (Hook 109-11). Never through an artistic continuum, but by emotional vicissitudes, Fitzball's style of showmanship offered themes for scrutiny and for enjoyment in a spectacle that all might accept on many levels. Certainly Fitzball's personality was not especially spectacular, a mixture of oddity, comicality, and pensiveness. Therefore, his works did have a personality of their own—an alter-ego to their creator. *The Devil's Elixir* was such paradox to Fitzball in its horrific and frenzied state. It was the virtuosity of the melodramatist, such as Fitzball, that gave the genre its flair. Nicholas Vardac concurs with this portrait of the melodramatist as popular artist:

The most popular single expression of the combined romantic and realistic theatrical modes of the nineteenth century is to be found in the melodrama. Writers of nineteenth-century melodrama were essentially men of the theatre, professionally aware of the potentiality of the stage for which they wrote. Their success as playwrights was measured by the degrees to which they exploited these capacities. (20)

Spectacle abounds in *The Devil's Elixir*. From the outset, the viewer is aware of Fitzball's aplomb and bravado. The opening scene at the Crystal Rock is gloomy and morbidly exciting with imps dancing and flying by wires; the fiery cliffs forbiddingly looming; and The Shadow King and Gortzburg chillingly evil. More than mere demonology, Fitzball has created a lore and world of wondrous monsters. Hell is cunningly drawn, within a Dore and Dante context. The stage is romantically and horribly stretched, with a touch of Fitzballian humor in all of its chaos: little demons flying though the air! One can sense Fitzball holding the wires and chuckling at himself and the viewers. The entire mise-en-scene evokes a cultivated gruesomeness with such gothic effects as the flickering lights, rolling thunder, and flashing lightning. But it is the monsters that hold one's attention the most. Leonard Wolf has written why ghosties, spooks, those things that go inevitably bump in the night, are so much a factor in human fantasy: "The monster is a message in our sleep from someone or Something trying to tell us how to love, or what to hate. Most of the time, the monster is fear, raw and hungry, taking shapes that almost teach us what we need to know" (8). Fitzball's gloriously hideous monster, Gortzburg, is

Francesco's dictator, if you will, that wrenched part of man's soul which restrains Jekyll and unleashes Hyde. For Fitzball, spectacle is a mise-en-scene in elaboration, but, moreover, it remains a metaphor for the possibility of Gortzburg's pending victory over Francesco, an eerie portent that vice always has the double-side of *Faust*. Fitzball's spectacle in hell is symbolic of one of those sides: the attraction of chaos.

Spectacle, if used for the macabre, is used by Fitzball for the serene, if ironically so. Francesco's reliquary is portrayed as medieval contemplation: painted windows on flats through which shines the sun, thus lighting the dimness of a monastery's solitude, as if God's grace is attempting to recall Francesco's soul; and, of course, there is the challenging and intriguing winding staircase ascending to that sunshine. Nature rebels at Gortzburg's appearance behind an transparent scrim which serves as an otherworldly vision. The detailed rectory is assaulted by winds and storms upon the demon's arrival. Demonically, a candlelight illuminates the monster, behind the scrim, to indicate his diabolic desires, or his continuing influence. The scrim announces that the monstrous in never far from the activities in the play. For graphic spectacle, Gortzburg's finish is a climactic piece of lavishness. Foiled in his attempt to corrupt Francesco, the demon is consumed by the fires of hell—in this case, the Land of the Shadows—as the stone stairwell crumbles underneath him! Fitzball has issued his moral: evil is damned and goodness saved. Such would be the precedent of Saturday cliffhangers and movie horrors yet to come. Fitzball's spectacle, as with all of his elements, is a litmus test for the audience. We know that he is toying with the macabre and with our seduction by it. Of note is the scrim, one of the highlights of his phantasmagoria. Writes Sybil Rosenfeld:

The development of the phantasmagoria consisted of the placement of a lantern behind a transparent screen let down after the lights wet out, the lantern being fitted with wheels so that it could be moved backwards and forwards, which caused the projected image to increase or diminish in size and brightness. (162)

Wonderful for a time, of not so very long ago, this special effect would cause Gortzburg's image to either grow or decrease, dependent upon his control in a given scene. Fitzball was careful in these prompt-books in transacting these effects, but critics may have added their own opinions later. Dependent upon his type of play, Fitzball saw spectacle as an intricate element in the melodrama, inasmuch as it impressed audiences with the force of some of the incredible activities of the stage. To be sure, Fitzball's use, or abuse, of the elements—and certainly the melodramatist did no more harm to these than did practitioners of other forms before and after him—fashioned them into a collage, a mosaic in the maze of Blood-and-Thunder. Spectacle's bluefire quality was a ploy for the audience. So were all of the elements ploys to satisfy those special needs relevant to each of the elements as viewed by the audience. Hence, the diction was lofty and thrilling, the plot predictable in outcome, and so on. The elements served Fitzball as he served the audiences, as partakers in his theatre of the macabre. Summarily, Gilbert Murray's musings about Euripides' mixture of the dramatic Real and Fantastic lends itself to a general comment about Fitzball's theory for the interplay between the normal and the bizarre. Since Fitzball has a linkage to Euripides, through the maneuvering of melodramatic intrigue, Murray's words about the Greek offer a relevancy to the styles of two writers separated by thousands of years, but yet strangely connected.

Fitzball's image of melodrama had its roots, seemingly, in that of Euripides. In *Euripides and His Age,* Gilbert Murray wrote that Euripides mixed the real and fantastic in much the same way as did Fitzball.

In this lies, for good or evil, his unique quality as a poet. To many readers it seems that his powers failed him; his mixture of real life and supernatural atmosphere, of wakeful thought and dreaming legend, remcions a discord, a mere jar of overwrought conventions and violent realism. To others it is because of this very quality that he has earned the tremendous rank accorded him by Goethe, and in a more limited sense by Aristotle, and still stand art, as he stood over two thousand years ago, "Even if faulty in various ways, at any rate clearly the most tragic of poets." (242-3)

Justification of the Elements

Neglectfully, theatre history and criticism have failed to mention that the melodramatist was privy to classic, dramatic technique, that Aristotle's elements were of value—and, in some instances, of more value—to him as artistry. Aristotle's elements supported classic melodrama as they were adapted to the genre's mission. Fitzball took the elements and wrapped them around his audience's cathartic attention, which translated into commercial profits. His best macabre plays also indicate that Fitzball was well aware of the potentiality and actuality of horror as a dramatic attention. In fact, the whole of his sensational triad was a compilation of an intricate networking of Aristotle's elements. Each element operated in tandem with the others in an intelligent and artistic way. It is for this reason that Fitzball rises above being just another *schlockmeister,* inasmuch as the latter uses graphic sensuality and shock for crude, entrepreneurial goals. And, since theatre has always been a public forum, the *schlockmeister* has availed himself of such gullibility in "artistic expression." Fitzball, for the sake of contemporary clarity, may best be compared to the film director James Whale, whose 1931 version of *Frankenstein* remains prototypical. It remains so because Whale combined intelligence, humor—always a factor necessary for macabre artistry—and showmanship in portraying the legendary monster. Fitzball's horrors contain the same, scrutinizing dimensions. Even 0. Smith as the the demon possessed some of the glaze of Boris Karloff's seminal creation in Whale's masterpiece. Even amidst Fitzball's glaring exhibitions, there always remains a grace of sorts: art and fine craftsmanship. After all, Fitzball was a hack. And how much art can a hack produce, churning out new plays almost constantly? Even the great Spanish dramatist Lope de Vega, given the epithet "el monstruo de la naturaleza" by Cervantes, and whose corpus has been estimated at between 400 and 1,000 comedias, did not yield classics with every stroke of the pen. And Lope wrote under quite accommodating circumstances. Fitzball did not always have that luxury.

Fitzball used, what Luzan termed, the "utile dulci," a literary approach that combined morality with enchanting beauty, and, in that direction, Fitzball appealed to the utilitarian side of theatrical commerce and to the middle-class values, hedonism included, of his audiences. The Freudian pleasure principle that zoned the pleasure seeking area of man may have played an active part in Fitzball's success, years before psychological foundations in drama became fashionable. It may be accurate to claim that Fitzball was a kind of psychologist, sociologist, and philosopher. His vocation and aesthetic inclinations demanded that he be. Theoretically, he took the realities of crime, horror, and madness and changed them into dramatic metaphors, whose amusement transcended the actual anxieties of life. Fitzball employed Aristotle's catharsis, if not medically, then emotionally, for the consumer theatre. Tom Hutchinson gives a poignant endowment to the *goblins Fitzballian* by offering a rationale for man's love for the uncanny as a psychological errantry.

The things that go bump in the night, beyond the light or our daytime comprehension, are creatures that have no form. It is for this reason that they are so frightening. The only remedy for us, therefore, is to get to grips with the fear by enjoying it. Through our shudders we are both entertained and still retain a sense of wonder at the way of the world. (13)

Fitzball's Triadic Expression

For Fitzball's world, the sensational triad was an exogenous experience, as much a part of reality as it was of theatricality. As such, the six elements were exoteric implementations in reality. Fitzball's drama of disaster, regardless of its fancy, had a visible core is society. But, of course, all drama has attempted to make its *memisis* recognizable. Melodrama has always done so beneath a layer of escapism, but that escapism has had roots in the public's perceptions of activities in life. Hence, melodrama's characteristic exaggerations are merely polarizations of that life, with which the public may easily identify. The popularity of the preposterous soap opera validates this theatricalism.

Making the sensational of his era tenable, moralizing, and spellbinding, Fitzball helped to set a custom which his modern innuendo, the adventure and horror film, continues to implement. His sort of melodramatic executions and trappings are allied today through the escapist films of Steven Spielberg, Wes Craven, and John Carpenter; Fitzball was ahead of his time by urging techniques now deemed cinematic. In the following chapter, his *opus magnum, Jonathan Bradford,* among other plays, will be analyzed as key examples of the theatre of the macabre, with the sensational triad as its main undercurrent. Fitzball's approach to the melodrama was an eclectic one, with Aristotle's elements as gifts to that artistry. Roy Huss has written that Gothic horror is expressionistic in style (23). It may be that Fitzballian luridness transcended styles and combined all: surrealism in its fantasy, realism in its production, and reminiscences of Euripidean psychology and Jacobean unsightliness. As such, Fitzballian dramaturgy has classic and modern relevance. The cavilling critics of the day failed to see this perspective in Fitzball's "common man's theatre," which possessed an individual artistic integrity and popular attraction—still a unique combination and one coveted.

Fitzball's virtuosity as an advocate of macabre art is in itself intriguing. His treatise sprang from a genuine ability, incandescent and ingenious, to create art from subjects often abused as decadent. A maverick, within a unbridled dramatic form, Fitzball raised Blood-and-Thunder, and all of its appendages, to a commercial and attractive *fin de siecle* theatrical art that became a theatrical bonanza. Fitzball saw theatre as an institution large enough even for hacks. His reputation is evidence of the truth and deception of such a conclusion. An insight into Fitzball's talents may vindicate the reputation of a dramatist who transformed, almost magically, the ghastly into the astonishing.

Chapter IV
Fitzball's Dramaturgy:
Analysis of Exemplary Plays

Virgil Aldrich has said that an artist reveals his artistry through the medium in which he works (30). Within the medium of theatre, Fitzball adapted his distinct philosophy to melodrama. Most of Fitzball's plays had macabre elements in them, but the ones presented in this chapter will be the outstanding examples, with *Jonathan Bradford* dominating this appraisal of Fitzball's dramaturgy. From Aristotle's *Poetics*, the six elements were drawn as the basic components for the drama. In this chapter, Fitzball's personal ideology about dramatic techniques will be assessed, as not only an entity in itself, but, moreover, as a melodrama reflective.

Whenever one experienced a Fitzballian play, he could expect to be thrust into a world of excitement where the imagination was free to roam at will. Fitzball was a playwright of combinations. Over other melodramas of the time, Fitzballian plays had a unique flair to them: they were not only horror, only escapism, only musicals. They told a memorable story and gave a sturdy philosophy of human values within the context of an exponential and extra-terrestrial plot. The feeling of the play was more important than the intellectualization of it. If compared to other stylists of his time, Fitzball emerged in covering the moral under the play's fantasy. In C.W. Taylor's *The Drunkard's Warning* (1856), as a contradictory example to Fitzball's style, the message was a heavy-handed temperance one about a drunkard's rehabilitation; Fitzball, if faulted for perhaps dealing with too much fantasy material, was never accused of moralizing without entertaining. This was perhaps, his unique flavor as a Blood-and-Thunder master of hallucinations-on-stage.

Beginning with *Jonathan Bradford*, the criticism will be two-fold: the plays as literature and the plays as theatre. It is only by this route that a controversial dramatist such as Fitzball may be properly judged. Frederick Crews has written that "good criticism appears to be largely a matter of sympathy, sensitivity, and pertinent learning..." (9). With Fitzball's dramatic conundrums, this exhortation is reliable.

109

Jonathan Bradford as A Triadic Example

Jonathan Bradford; or, Murder at the Roadside Inn was two-act play, first performed at the Surrey Theatre on Wednesday, June 12, 1833. It was inspired by an actual crime committed at the Roadside Inn, not far from London, under the proprietorship of one Jonathan Bradford and his wife. In a primitive way, the play may be discerned as a type of docudrama, with the murder and robbery instilled relatively unblemished as facts. The plot goes as follows. In Bradford"s establishment are several lodgers there for pleasure and business. However, into the center of this domestic bliss—and bliss is very important, as the initial melodramatic atmosphere, that must be polluted by the conflict later—come the villains: the leader, Dan Macraisy; and his henchmen, the doltish Caleb Scrummige. Immediately, Fitzball, in a Restoration-like, homophonic artifice, gives the miscreants names which sound very much like *crazy* and *scum*. Fitzball is always aware of sensory trickery. Hearing that the wealthy tenet Mr. Hayes is retiring, Macraisy steals into his room that stormy night, stabs the shrieking Hayes, and flees through the open window. Awakened by the scream, Bradford and his wife rush into the room only to discover Hayes mortally wounded. Picking up the bloody knife, Bradford is, thereupon, accused by the entering guests as the perpetrator of this deed most foul and is taken to trial and condemned. Bradford's comical servant, Jack Rockbottle, contrives his master's escape from jail, and the two of them track down the real culprits, who are hiding in the countryside. As would be expected, the fiendish Macraisy is attempting to have Caleb sign a confession to the murder, which would, therefore, exonerate Macraisy.

Bradford confronts the killer and wrenches from him the truth; however, Macraisy is impenitent. Frustrated that Macraisy will not accept his just due, Bradford returns to jail, knowing, at least, that Macraisy realizes that he has been found out. On the morning of Bradford's hanging, Hayes' funeral procession passes by the rogues' concealment. Seeing the morbid sight drives Macraisy, who is fairly-well crazed anyway, mad with quilt. The moral of one's sins finding one out is consummated in the killer, who, in a wonderfully mounted climax, literally writhes in soulful agony. All of his crimes have come home to haunt him and he can stand himself no longer. Rushing into the graveyard, after Hayes' burial party has left, the archfiend stabs himself—a usual melodramatic way of suicide—with the same dagger and in the same fashion relevant to Hayes. It was because of such outbursts of spectacular violence and stage madness that A.E. Wilson noted that Fitzball was popular with audiences (60). The cliff-hanger has Macraisy stumbling into the crowd, awaiting Bradford's hanging, at the gallows. Screaming his guilt in the crime, the villain repents and swoons at the feet of the gibbet. Justice confirmed, Bradford is reunited with his wife and with his respected name. The reparation complete, Macraisy, bleeding, dies. A drama begun with high-pitched tension ends with the same acme of emotionalism.

Knox Hill reminds the able critic to use emotion in validating a work's structure, and, to be sure, emotionalism runs high in this macabre action (53). Concerning this frenzied plot, Booth acknowledges, "The most vivid melodrama concerns crime and drink. Then as now the public were avid followers of murder cases, the bloodier the better. The sensational element of crime suited it ideally to the melodramatic stage" (*Villain* 28). Booth's summation justified the thematic premise that indeed the sensational triad was a human factor before Fitzball transferred it to the stage. From the Greeks onward, drama found its impetus through human institutions and social circumstances before it was transported to the stage by the great playwrights. Melodrama, for all of its uproariousness, was no different. As a paradigm of the crime drama, *Jonathan Bradford* had its share of the sensational triad, which for Fitzball was always a physical reality before it became a metaphorical one: horror in the bloody murder, crime in the murder itself, and terror and madness in Macraisy's acts and delirium. Unlike *The Devil's Elixir*, a collate between the two plays indicate that Fitzball was pliable in his largess of macabre ingredients. There is a supernatural network in *The Devil's Elixir* that is lacking in *Bradford*, but the latter drama is no less disturbing. Perhaps it is more so because there are, in truth, *Macraisys* in all society. Possible horrors always make one more squeamish than do fantastic horrors because they are possible. Macraisys are now the modern terrorists, while Gortzburg remains a bogeyman. The versatility of Fitzball lay in his descriptions of the macabre and his thoughts about it—at once, the horror is real; at once, it is incredible. It is always terrifying—and wonderfully so.

Prototypical of the episodic-climactic play structure in melodrama, the Exposition, or Introduction, quickly moves into action. True to form, the tone, mood, and unity of design are established: a lonely inn, its strolling guests, and the arrival of Macraisy and Caleb set the above traits into play. In Act 1, I, Bradford; his wife, Ann; and the comic servants, Jack and Sally, are presented. Leaving nothing to chance, Fitzball's characters represent, of course, stock figures, with, however, distinguishing features all their own. It is the disruption of the stock-value system of common life that makes for a drama of disaster. Bradford and Ann are responsible citizens, the prey of villains; the servants are funny; the guests Chaucerian: they come from different walks of life and seem gregarious and fairly innocent; and the villains are just that, villains. The viewers can easily distinguish the good from the bad. In scene ii, the rogues mysteriously enter. Again, Fitzball cleverly instills the pun in Macraisy's name, which could be discerned as *Ma' crazy*, inasmuch as he does go berserk in the denouement. The conversant dialogue and the comfortable inn setting give the atmosphere a relaxed aura soon to be violated by murder. When the murder is committed, for spectacular effect, a storm arises, thus suggesting that heaven itself is denouncing the misdeed. Again, melodrama's alliance to spiritual conventions is substantiated by Fitzball, even if fleetingly. The macabre attitude in the play is thus fixed. An indication of Fitzball's reliance upon a stark characterization comes whenever Macraisy indicates his intentions by his very words. With an Irish brogue, he mutters to Caleb,

Haven't I a schame to make your fortune?—haven't I heard that Mr. Hayes slapes there at the George Inn tonight, with a big purse of money in his pocket...and won't I transmorgify that bit of a bit purse into my own pocket, as neatly as if it was made to fit—eh? (*Jonathan Bradford* 9)

This sudden exposition of the play's essential plot and the delineation of the characters, here in particular Macraisy as the villain, indicates the violence to come. Violence was very much an undergirding of the triad, and Fitzball made the most of it. Macraisy is one of Fitzball's most interesting characters because his portrait is of brutish turbulence, symbolic of the violence in nineteenth-century London and of brutality universal. Within Macraisy resides all the properties of the triad, volatile and arresting; he is a symbol of that mad carnage that has scarred history and that has given interesting dimensions to evil as a dramatic force. We have all encountered, if indirectly, Macraisys: they are the nameless and faceless brigands of prisons and death chambers.

In keeping with Richard Hofstandter's conclusions that most violence is a multi-faceted phenomenon, processed by varying social forces against mankind, it is easy to see that Macraisy, theoretically, may have been a product of London's criminal counterculture (4). With dexterity, Fitzball carefully configures Macraisy as a complex creation. He is no ordinary thug, but, in Kanfer's epithet about forces of evil, a so-called "twin-terror," an appearance of evil predisposed to enact crime (83). This reminds us of Ellis' classic portrait of the habitual felon: that crime is a result of physiological influences. Within melodrama's meandering world of logical upset, Macraisy repents, at the *non secruiter* last minute, so that the standard "happy ending" might be effected.

Such was a conjoint convention to make morality plausible in a highly implausible situation. But plausibility is relative in melodrama. Lawrence Ferlinghetti once said that fantasy "constantly risks absurdity" (Watson 483). Absurd endings, frenzied characters, and chaotic plots assert Ferlinghetti's pronouncement; in melodrama, particularly in Fitzballian fare, inharmoniousness is acceptable, even so designed, as long as a moral is given. Fitzball ruminates in *Bradford* a reversal of what David Daiches says about the populace imitating the art of the creator (59). *Bradford,* conversely, imitates society in its crime and violence with goodness battling evil. Fitzball's protagonist and antagonist represent more than hero and villain. They are romantic creations of literary and dramatic sublimity and grotesquerie (Hall, Jr. 89). Such universal symbolism is the difference between art and ersatz.

And because of art's universality and philosophical relation to life, Fitzball, true to form, quickly exposes the duality between good and evil by providing the classical device of Recognition. In a powerful scene, the villain shows his menace, or his true motives, by pulling a gun on his henchman, Caleb. Posing as a landowner, one "Janus O'Conner," Macraisy's warped mentality cannot stay hidden for very long, and, although this act is intended as a jocular demonstration of manly bravado, Fitzball startles his audience with a taste of the horror to come. Hence, the battleground between evil and good has been set. Also, Spencer's philosophical idea of Natural Selection is hinted, inasmuch as Macraisy is a predator upon the weak of his own species. Pity and fear, the two Aristotelean emotions, are aroused for two reasons: 1) the audience was aware of the genuine crime at the inn as fact and 2) the audience knew that Bradford and Macraisy must collide. Aristotle saw pity as upsetting empathy on the viewer's part, concerning the suffering circumstances forced on the hero, and fear as terror felt by the presence of evil forces (256). Bradford's pending dilemma will arise as a fine example of the cathartic condition as envisioned by Fitzball.

More than escapism, *Jonathan Bradford,* by offering the protagonist at the hands of a criminal, parallels life. Man threatens and is threatened. "The strong winds of intensity upon which melodrama depends" underlie *Bradford* because the play never relinquishes the ardent sense of intensity throughout its plot (Beckerman 100). With the point of attack (the crime) accomplished early in the play, Fitzball takes on the task of interpreting the individual psychologies of his main characters, Bradford and Macraisy. The sensational triad reaches an important position in a matrix well beyond sensationalism and exploitation. Redolent of melodrama's interest in the Grand Guignol tradition of gore and horror, the murder itself is a telling factor in Fitzball's dramaturgy. An inspection of this thrilling scene will endorse these remarks.

The heavens screaming and the background music swelling to a crescendo, the murder is accomplished. For every physical act, Fitzball, as psychologist, balances the actual with the emotional. In short, one may look into a Fitzballian character's very soul when an act is done. The diction is quickening and unnerving. Hayes implores, "Who is there? What hands grasp my throat? Landlord! Villain! Plunderer! my money or this knife (Hayes has a weapon for protection)" (*Jonathan Bradford* 18). This desperate monologue has a reference similar to a Poesque tone, as in his story "The Tell-Tale Heart," wherein the blind man is murdered by his servant. Also, Fitzball naturally clouds his more animated diction with an abundance of exclamation marks and nominal expletives. Countering Hayes' monody, Macraisy intimidates his victim thusly: "Knife! in my own defense then. Devil, where's the purse" (Jonathan Bradford 19). Leaving the dying man, Macraisy and Caleb escape through the window as Bradford enters. Hayes resurges momentarily, and, in an elegy worthy of a length in *Hamlet,* groans, "A Light—ah! my purse—that knife in his hands! my assassin" (*Jonathan Bradford* 19). Fitzball's complication and point-of-attack are usually synonymous. Generally, the hero was not the most intellectual of characters in melodrama, so Bradford's infelicitous grasping of the murder weapon seals his fate, but this was part-and-parcel for melodrama's plotful absurdities where normal logic had no place. Gingerly, Fitzball has woven the technique of Recognition into the complication level of dramatic structure. The complication is always dramaturgically sudden in the scheme of the plot, even if it is unpremeditated by actions done beforehand. In this case, Macraisy's crime sets the tempo of the plot, but melodramatic conflict may sometimes appear for no other discernible reason than to initiate action. Such a process was usually found in inferior melodrama. However, we must realize that a hack's patrons came to the theatre for sudden action, not for any drawn-out rationale leading to the conflict or point-of-attack.

In melodrama the climax is the most important level of dramatic structuring, and all action must lead to a high-pitched climactic encounter. The confrontation between Bradford, the moral sublimity, and Macraisy, the immoral grotesquerie, is eagerly anticipated for the cliff-hanging suspense. Brander Mathews' idea that melodrama has "a tense conflict of contending determination" is proved correct in the confrontation (104). Though Bradford has honor and Macraisy has disesteem, Fitzball has given his main characters dramatic depth beyond the usual one-dimensionality current in melodrama. If only marginally so—and, again, one has to appreciate Fitzball's audience—Anne and Macraisy possess some depth: she is strong and he is a villain psychologically troubled by his life of crime. Bradford is less interesting, partly because he is a stereotypical hero. Yet, he does not duel with Macraisy, as do most heroes with villains. He takes his nobility to his death sentence. That characteristic, while improbable, does add another scale to the character.

Of curious interest is the role of Ann. Typically, the heroine was an almost-caricatured persona, as were the hero and villain. However, Ann emerges as strong, faithful, and defending. At every opportunity, she boldly advocates Bradford's innocence. Macraisy's lifelong insurgency against society transforms into a restitution before death, and one may imagine that this villain, for all of his criminality, was a victim of Spencer's "survival of the fittest" social philosophy. Although Fitzball does not give a social reason for Macraisy's criminal behavior, it is possible that the rogue's predatorship has come from a society alien to his comprehension. His climactic indignation of self, during the burial sequence and at the gallows scene, indicates that the monster did have a moral dimension about him if only slightly. With Macraisy his sense of self worth may only be realized by a perverted challenge to a pristine lifestyle from which he will always be ostracized. As modern criminology supports, the criminal often acts out of frustration against a social norm foreign to him. Bradford emerges as the most stereotypical of the characters. His stalwart position, to the degree that he tends to be almost sanctimonious about his death, is a bit much even for a melodramatic hero. Nonetheless, the confrontation scene does put some vigor in him.

In Act II, Scene Fourth (as Fitzball has loftily named the scenes in ordinal numbers), Bradford charges Macraisy near the flickering campfire thusly: "Yes, monster! Heaven hath heard my prayers—low shall thy body lie...in eternal flames" (*Jonathan Bradford* 301). Without fisticuffs, or even a verbal insistence that Macraisy return to exonerate him, Bradford marches back to town and the hangman. In the following sequence, Macraisy startles Caleb with that tint of morality referred to earlier. Remorseful of his crime, Macraisy goes mad upon hearing the funeral dirge and stabs himself. It is one of Fitzball's most invigorating scenes. Bleeding and insane, Macraisy has become a personification of the sensational triad: "They are singing the anthem of the dead! I'll not hear it—Horror! I cannot bear it—no; rather than that I'll die I'll die—die (stabs himself) Ha, ha, ha, ha, die! Ha, ha, ha" (*Jonathan Bradford* 31). The *ha, ha's* were a standard diction in showing insanity or villainy. Unlike camp, such grammatical idiosyncrasies were purposely enacted as tools to convince the audience of the emotionalism on stage.

Because Macraisy is the dramatic interest in the play—and the villain always is—a psychological sketch of him may prove interesting. Obviously, he has delusions of grandeur: his life of crime a battle for supremacy, his psychotic schemes directives to enhance that supremacy at any fascist cost. All of these are psychological foundations for terrorism (Coville, Costello, and Rouke 121-2). Nevertheless, within Macraisy's dementia, there is the tendency for self-destruction. In rushing to the gallows, Macraisy screams, "It's a villain I've been—a bad, heartless villain—but I am punished. Pardon! Pardon" (*Jonathan Bradford* 28). His immolation is a romantic act to be sure. But Fitzball's theatre was just that, romantic, unrealistic art. In this forte, Fitzball shared with Euripides a drama called "the romantic or melodramatic kind" (Murray 241). Therefore, spectacle became for Fitzball not only an ingredient for sets and production, but an ingredient in characterization as well. Macraisy, ironically, is the seal for the moral lesson of the play. He did not have to intervene in Bradford's execution, but his conscience forced him. Fitzball is symbolizing hope for virtue, through one of his most diabolical characters.

Fitzball's criminals symbolized, in the words of social scientists Merton and Nisbett, "the inevitable conflict between man's biological nature and the demands placed on that nature by society" (87). Again, Fitzball was not a social-thesis dramatist. Yet, Fitzball's characters, in several of his plays, do rise above the expected. And, knowing the emphasis of Blood-and-Thunder excitement, for the rousing sake of thrills, Fitzball's care in writing some interesting characters, especially the villains, must go to his credit. To reiterate, the development of psychological criticism has more to say to a play than perhaps the era in which the art was formed. Since this method of criticism has run the gamut from Aeschylus to Sam Shepard, the psychological complex found in *Oedipus Rex*, to the social freedom in *Hair*, all art, including theatre, has become transfixed by psychological criticism-interpretation. Only classic melodrama has been ignored as having psychological overtones. Poignantly, Fitzball's *Bradford* was based on a true crime; Macraisy could be a reflection of the type of criminal one might encounter in a city's mean streets—especially based upon the determinants of nineteenth-century criminology; and the sensational triad had a basis in the chaos of the urban life. All of these theatrical entities seem to command a psychological evaluation. The moral factor represents a interpretive yearning, at the very least. Fitzball's dramaturgy was colored by the actions of his personas. It was as if Fitzball created the characters and then the dramatic structure, inasmuch as his characters tended to overwhelm all other facets in a given drama.

Recapitulating the basic levels of *Bradford's* structure (level), the play emerges as paradigmatic of Fitzballian dramaturgy. The levels, sometimes called the dramatic pyramid, are as follows: the exposition, the rising action, the climax, the falling action, and denouement. Within this matrix is Fitzball's consistent hope above all others: to please and to moralize to the viewer. In appreciating Fitzballian dramaturgy, one must bear a single directive in mind: Fitzball's artistry is aesthetically between that of a thinker and of a joker. Bernard Cohen reminds the critic that he must see literature's relationship of ideas in order to perceive a "totality of meaning" (1). This is essential in reading Fitzball. More than that, it is a veritable anchor for the critic's comprehension. For a while Fitzball will delineate a solidly planned string of events. Then, quirkily, this elf of the uncanny will inject a happening that throws the reader and viewer into mental consternation. The relationship between ideas seem untied and carousing. For instance, in *Joan of Arc*, Joan is saved form death by the arrival of Charles, her savior. The executioner had already torched the pyre. Joan's death would have had a solemn, martyring effect if left alone. However, Fitzball, seemingly to end the drama quickly, as melodrama, injected the rescue. One can sense his attitude by the brevity of the stage direction.

Music. The Executioner sets fire to the pile—at this moment the gates are thrown open and Charles, Florine, and soldiers rush on and liberate Joan. Beauvais, Richmont and Chalons, taken prisoners. Tumult. A general picture is formed and the curtain falls. (29)

Almost magically, Fitzball, the sorcerer of dramatic mayhem, brings his "unity of design" in to conclude the work's "totality of meaning." This, of course, was Fitzball's aesthetic charm and vocational kudo; his menagerie of theatrical and dramatic trickery was also the source of some discommendation from critics put out by such whimsy. To follow Fitzball, then, one must realize that he is on a roller coaster path, which, at anytime, may twist and turn.

In the exposition, the plot, the murder, and, most importantly, the characters were presented. In the rising action, the innocence of Bradford and the guilt of Macraisy were established as issues to be confronted. In the climax, and this is melodrama's most pungent level, the combat between the protagonist and antagonist was brought to bear, with implications for the future. In the falling action, Macraisy's mortal stabbing and his wild repentance were enacted. In the denouement, Macraisy sets Bradford free in the nick-of-time, dies, and Bradford's virtue triumphs. Although these divisions do overlap with one another, the demarcations in transpontine and, to an extent, modern melodrama have remained fairly well consistent. The paradigm may not vary too greatly, or the moral lesson will become obscured, and audience interest will become confused. The masses have come to expect these levels, so the genre does not deviate too much from this pattern. Fitzball uses the paradigm as a continuing layer to build moral interest and dramatic qualification. Quantitatively, Fitzball's plays are usually divided along these levels. In *Bradford*, the crime sets in motion the demarcations because each level of the paradigm rests upon a certain reflection of the crime. The implications and ramifications from it branch out. Wrote Fitzball of the success of the play, in which these levels played no small part in the audience's abilities to follow the action:

It was the hundredth reception of "Jonathan Bradford." Mr. Osbaldiston, who played Jonathan, gave sumptuous de jeuner on the stage, to his performances, on which occasion, to my utter surprise, I was presented with a costly silver cup. (1: 249)

Of importance to the play's physical setting, Fitzball envisioned a deft procedure of stating the numerous kinds of action. The usual box set was staged, within the proscenium four-wall setting. Of course, the spectator would see the action through the invisible wall facing him. However, multiple settings were implemented: one room was above the living room of the inn. This was an innovation since audiences, especially those of melodrama, were used to seeing only one set at a time. Fitzball must have reasoned that the more spectacular—and any deviation in normal theatrical procedure was spectacular—he was in depicting action and mystery, the more intriguing his art would become. Herein, the murder could be enacted while serenity was simultaneously seen in the downstairs area. Hence, the irony of complacency and violence would be set in motion physically and emotionally. In addition to the multiple setting, the play had six locations, usually accomplished by rolling flats: the interior and exterior of the inn; the interior and exterior of Farmer Nelson's home—he was Bradford's father-in-law who thought him guilty; the cemetery; and the gallows. The unities of Aristotle, which have become part of drama's encompassing and overall presentational aesthetic, are direct in *Bradford*. They are mentioned only because of their cohesive effects in dramatic terms.

The unity of place, that the action should be confined to a singular or general locale, is fairly precise, although Fitzball was given to jumping from one location to another, as the action dictated. The unity of action, that there should be one dominating plot, not a potpourri of plots, is established in the murder itself. And the unity of time, that the play's action should be accomplished in a 24-hour period, or within a logical time span, could have been easily accomplished. For Fitzball the unities were, at best, only contingent upon the dramatic elements and what the writer fancied as logical to the aesthetics of the play.

Fitzball patted himself on the back by remarking of the play, "...here was a dramatic magic" (1: 257). The critic Bartone Baker countered, "No poorer specimen of dramatic work was ever given to the on the stage of a traspontine theatre" (1: 257). This argument evidences Fitzball's running battle with critics. Nevertheless, as they were wont to do concerning Fitzballian fare, especially with the macabre kind, the audiences confounded the critics by turning out in throngs to see the play. It ran 264 consecutive nights and netted for a happy manager, who was also the play's star, David Osbaldiston, a hefty 8,000 pounds (Byrne 64). However, with the set innovation, the profits, and the viewer response, Fitzball outdid himself with characterization and acting technique. Without a brief understanding of what nineteenth-century, melodramatic acting was, one cannot enjoy the luster of the genre. Victorian dramaturgy was very much emphasized through its sensational and ornate production, in which acting played no little role. It would be well to continue our inspection of *Jonathan Bradford* from this angle: how did characterization motivate the dramatic aesthetic? The answer to this question will reveal much about the way Fitzball saw the total function of dramaturgy.

Though his characters, at least the main ones, are not purely stock figures, the comic servants are reminiscent of the Roman theatre stock characters whose "lines of business" provided comic relief. Such "lines of business" were in keeping with the lazzi, or 'bits of comic business, or action, used by the performers in the comedia dell'arte during the Italian Renaissance" (Roberts 514). The comic servants' song and merry intercessions about marriage, in the first act of *Bradford*, were given by Fitzball as standard comic relief and may have been precursors of vaudevillian routines. Melodrama always had comedic characters to offset the seriousness of the lurid plays. Unlike the improvisational forms in the commedia, the melodramatic lazzi were staged as part of the drama. One of the distinguishing features of the characters is that of workingman stock. Bradford maintains a discernible aura of middle-class functions and, thereby, makes audience empathy the more potent. Bradford is a common landlord and Macraisy is a criminal, the type of creature in London's jails, streets, and "pennydreadfuls." The melodramatist, with his moral to tell, always made the most of subjectivity in dramatic purpose. Wrote Fitzball about characterization. "All art has a purpose. The purpose of drama is to entertain;

the aim of drama is to tell a story. The enactment of the story by a group of characters is the special province of drama" (1: 243). Fitzball's dramatic theorem was to combine purpose, aim, and enactment in insuring that the play bolstered entertainment with morality. All three entities in *Bradford* are enlarged by Macraisy's challenge to Bradford's middle-class set of values and ethics. With apostrophes to heaven, references to sin, and spiritual ordeals, the macabre tone of the play takes on an eerie, folk-tale quality, similar to those tales woven by Hawthorne and Cooper. Fitzball does not attempt a cosmic presumption, but the war of ethics has a grand, theatrical flavor to it, with the theological undertones in most melodramas.

The Acting of Melodrama

Since acting is at the heart of all drama, a word should be said about the style of acting present during Fitzball's age. Certainly this has pertinence to melodrama, since melodrama is largely remembered for its specific mode of volatile histrionics. An example of the flavor in the acting of the period is found in a review of Fitzball's *The Inchcage Bell* (May 26, 1822). David Osbaldiston played the hero, Hans Hatton, a role not unlike Bradford, in this nautical drama. The *Examiner* lauded, "There is a gaiety together with forcible expression—a spring of spirits, an elasticity combined with power, in this performer, which we rarely see and which denoted no ordinary capacity" (436). Spirited, elastic power was the foundation of the age's acting.

Melodramatic acting, like melodrama itself, placed emphasis upon stereotyping of characterization and predicaments. As has been asserted, the literature had to make its premise simple and stark enough for the masses; the acting skills were no less demanding. We must remember the times' social circumstances: the working class was largely unsophisticated and the intelligensia wanted entertainment. The acting style had to suit both needs. Fitzball's villains—the personification of the triad in deed or in mood—were as black as double-dyed villainy would permit. For instance, 0. Smith's enactment of the monster in *The Black Vulture* was seen as being able to "...freeze the spectator with his weird appearance and action" (Marston 19). His griffin-like character was something akin to an alien *Thing* from another world. Fitzball knew that fright meant commerce. Caesar Bonesana once wrote that crime was an immediate attack upon society (36). What Fitzball did with the grotesque, through acting, was to create an attack upon a society's malaise by metaphor. Checkland notes,

In the thirties and forties (of the nineteenth-century), male youth and adulthood buried themselves in penny-dreadfuls, wherein they might sup upon the horrors of the gothic romance with its deathsheads and spectres. (269)

Acting brought these fears, and their opposites, virtue and daring, to life. The actor made the dream world of the melodrama come to life. Buss' feeling that man has a need to be frightened safely was the priority of Fitzball's whole perspective in the triad (48).

Fitzball was an advocate of good acting skills, with a goodly amount of blue-fire bravado thrown in for good measure: "Fine acting was enough for the great authors, but a little blue-fire, and to know when and where to use it, was necessary for me" (11: 12). About *Bradford*, with its shadowy rooms, gory murder, and whailing storms, the *Atlas* named it "fine drama" (1: 253). For Fitzball, his grandiose dramas had to be magical. It is no wonder that Fitzball, his genre, and its acting style have been rebuked. The reprimand comes from ignorance about all three. It is true that cheap exploiters of melodrama aided in such dramatic mockery. Upon examination, however, Delsartian acting will be shown as having integrity and worth. To be sure, Francois Delsarte influenced generations of actors, and some of the best that the theatre has ever seen.

Fitzball did not write plays to be read; the hack had to write for performance. Blood-and-Thunder relied on performance for its artistic and economic well-being. Brockett praises Delsarte (1811-1871) as being most aware of the actor's entire being. For Delsarte, the actor commanded in body that which was in the soul.

(Francois) Delsarte sought to analyze emotions and ideas and to determine how they are outwardly expressed. He divided human experience and behavior into the physical, mental, and emotional-spirited, and he related these to each action, thought, and emotion. By the end of the 19th century it was being taught all over the world...to most subsequent attempts to formulate training programs for actors. (*History* 388)

The legendary Henry Irving, one of classic melodrama's best interpreters, was a Delsartian. In his historic portrayal of *Dr. Jekyll and Mr. Hyde,* the actor's transmutation was thusly critiqued:

Henry Irving, who would turn the screw more surely than any of his contemporaries, was never more chilling than in what his son called the physical change from the tall, austure Jekyll to the dwarfish creature of unmitigated evil. *(Edwardian Theatre* 170)

A very physical form of acting, not in the least shoddy or haphazard, the

Delsartian technique demanded that the internal become external; that the actor vigorously demonstrate his command of body, diction, and thought; that the theatre experience, by way of the actor, be one of spiritual, as well as artistic, greatness and expression. Ewin Duerr notes that the legendary teacher encouraged his actors to see art as a combination of life, mind, and soul and its goal as emotional movement, interest, and persuasion (326). When one saw a play, such as *Jonathan Bradford,* he was aware, through the acting itself, on the sheer physicality and emotion in the theatrical experience. Certainly Fitzball's plays relied on an intriguing system of acting to get its theatricality across. With an impetus from English "dumb shows" (pantomime) and the reflections of the lavish dramas from Shakespeare's era, Fitzball was aware of what constituted fine acting, even if he did accentuate histrionic bravado.

In his seminal book on Delsarte, *Every Little Movement,* Ted Shawn writes that Delsarte was more than an innovator of acting. This misunderstood tutor was a philosopher, multi-talented artist, and virtuoso. He was also ahead of his time, with many a critic desperately attempting to fathom his thought. Delsarte's reflections imply a commonality with those of Fitzball:

Art is divine in its principles, divine in its essence, divine in its action, divine in its end. And what are, in effect, the essential principles of art? Are they not, taking them together, the Good, the True, and the Beautiful.... Movement is the direct agent of the heart, the most powerful means by which emotion is expressed. In a work, it is the spirit of which the work is only the letter. (23)

Delsarte's exhortative content, *a fortiori,* implied the message and ontology of melodrama. Henry Wallack's portrayal of Macraisy says much about the principled vigor in a finely etched, melodramatic persona, brought to life by an acting style of magnetic persuasion. Fitzball happily reflected:

In Dan Macraisy, Henry Wallack made a most unlooked for impression. He suddenly, as the rehearsal proceeded, seemed to launch into the character and to discover its opportunities by degrees as a boy discovers a problem in mathematics. The low cunning which built itself upon the exterior of an Irish gentleman-not an exquisite conception of the part of Macraisy. The audience testified their appreciation of Wallack's performance by calling him at the fall of the curtain night after night which was a very unusual compliment in those days. (1: 249)

Again, the idea of Aristotle's mimesis comes to mind: that the dramatic imitation of life is an embellishment of that life. Victorian (Delasartian) acting was not some distortion of dramatic imitation. Rather, it was a style of acting that stressed "intense emotional expression; rhythmic, melodic, poetic vocal delivery....and sweeping, flowing gestures" (Crawford 267).

Probably Victorian acting was seen at its most characteristic not in tragedy or comedy, but in melodrama, the characteristic entertainment of the age. Melodrama demanded of its exponents a singular combination of athleticism and bravado which was instinctive rather than interpretive, but which bloomed profusely in the forcing grounds of the minor theatres.... Without some conception of the vigor and appeal of their acting it is impossible to account for the success of the countless threadbare melodramas, concocted by men happy in the knowledge of such methods and themselves willing victims of their magic. There was acting to raise the emotions without troubling the mind, and as such was admirably designed to carry the bulk of the Victorian audience into the gas-lit world of Victorian drama. (*The Victorian Theatre* 26)

Unfortunately, Fitzball's *Agamemnon* became his only work revived—and only as closet drama—after his death, perhaps because of encroaching realism in dramaturgy, theatricalization, and audience responses. However the Edwardian Theatre maintained an interest in the type of play theatricalized by Fitzball: grandiose sets; presentational acting; exciting, cliff-hanging episodes. Perhaps, unconsciously, this evolving theatre was carrying on the milieu so well marked by Fitzball. As was earlier stated, the devotee of melodrama was/is relentless in the emotional response of the genre.

Perhaps Disher best summarized the overpowering attraction of melodrama, in its most Fitzballain grotesquerie, when he wrote of its histrionic specialties:

Popular imagination creates its new fashions out of old ideas. You may see the bugbear in the demonic, for these monsters in superhuman shapes are given to crying, "Ha, ha!" with the joy of evildoing, and in the early nineteenth-century fiction your demon is your only eager evil-doer...They did not become exultant until actors had exhibited Shylock, Iago, and Richard III as fiends incarnate, and in this way the theatre outstripped other imaginative forces in reflecting what was happening in the great world beyond playhouse walls. Evildoers who repented of their sins and seducers who were in the end only to glad to marry the girl were the vogue. Demons, vampires, and hobgoblims of land and sea committed crimes too awful for human agency. "Moralizing on stage" depicted villains, who sometimes repented before death, but the triumph of virtue over vice, spirit over the demonic, was the enchantment of the genre. (113-8)

"The enchantment of the genre" was melodrama's guises of the morality play, Francisco's salvation from Gortzburg, and Bradford's triumph over a fallen

Macraisy. "The enchantment of the genre" were all of these plots and ideas. And "the enchantment" was physicalized before an "enchanted" audience by "enchanting" actors, who knew their craft, their theatre, and, most importantly, their spectators. These figures possessed a flair and frenzy about them that was emotional and dynamic outwardly, not inwardly. For this reason, in developing a great and poignant characterization, many playwrights will effect a certain melodramatic nuance. It simply makes the character larger-than-life and, henceforth, memorable. The spectator of melodrama experienced catharsis in watching raw, human emotion rigorously portrayed on the stage. The influence of romanticism, as both a literary, philosophical, and theatrical impulse, was too strongly felt and urged to be ignored. Hence, to see any type of nineteenth-century melodrama—Fitzballian drama—eminent was to see romanticism concretized for the masses' vision, as well as for their stirred emotions.

The Elements in Jonathan Bradford

Hull's notice that melodrama's well-constructed plot must deal with "a brisk conflict of good against evil" is a testimony to *Jonathan Bradford* (209). In all of Fitzball's extant works, none is more satisfactorily drawn, especially within the framework of "moralising language" (Fitzball's term), than is *Bradford*. Knowing Fitzball's nature for the theatrical and for the thoughtful, within the moral scope of the genre, such kudos are not unwarranted. The macabre elements of the play have just enough power to keep suspense high, and the triadic qualities of Macraisy are never used only for the sake of shock effect: they are part of the character's fibre, just as honor is part of Bradford's. The *scene a faire* is Fitzball's dogma; it is the obligatory scene wherein all the patterns of the unity of design come together. Within this gallant situation of theatrical realities, Fitzball found his audience "...crying and laughing to supply the exhaustion of both mind and body" (11: 336). Cathartic integration was for Fitzball not simply a theory; it was an artistic and emotional destiny.

Diction

Much of *Jonathan Bradford*'s fame rests with its splendid dialogue. Mused Fitzball about his skills, "A man must be born an actor, as well as a poet" (1: 394). He also concluded, and not so timidly that, "My poetry, however, was my brightest plume; my greenest laurel" (1: 15). Sometimes the peacock, Fitzball indulged himself: "As a melodramatic writer, with what was called the freshness of style, 'I became at once popular' " (1: 94). The actor Frederick Robson mentioned Fitzball's literary finesse with respect, if not exultation: "Edward Fitzball was writing verses in Fanny Robson's Album to celebrated her sixteenth birthday, addressing her as 'Young lovely rose of Amphill Square' " (Sands 110). A dedicated and sincere poet, perhaps in the "Hallmark Card" variety, Fitzball's diction could range from the sweet to the rugged at a whim, while maintaining its individuality and rapture. In *Bradford* his diction has the full-blooded zealousness which would snare the attention of the spectator and keep it. In the confrontation scene, Bradford steadfastly accuses his foe and threatens Macraisy with a punishment far worse than the gallows:

Yes, monster; that Jonathan whom you would so want only have sacrificed: the husband of a devoted wife, the father of children, whom you have plunged in to irretrievable infamy. Heaven hath heard my prayers to avenge and punish. (1: 244)

The Devil's Elixir and *Jonathan Bradford* are key examples of Fitzballian diction at its best. If diction were an affirmation of style, then music was Fitzball's shine of feeling.

Music

Since Aristotle deigned that music was primarily adjunct to drama, he would never have guessed the effectiveness of melodrama's generic usage of the lagging element. Concerning music's place in *Bradford,* one notices immediately that it is not forced or cumbersome, but always placed for the ultimate in emotional response. *Bradford* is not a burletta, as Fitzball was wont to write. Rather, the musical instances served a more incidental nature. Whenever sensational scenes would arise, as in the storm during the murder, the music would reach a fervent pitch, thereby propelling the audience into yet another dimension of emotional involvement. For Fitzball, music-in-drama, created the final thought for, what Rowell described as, an "artistic world entirely different from our own" (*Theatre in the Age of Irving* ix). The howling wind, mixed with the eerie cadence of a musical motif, brought the macabre mood to an emotional acme. Bradford's natural, dramatic rhythm is indebted to the musical interludes, which pull the viewer further into the play's force.

The opening scene has Jack Rockbottle, the comedic manservant, singing a ditty about unrequited love. Such merry tunes were popular with audiences, and they formed a basis for future burlesque and vaudeville routines. In a smattering of Fitzball's plays, there are attached scores. For instance, *Esmeralda* (1834), the dramatization of Victor Hugo's *The Hunchback of Notre Dame* (*Notre Dame de Paris*, 1831), has a sibling libretto, *Ouasimodo; or, The*

Gypsy Girl of Notre Dame, which was premiered on February 2, 1836. Notice that Fitzball appealed to the manly love of the feminine mystique by the title and subtitle. He knew the perfunctory attraction of "a dancing girl" would enhance a public attraction to the classics, in which he mixed art with sensuality. In his macabre plays, music was essential for mood effects. *Paul Clifford,* a fine example of the criminous portion of the triad as theme, was termed, in an unsure way, as either burletta, opera, or tragedy. With an exciting score by Redwell, Fitzball exclaimed that the 1835 work was "...a musical burletta" (11: 38). In his eight years at the Drury Lane, Fitzball was engaged by the musical producer Alfre Bunn to write numerous light musicals (Hartnoll 320). Of his interest in musical theatre, Fitzball noted,

I had, it was quite evident, created an audience of my own (i.e. at the minor houses), who seemed to follow me ...my dramas, such as they were, pleases greatly a large portion of the public, and were the fashion with the middling classes. (11: 14-5)

The difference between Fitzball's musical theatre and our contemporary one, chiefly initiated by the revolutionary *Oklahoma,* resides in the function of music. For Fitzball, music was primarily an instrument for emotional discharge. Today, musical theatre seems to integrate song and tune unavoidably as intrinsic ingredients in the play. *The Devil's Elixir* could be played effectively without its musical incidentals; though another melodrama, *West Side Story,* could not survive, with any distinction, as a play void of music and song. Therefore, melodramatic music was effected for emotionalism; whereas, contemporary musical theatre uses music as a much more implanted element in the narrative, an element necessary for the fantasy portion of a usually realistic plot.

　　In all, Fitzball composed 500 tunes, and most of his 170 plays, whether afterpieces or main attractions, had musical interludes. As part of the music in *Bradford,* Fitzball introduced the song, "A Kind Old Man Came Wooing," which Sally, the maid, chortled. As examples of Fitzball's musical range, *Bradford* had the following: Sally's song; Caleb's song about a sailor's freedom; the weird, musical accompaniment to the clock striking midnight before Hayes murder, a melodramatic technique carried on today as a hint of foreboding; and the exciting, thrilling, and suspenseful leitmotif flanking Bradford's escape form jail, again another transposed aesthetic of music underlying adventure scenes, still used in contemporary, melodramatic media. Interestingly enough, Fitzball forewent a final score. Fitzball's musical interludes possessed an "imagery of feeling and sense" (Peacock 156). Such may be gleaned form Macraisy's canzonet, set to the tune of "St. Partrick was a Gentleman, " which has the burletta style seen in two of Fitzball's most deft burlettas, *The Barber* and *The Three Hunchbacks*. The song is particularly ironic in that Macraisy is no gentleman, and that his victim was very much a man of dignity. The song divulges much about the villain's imagery of self: "We independent gentlemen,/ We stayed at home at sea,/ We kiss the girls, and kick the man,/ And do just as we please" (*Jonathan Bradford* 18). From this song, Macraisy's lust, anarchy, and ruthlessness—in fact, the triad itself—are revealed in this happy tune, a subtle divarication used by Fitzball in furthering characterization. Summarily, Fitzball's music in *Bradford* was used sparingly and always for a point: emotional interest that would aid in a cathartic response. Whenever the audience would cry, or be frightened by music's enhancement of a given stage circumstance, Fitzball ushered in catharsis a little more, until the effect was ultimately accomplished.

Spectacle

Concerning spectacle, *Jonathan Bradford's* use of that element is incomparable to that of *The Devil's Elixir*'s usage. In the first place, *Bradford's* haunting skies, roaring thunder, fulgurous explosions, terrifying murder room, and graveyard scene evoke the macabre atmosphere for the sake of mystery, while the spooky occurrences in *The Devil's Elixir* have their impetus from an unearthly encounter. And, in the second place, Macraisy is himself a human personification of the triad, with whom audiences may more readily empathize as a figure in society, while Gortzburg is a demon, a literary metaphor of evil. In short, Fitzball, with care and wit, has shown two sides of the triad and the macabre theatre: the human and the supernatural. On the other hand, the theatricality of spectacle, in either case, projects upon the spectator a feeling of allurement to a circumstance made overwhelmingly enveloping. Fitzballian spectacle was always a product of episodic scripting: the horror of the murder and the stichomythic dialogue, between hero and villain, had a darkening atmospheric tone and mood to them, with a portent of more action to come. The climax and its aftermath had an athletic and grandiose simulacrum about them, within the context of the chilling graveyard and forbidding gallows; and, of course, the conflict between Bradford and Macraisy became metaphorical. The sun rises to set this morbidity aright at the denouement, and the tone of spectacle takes on a hopeful and positive illumination. In all of his plays, Fitzball saw spectacle as the brush with which to paint his action. The strokes are long in *Bradford,* whose fate, Fitzball lamented, seemed doomed to minor houses (1: 250) The play's revivals dispelled that disparagement.

Jonathan Bradford as Prototypical Fitzball

Figaro criticized Fitzball's mass-motivating appeal when it noted, "Fitzball's brain has a strong attractive power, and the gallery has overflowed more than ever. Fitzball is, after all, a clever man if he answers his own purpose and that of the manager" (180). Again, the critics failed to consider what Fitzball, theoretically and practically, was attempting: the presentation of a play for public consumption which met the mentality of those in attendance. A hack could not write a play over the paying customer's head and expect to keep his job or see his plays revived. I have used *Jonathan Bradford* as prototypical Fitzball for two reasons: 1) to demonstrate that its dramatic and theatrical composition is exemplary and critically attractive as classic melodrama and 2) to assert that Fitzball's theatre of the macabre can use the sensational triad in a social frame of reference. In the long run, *Bradford* may be contextually seen as a fine example of the crime play, in the literary tradition of such works. Fitzball's romances have their germination in reality. Booth reports that at least 50 plays during the nineteenth century had murder in their titles. "Many plays of this kind were hastily prepared versions of actual crimes, sometimes purely local in origin" (*English Melodrama* 51) *Bradford* was exemplary of this type of dramatization.

In a summary reflection of the crime play, Fitzball was part of a literary fascination with macabre felonies, which seemed to include all types of literature, stretching from the novelist Gerald Griffin, whose work *The Collegians* (1829) told of the murder of Ellen Scanlin, by one Stephen Sullivan, at the behest of her husband, John; to the crime's dramatization by Dion Boucicault in 1859; to its operatic treatment by Julius Benedict in 1863. William Corder's confession to murdering his mistress, Maria Marten, was used as the text for the melodrama *The Murder in the Red Barn* in 1828 (Nash 1502). These artistic examples were given to indicate that Fitzball's era was much interested in such macabre goings-on in all manner of artistic expression. *Jonathan Bradford* was Fitzball's well-crafted gift of man's eternal fascination with the crime and the sensational triad.

It may be well to elucidate the facts behind this primitive type of docudrama. In his autobiography, Fitzball recounted the nature of the grisly crime that he dramatized so well.

JONATHAN BRADFORD

OR,

The Murder at the Roadside Inn.

The scenery by Marshall. Music by Jolly.

This Original Drama

Is founded on real facts: Jonathan Bradford actually kept an inn on the London road to Oxford and bore an unexceptionable character. The extraordinary affair which led to the construction of this drama, was the conversation of the whole kingdom. The innocent and unfortunate landlord, accused of a cruel murder, perpetrated under his very roof, and, borne down by a train of overwhelming circumstantial evidence, in vain pleaded not guilty. All conspired to condemn him; his assertions were of no avail; never was presumptive conviction more strong. There was little need of comment from the judge, in summing up evidence, and the jury brought in the prisoner guilty without going out of the box. He was hanged; and he was innocent. (1: 241-2)

In keeping with the happy ending ploy, Fitzball exonerated Bradford theatrically, by way of including a *peripeteia*, thereby making a plea for social and legal justice. If for nothing else, this play, thereby, rises above exploitation. The play, compounded with Fitzball's politically-conscientious handling of a real case, was a type of precursor, somewhat, to Maxwell Anderson's satire on the miscarriage of justice in *Gods of Lightning* (1928). This gives Fitzball an integrity and dignity beyond stage pyrotechnics and monsters. It is because of this play's maturity that Fitzball's corpus deserved "better press." He may have churned out hack potboilers, but, when artistry demanded it, he was capable of much more. Wrote Fitzball:

On perusal, I found that Jonathan Bradford contained the essence of what I required, and I could draw upon my imagination to do the rest; which I determined to do...to re-establish my credit in the theatre, once so full of approval, yet, where my last work was received so coldly (Andreas Hofer). How was all of this to be accomplished? and with what magic? It was not by literature!—it was not by poetry! it was not by mirth—it was not by tears!—all of which had been tried in Hofer. It might be by the harmony of the whole; with a spice or two of original effect, thrown in at intervals...the effect succeeded, in its results, beyond any drama that I had yet presented to the public! (1: 324-35)

Faced with critical attacks, but supported by audience sympathy and commercial appeal for the most part, Fitzball saw in *Jonathan Bradford* his vindication. As did Shakespeare, Fitzball attracted the regular playgoer. The play witnessed that "harmony of the whole" artistry when he wrote:

...at least 4,000 of the public witnessed its representation; and that, not merely confined to the middling, or working classes, but contained, within its numbers, some thousands of the highest order of intellect and society...this play, for its was, unquestionably, legitimate, contained, without partiality, or weakness, a peculiar claim to our prolonged attention and remark...by public voice. Mr. Cobdin would say, "...simply because it came so closely home to English feeling." (1: 257)

With intelligence and artistry, complemented by that English feeling, always a strong identity for Fitzballian drama with the public, *Bradford* emerged as Fitzball's most engrossing play. As Peter Brook has noticed, "It is always the popular theatre that saves the day" (65). Within that spectrum, Fitzball managed to assuage even several of the critical bigots who though that his Blood-and-Thunder was only the stuff of blue-fire bogeymen. Montrose J. Moses once wrote that a dramatist is always part of a play's development (2). *Jonathan Bradford* became Fitzball's prized play due to that awareness being poignant in every aspect of its conception and production. Rowell gave the play its influential and artistic benediction thusly:

Fitzball devised in *Jonathan Bradford* a play whose technical daring in showing four of the Inn's rooms simultaneously...provided stories of crime in low life. It was not long before the annals of the police court were being searched for cases of sensational as those of Maria Marten and Sweeny Todd, the Demon of Fleet Street. (*The Victorian Theatre* 50)

Exemplary Plays of the Sensational Triad
The other plays to be examined will have their highlights as examples of Fitzballian sensationalism extolled. A close race for the fame of *Jonathan* is that of Fitzball's most celebrated monster play, *The Flying Dutchman*; or, *The Phantom Ship*. Premiering at the Adelphi Theatre on January 8, 1827, the play was definitive Blood-and-Thunder-blue-fire-fright. Inspired by the French melodramatist J.R. Planche, whose *Vampyre* had scared the very wits out of an hypnotized audience in the best of Grand Guignol horror, Fitzball was determined to do the some with *Dutchman*. George Rowell recalls criticism about one of Fitzball's grandest creations, the monstrous Vanderdecken, in *The Flying Dutchman:* "Edward Fitzball profited by Planche's *Vampyre* to write *The Flying Dutchman,* which introduced to the stage the perennially popular figure of the accursed Vanderdecken" (*The Victorian Theatre* 45). Starring as

the ghostly figure was none other than that venerable portrayer of monsters, O. Smith. Another actor of distinction in the cast was Frederick Yates, whose "star" role of the sailor Toby Varnish, was outstanding. Having every conceivable type of triadic nuance in it, the play's haunting imagery of monsters and mayhem was its main attraction, with all of the dramatic elements hard at work. From its opening night, *Dutchman* was a worthy companion to *Frankenstein, The Vampyre, The Castle Spectre* and the other macabre entries of this ilk. Disher concludes, "In the Adelphi Fitzball now designed a piece of Diabaldrie which should not be by any means behind even Frankenstein in horror and blue fire—*The Flying Dutchman; or, The Phantom Ship*" (98). If *Bradford* were his masterpiece of dramaturgic skill, then *Dutchman* was Fitzball's prize for naked horror.

Letting out all stops for his theatre of the macabre, both theatrically and dramatically, Fitzball's sensationalism was personified by O. Smith. His career would include starring roles as fiends in *The Devil's Elixir, The Black Vulture,* and in *Esmeralda*. Of him Fitzball would laud, "His acting of Vanderdecken had in it sublimity of awful mystery, which those who have seen him in the part can alone comprehend" (1: 171). Often played against *Frankenstein, Dutchman* was a *coup de theatre* of tremendous power. Because his monsters bedazzled creation through art, Fitzball may have agreed with J.E. Cirlot, who saw the monster as "...symbolic of the cosmic forces at a stage one step removed form chaos...base powers which constitute the deepest strata of spiritual geology... eruptions of some monstrous apparition or activity" (213). There is more to Vanderdecken than rampage; Fitzball drew him not as a created monster, as was the Black Vulture, but as a man-cum-monster. Within that paradox, there is another plane to his being, just because he knew once the dimensions of being human. A spiritual chaos is a featured part of his character.

Begging permission to ascend from the "Evil Spirit of the Deep," Rockala, Vanderdecken rises from the murky depths to plague the robust sailor, Toby Varnish. The blue-fire syndrome, critically, is observed as the monster flamboyantly rises form the churning and darkened sea. The skies sense this blasphemy and storm. Vanderdecken arrives, with a ghostly, cyan tint about him, wearing a dark garb and an even darker expression. With parallels to Gortzburg in his ascension from hell to earth; his alliance with a superior devil-in-charge; and in his association with a maiden fair, all typical of a Fitzballan schema—the monster is in want of the lovely heroine, Lestelle. Notice should be taken of Fitzball's pun in this name, which is redolent of star, the fairest of celestial bodies. Episodically, the suspense mounts as the ghost steals about the ship. The confrontation scene comes in Act III between Vanderdecken and Toby, his nemesis. In order to save Lestelle from the clutches of the fiend, Toby suddenly burns the "mystical book" that is in the monster's cave. The destruction of the book, which contains magical incantations that allow evil to succeed, causes the destruction of Vanderdecken, who then plunges into the sea, defeated and lost to hell. Toby comforts Lestelle, as the seas rush into the cove, destroying all, as the good characters escape the monster's sinking lair.

In all of Fitzball's examples of the theatre of the macabre, there are three essential points concerning theology, ethics, and morality. First, Fitzball usually has the salvation of someone's soul, the cosmic/theological instance, as a stake in his most macabre dramas. Second, there is a robbery of some type, thereby undermining ethical values. The robbery may be kidnapping or plain stealing, but this crime is often a integral part of the villain's plan. And, third, there is oftentimes a seduction or allusion to the seduction of a heroine by the villain, which is a standard ploy in classic melodrama. Of course, these three entities all combine as the moral hallmark against which the sensational triad will rail. These are certainly present in *The Devil's Elixir* and *Dutchman* and seem emphasized where the supernatural is concerned, chiefly because this type of melodrama creates a world of stark, spiritual contrasts.

The outstanding character in *Dutchman* is Vanderdecken. Though not so physically menacing as the Vulture in appearance, he is a blue-fire wonder, dressed in the garb of the sailor that he was before drowning with his crew aboard the Flying Dutchman. Wischhusen describes the creature's captain garb as "Green old fashioned dress, with white sugar loaf buttons—belt—high boots—old English hatred hat—red feather" (8). More of a ghostly pirate, than an explicit monster of the ogreish type, Vanderdecken's *monstrosity* is as much one of supernaturalness in personality, as in appearance. He is personally evil, even if his countenance is not terrifically hideous. As the Vulture, Smith's unearthly decorum was the main attraction, not his inner corruption: "a gigantic Turkey buzzard with wings lined with silk" (*Spectator* 797). Wrote *Dramatic Magazine*, "Smith cut a most extraordinary figure with his plumage and beak" (317). All of this criticism attests to the finesse of Smith's impersonations of evil, which is one of *Dutchman's* primary strengths. Baker summed up the actor's extraordinary penchant for protean characterizations of the uncanny, with the Vulture as an example: "It was grim, horrible if you will, but it was picturesque and imaginative, and therefore not revolting" (77) Fitzball's Vanderdecken was a ghostly manifestation of fear in the spectators' unconscious irrationality, based upon life's anxieties, which Arnheim suggests as primary reasons for the monstrous in art (256) .

Dutchman's main strength lies in its uncomplicated use of the triad. There is not the overt Faustian theme as in *The Devil's Elixir.* Vanderdecken creates the triad as a battle between fantasy and reality. The spectacle of the ship, the Fortress, and the eerie cave set the tone and mood for the battles between the earthly and the unearthly. The *Dutchman* is as fine an example of Fitzball's playing with the macabre as one may get. Fitzball's pre-eminence as the master of the blue-fire theatre of the macabre may be justified by comparing him to another exponent of that mode of melodrama, H.M. Milner. Both dealt with "the menace of Nature and the ferocity of the beast" in their blue fire sagas (King 23). Therefore, it seems natural to compare *Dutchman* with *Frankenstein,* inasmuch as both plays deal with the supernatural, the natural, the bestial, and the ferocity in dramatic art.

Fitzball and Milner

There is no doubt that both plays were gothic in their orientation, and, thematically, the Gothic play provided chills through suggestions and implementations of the supernatural (Bailey 23). There is also no doubt that both plays met this expectation of macabre delight. *Frankenstein; or, The Man and the Monster! A Peculiar, Romantic Melo-Dramatic Pantomimic Spectacle in Two Acts* was Milner's titular ascription to the Elizbethan practice of lengthy titles. It should be remembered that classic melodrama used titles as an encompassing feature as to what the play was about, thereby whetting the appetite of the potential viewer. The practice, which had its start in the sixteenth century, was standard dramatic usage well into the twentieth-century. Milner, in addition to adapting the Shelley novel, also *borrowed* material from a French romance, *The Magician and the Monster.* As a hack himself, Milner, who was once replaced by Fitzball in that capacity, knew all the tricks of that trade. Beyond the macabre essence in the play, which 0. Smith, as the original monster in the 1826 version, had characterfully sown, was the usual moral value of melodrama. This value stressed, in a word, the Aeschylean edict of "moral law overcoming passion" (Wright 182). Originated at the Coburg Theatre on July 3, 1826, the play spawned imitators, the most famous of which was R.B. Peake's *The Fate of Frankenstein,* in which 0. Smith again donned the role of the creature, after he had left the cast of Milner's classic. It must be noted here that sequels and imitations of plays were always being done. As with *Uncle Tom's Cabin* in America, there were many companies enacting the same play throughout the provinces. That tradition remains one of the theatre's most obvious; therefore, as in Smith's case, it was not unusual at all for an actor to create a role then later leave for another part. Smith would do just that in the role of Vanderdecken in 1827.

Without savoring diction to the degree of the poet Fitzball, Milner, who was a sturdy journeyman-dramatist, gives little exposition to the play. Rather, he begins the action almost at once. Distraught over the misshapened creation, Baron Frankenstein plans to destroy the brute. In fact, this one motif is the controlling idea in the drama: creator against monster. Milner accentuates a maelstrom of action, a concern for characterization, and the evocation of melodrama's dream world as his most obvious interest. Although Milner does not have Fitzball's penchant for poetic dialogue, he does create a dictional imagery of note. Frankenstein laments over his creation in a telling way, "Is my fairest model of perfection come to this—a hideous monster, a loathsome mass of animated putrefaction, whom just to gaze on, chills with horror even me, the creator" (Wischhusen 11). Surely, Delsartian acting would be the only conduit for such a piece of dialogue. In fact—and this has always been one of classic melodrama's stronger points—the reader must use his imagination in seeing how such lines would have been delivered on stage in that bygone time. Rich acting had to accompany rich dialogue. When Frankenstein's awful discovery is made, Milner injects the atmosphere with thunder and lightening. Blue-fire horror was always used whenever the opportunity arose. Milner, for all of his generic fervor, instills in the monster a hint of humanity. After all, Frankenstein's botched efforts were in creating a man. In this attitude of monster characterization, Fitzball and Milner have similarities. The monster's picking up of the fainted Emmeline is strongly, and humanly, gentle.

Milner's tempo is faster than Fitzball's *Dutchman*. Milner does not give the spectator any time for respite. After the monster has murdered, Frankenstein shakes his fist towards heaven, exclaiming, "Eternal Heaven!—that fiend has perpetrated it" (Wischhusen 16). With the customary, grammatical idiosyncrasies of melodrama, but void of Fitzball's ubiquitous, poetic leanings, Milner does create good imagery through *fiend* and *perpetration*. Another example of this dictional panache is in the creator's pursuit of the monster: "Ha! 'tis that hideous voice! Quick, quick, let us fly! His hellish malice still pursues me..."(Wischhusen 22). Milner wastes no time in the accusation of the monster's triadic nature, which is reminiscent of J.O. Bailey's admonition about Gothic drama's motif in the supernatural.

Frantic, invigorating, and, sometimes, anomalous in its odd logic and dramatic situations, *Frankenstein* is never decadent, though Milner does not have the humor of Fitzball's stage madness. He is also more reserved in his approach to the macabre theatre, inasmuch as his moralizing often seems to reduce the innate fun of *Frankenstein*. This may be because Milner has taken Shelley's theme of *"The Modern Prometheus"* to heart. Milner is concerned with a serious overtone in that hapless theme; whereas, Fitzball's thematic seriousness is always balanced by dramatic ovations and theatrical extravaganzas. Nonetheless, in deference to Milner, he does permit the innate absurdity of classic melodrama to climax chaotically. Like Fitzball in this instance, Milner makes no apologies—and gives no rationale—for the illogical ending of the monster. In the finest tradition of transpontine theatre, Milner devises an ending that is a tour-de-force.

In keeping with Thalbitzer's observation that maniacs are quicker in their actions than are normal people, Milner applies that observation literally to the revenge of the monster upon its master (47). Within a gothic setting of cliffs, crags, and mountains, the final battle between forces of created evil and scientific megalomania is enacted. Rather than a conflict between overt powers of good and evil, Milner endorses the theme that neither character, monster nor Frankenstein, may represent good, inasmuch as both represent degrees of transgression. Perhaps the monster is less guilty because he was formed as he is, innocent of any conceit or destructive forethought. Frankenstein's destructive madness is the underlying theme in the play. In close proximity to Mt. Etna, since the play takes place in exotic Italy, rather than dreary England, the monster has been stabbed by Frankenstein and chased into the cliffs of the mountain. Without dialogue—hence, the title's reference to pantomime—the *Coup-de-Theatre* climax is swiftly raised. Like Gortzburg and Vanderdecken, the monster moves speedily, its maniacal energy at top form, but, so does Dr. Frankenstein, with frantic delirium. The stage directions tell that the bloody dagger is to be left in the monster's gushing wound, thereby retaining the gory aesthetic of the Grand Guignol conventions of stark horror. Skulking behind a crag, the monster confronts Frankenstein in pursuit and, pulling the knife from the wound, stabs its creator. Incidentally, the monster's attack on his creator has, of course, poetic justice: the dagger was the one Frankenstein used to stab the monster earlier. Staring at this creation, Frankenstein plunges from the cliff, and the monster, now quite berserk, leaps into Etna's fiery crater. Both are damned in the victory of Good over man's mishandling of nature.

While stressing the novel's moral of evil haunting its exponent, Milner took extreme measures in dramatic license by way of location, characters, and ending. With these arbitrary transformations, Milner shared much in common with Fitzball. There are, however, problems in comparing and contrasting classic melodramatists for two reasons: 1) classic melodrama's formulaic composition is consistent with all stylists and 2) it's basic freedom in how that formula (virtue triumphant over evil) is to be imagined, plotted, and deduced by a writer prohibits deep scrutiny. This poses a critical problem unlike the freedom in interpretation of tragedy, comedy, and farce. These genres are susceptible to novel approaches to their meaning because they deal in universal symbols, and each succeeding generation may see that symbolism differently, based upon novel approaches to psychological and sociological dimensions. For instance, Sophoclean and Shakespearean tragedy has been re-evaluated constantly as to theme and dramatic composition. There is a reversal in the makeup of tragedy to melodrama. Tragedy keeps its dramatic quintessence, yet is open to new methods of theatricalization and interpretation. Melodrama is open to all kinds of fanciful plots, but it follows such a formulaic regimen that an interpreter cannot ignore that scheme. Orson Welles' radical interpretation of *Julius Ceaser*, in modern dress, retained the political theme of Shakespeare's play. One cannot produce classical melodrama without following its historical usage of the elements and be effective: the genre is dependent upon its historic flavor, without which parody results.

I have mentioned this because Milner and Fitzball remain products of their time and are not open to thematic criticism, since classic melodrama had only one: virtue triumphant. However, the two may be compared on their individual uses of the dramatic elements. Fitzball is superior to Milner in the use of poetic diction. *Dutchman* and *Elixir* both have a distinct flair in an internal rhythm. Milner uses dialogue for the furthering of the plot. He is not caught up in language for its own sake although the style of the day was inflated and euphemistic. Fitzball urges special effects whenever he can; his reliance upon spectacle, in all of its wildly blue-fire degrees, was famous. In fact, Fitzball was such a virtuoso that one gets the feeling that he is just waiting for an opportunity to display his razzle-dazzle theatricality. Milner uses spectacle when only necessary, thus permitting the plot to stand on its own. For instance, had Fitzball written *Frankenstein*, there world have been indulgent disclosures of more physical action and suspense: the climax would have been, perhaps, more violent and grandiose, with Frankenstein having a heroic element to him. Horror would have been more directly consuming. Milner does not inject enough horror in his monster, nor any humor in the play. Fitzball would have done both. Aside form speculation, Fitzball bettered his peers not because his plots were better; (in fact, many of them were adapted and hurried), but Fitzball betters Milner because of his showmanship, a trait almost impermeable to others. Plus, Fitzball's artistic versatility, especially with music and diction, and the uncanny knowledge of audience psychology, made him an *impresario-dramatist.*

Of course, Fitzball has dramaturgic faults: he is verbose and some of his plots are labyrinthian. Exacerbating these vices, Fitzball often gets so carried away with the image of spectacle that the drama seems lost in the helter-skelter of it all. Nevertheless, he uses the dramatic elements, for the most part, cleverly. He may best be described as the *Florenz Ziegfeld* of blue-fire, who could write music, compose poetry, and, most importantly, turn the theatre into a circus, even when Vanderdecken was at his most fiendish. The critics could not gloss over his popular and commercial appeal. Limited thematically, Fitzballian fare knew no prison in plot and theatricality. The following remarks about his plays of the macabre will demonstrate that thrilling escapism which was Fitzballian.

Remaining Examples of Macabre Drama

As has been established, Fitzball used theatre as a means of introducing the working class to the dramatic arts by way of the macabre. As an aside to this inclination, one need look no further than the services of the actor T.P. Cooke in Fitzballian fare. This extraordinary character star, like 0. Smith, was given to masterful creations of the bizarre, creations that were in line with Fitzball's theatre of shock and delight. A word about Cooke's playing skill will provide a reason why Fitzball found his services so valuable. As the original monster in the Lyceum Theatre's *Presumption; or, The Fate of Frankenstein* in 1823, some three years before 0. Smith's interpretation, Cooke went on to play the marauding creature some 365 times, with the fine thespian James Wallack enacting the role of Dr. Frankenstein in many of those instances (Mank 12). This was an era of popular adaptations of plays, such as *The Fate of Frankenstein,* which was presented at the Coburg in 1826. The troupes of Frankenstein dramas seemed to be everywhere, so popular was Mrs. Shelley's monster. In any event, Cooke was just the type of actor for Fitzball, especially in light of the recollection of his performance, along with a comparable notice of Smith's style. Such excitement colors the following dramas.

T.P. Cooke gave the charnel house monster a green, Putrescent hue. "What," asked Oxenburry, the actor, in his Dramatic Biography, "can be more dreadful than his manner of walking against the balustrade.... For monsters without any conscience the playgoers had only to look for the name of 0. Smith on the bill." (Disher 96-130)

In *Mary Glastonbury; or, The Dream Girl of the Devil Hall—A Romantic Drama in Two Acts*, there is a character named Mad Jack, who is in stride with the best type of monsters created by the likes of Cooke and Smith, although he is a human devil. The above notice about Cooke and Smith apply essentially to the wonderful sense of fear and dreadfulness in Fitzball's best, triadic villains. And the sensational triad is personified in Mad Jack. Debuted at the Surrey Theatre, on September 28, 1833, Fitzball used a dream for the foundation of horror. Through this fantasia, Lucy Laurel sees her lover, Frank, stabbing an intruder in the house. Awaking, and discovering the oneiric experience accurate, she insists that Mary, her friend, accompany her across the moors, known as Devil's Hall, with blue-light (a special effect) shining about, to find a doctor for the ailing intruder. They stop for help at the shack of Mad Jack, whose lustful advances they must battle to escape. Finally, fleeing from Jack's murderous intentions, they arrive at the home of Aristotle Jede Kiah, one of the best caricatures ever drawn about a physician. With him, they return to nurse the burglar back to health, thereby saving Frank's reputation and reuniting him with his beloved Lucy. Based on "an old black letterballad, the scenery by Marshall, and the music by Jolly, including 'Leader of the Band' made this piece worthy" (*Mary Glastonbury* 1). A vanguard of the play is its gothic atmosphere, redolent of *Jane Eyre,* with its sudden escapes, mystery, danger, and reuniting love. Fitzball has given Mary clearly a secondary role, but such a designation was usual in literature of the era. For instance William Godwin's psychological thriller, *The Adventures of Caleb Williams* (1794), used the titular figure as a catalyzer for all of the characters and actions in the book. Poe was another author given to this proclivity. The *Narrative of A. Gordom Pym* is such an example. Therefore, Fitzball's usage of Mary as a static character and symbol was understandable and in vogue.

As I have mentioned before, only the "acting versions (prompt books)" of Fitzball's plays are available in print or on microfilm. Many of them, including the ones to be used as examples of his diversity in the macabre, have initial critiques in the front of each copy. The critic, who went by the cryptic pen-name of "D-K," will be referred to for his remarks about the plays at the time of their presentation. The strength of *Mary Glastonbury* lies within the morbid environ, wherein the women must persist, and in the brutish villainy of Mad Jack. Frank's attack pales beside Jack's evil. The play boasts a womanly strength, not uncommon for Fitzball, as *Bradford's* Ann demonstrated. "D-K" applauds Fitzball:

The grave physiognomy and sober bearing of Mr. Fitzball proclaim him an exception to "Sigh no more ladies; men are deceivers,—one foot one sea, and the other on shore." We suspect, however, that this predilection of the sea arises from a desire to live comfortably on the shore...and conjures up monsters by sea and land, as we poor critics write. Mr. Fitzball is said to possess a greater share of imagination than most of his contemporaries; yet here is one thing he can't imagine—a playwright simple enough to forego solid pudding for empty praise—Mr. Fitzball is wise in his generation, and we applaud him for it. The very nature of this drama...is a passport to popularity. In this art and mystery, Mr. Fitzball is more than commonly successful. His title fits well, and his ball hits the right mark. Did Mr. Fitzball's forte lie in fun, he would be the death of us. (*Mary Glastonbury* 3)

One of Fitzball's best gothic entries was *Margaret's Ghost: or, The Libertine's Ship,* a play in two acts, presented at the Victoria Theatre on October 14, 1833. William has murdered his wife, Margaret, for her money. To his dismay, she returns from the grave "in a whirlwind, like a Lapland witch!" (II,ii) to set his ship ablaze. In a spellbinding scene, in which the ghost rises form her watery grave, redolent of Vanderdecken's arrival from the deep, William recants; he then rushes to Margaret's grave, wherein the corpse was put after drowning; and, now insane, he falls dead. In a perverse way, through a ghost, usually seen as evil, Fitzball has re-established morality in William's obligatory death at the hands of a spectre. Here, it is the human, and not the ghost, who is hedonistic and immoral. The overall, frantic tone of the work is exemplified by the sailors' fear of the ghost while the ship burns. The crime of murder, the terror of exposure (by a ghost), and the madness of William's reaction to his misdeed make this play an outstanding example of the Blood Revenge type of romantic tragedy. Directly enacted, the play does not have some of Fitzball's more notable verbosity; it relies on action and mood. Fitzball's love of stage fire is a significant feature in the play. Astonishingly enough, Fitzball's pyrotechnics were never responsible for any theatrical conflagration, so precise were his special effects.

"D-K" introduces the next play. *The Haunted Hulk* remains one of Fitzball's satisfying journeys into the macabre. It is also one of his most regal, with the wonderful T.P. Cooke and O. Smith joining forces.

"The Haunted Hulk" is one of that particular species of drama, which, of late years, has proved popular in the minor theatres; where the sea is the principle scene of action, and the sailor the principle character; where a supernatural interest is cast over the plot, and fire and water are pressed into the service to heighten effect. Two actors of original genius have mainly contributed to the success of these ventures—T.P. Cooke and 0.

Smith. The former, justly celebrated for his bold, vigorous, and romantic picture of the British tar...dashes of pathos that he mingles with his good humour and jollity. The latter, for the mysterious, abstracted, half-crazed looked and manner; that ominous, hollow voice, stealthy step, and subtle delivery, so peculiar to him. We have longed to shake hands with this warmhearted seaman. Not so with 0. Smith...the incarnation of fire and brimstone, breathing combustion and blue flame...a spirit of mischief in earthly costume; which makes us keep a sharp look out for his hoofs and tail! (*The Haunted Hulk* 12)

Inchoately, we observe that Fitzball had fans and that actors, in this Golden Age of Acting, had the same. They also suffered from a stereotyping and confusion between reality and fiction on the part of those fans. The blue-flame allusion to the play was typical of critics forever looking for Fitzball's blue-red fire trademark. More than the power of these actors involved in the macabre, the play was also one of Fitzball's better nautical dramas. In the plot, evil Caleb (Smith) is a smuggler, whose contraband is hidden in a supposedly haunted ship's hulk, which, of course, terrifies any interloper. For power, this terrorist slyly kidnaps the heroine, Suzette, after failing to do the same to young Stephen Barncliff, who, with the help of sailor Oakum (Cooke), foils the ransom scheme. His plans upset, Caleb is overpowered by Oakum and Barncliff, who rescue the girl. Caleb rushes from his cave hideaway into the bowels of the hulk, where, in addition to stolen booty, rests explosive materials. His majordomo, Caulder, rushes onto the ship, having been targeted by the policeman Raker, who shoots down the henchman. With torch in hand, Caulder falls into the galley where Caleb is planning his escape. The finale is an acme of blue-fire zest. Caulder drops the torch as he falls, thereby igniting the explosives and blowing both villains and hulk into oblivion. Fitzball uses the magic of melodramatic diction to its utmost with Caleb, who, at one point towards the end, shouts, "Never! while revenge is in my power! Sooner with the torch will I fire the vessel and perish in flames." The line was prophetic (*Hulk* 25).

The entire play issues the macabre sense of evil and horror. Caleb is mad, terrifying, and violent. The gloomy settings among caves and the ship are pertinently frightening. The moral is exacted in the full measure of high adventure, whose structural pace never falls into lethargy. Fitzball's dramatic levels are clear and his purgation of the spectators' emotions complete. Opening at the Adelphi Theatre on July 12, 1831, "D-K's" comments were indicative of its fine reception. The play is the cliff-hanging *stuff* of the best in romantic drama.

Fitzball's enjoyment of exotica and special effects was the undercurrent for *The Earthquake*; *or, The Spectre of the Nile*, produced at the Adelphi Theatre on December 8, 1828. This holiday season entry had music by G.H. Redwell and its scenic designs were made by Mr. Bonner, based upon the drawings of Cruikshank (*The Earthquake* 1). Because the play had been devised for sheer entertainment, critics lambasted the *bete noire* essence of the play's escapism. These judges of art had apparently missed the fact that melodrama was famous for its abilities to put train wrecks and even earthquakes on stage (Gielgud 131). However, Fitzball had not forgotten the desideratum of his audiences who flocked to plays that gave them sensationalism in spades. Moreover, "D-K" agreed with the masses and exclaimed, "The scenes of hail, rain, thunder, and lightning, that occur in *Macbeth* and *Lear,* are beheld in admiration" (*Earthquake* 3). If Shakespeare could fill his tragedies with afflictions from heaven, could not Fitzball be so bold? "D-K" went on to praise the play as therapeutic. Simply, the viewer was able to release his repressed tensions by seeing a receptive tension in the drama, wherein he could vicariously deposit his own anxiety, ridding himself of the need "of overt expression of such emotions in actual life" (Fairchild 34) It seems appropriate to remind us of the catharsis factor in Fitzball, inasmuch as *Earthquake* was attacked for doing just that. Wrote "D-K":

The propriety of presenting the earthquake scene is calculated to show nature at its most combustive cataclysmic. The Adelphi stage is conducive by machinery to special effects. Sensationalism lifts the souls above the dull drudgery of mere animal existence. It would be unjust to judge a spectacle by the rules of criticism. (*Earthquake* 3)

Fitzball's format for the play, which would always entice his uneducated viewers, was an exotic locale almost out of *The Arabian Knights*. Music was a part of this extravaganza in the forms of duets and quartets. However, the wired flying chair, instead of the usual carpet, was a highlight, second only to the earthquake itself. Cooke played Galzetto, the cunning slave, with a grandness which, ironically, has been ignored in theatre history texts. But, then, he and Smith, because of their association with the more lurid examples of melodrama, never received the historical recognition due them as actors. Fitzball traded in a complex plot for the rousing fun of spectacle. The plot mundanely involved an earthquake coming as a climax in a land filled with political intrigue. Fitzball knew that an effect of this magnitude would be the center of attention anyway; therefore, he merely tacked on a plot. A collate may be made between the play and many of the *Hercules* films of the 1960s: the plots were always similar and subordinated by sheer spectacle. *The Earthquake* was a similar frolic.

Galzetto's knowledge of the black arts saves the kingdom from anarchists. However, in deference to the plot, it must be conceded that Fitzball did pace it well, but then a cabal and an earthquake naturally moved themselves along, especially whenever the audience was waiting for the climax literally to erupt. Criminal intrigue was the triadic force in this play, and macabre elements surrounded Galzetto's magic. The play, almost as an afterthought, boasts one of Fitzball's best songs, a clever, little tune that is sung by the comedic Dr. Kalliboss, inventor of the elixir of life. Potions and magic books were pet props for Fitzball, who used them anytime he could. The song is lazily sung by the funny character as he relaxes:

> There's a balm for every blossom
> Essence bright at holy dew (Doctor exults)
> Soft as evening sunlight falling
> On the lake's eternal bind
> Near his bower our rest shall be, (Doctor begins to sleep)
> Under the Ahyssinizn tree
> When the nightingale is singing. (Doctor sleeps)

Just as The Earthquake was designed to showcase Fitzballian spectacle and exotica, so *Carmilhan; or, The Drowned Crew*, presented on April 21, 1835, was specifically prompted by the playwright's interest in attracting children to his fare. Reminiscent of *Dutchman*, this ghost play was an example of how the masterful Fitzball could be versatile enough to pen a play for a targeted audience. The penny dreadful had all of the macabre panache of a traditional "Ghostie saga," but, as juvenilia, it had an added magnetism, a style for young people to enjoy, as well as adventure enough to keep the attention of the usual mature spectator. Inordinately, the play was successful on all levels of enjoyment.

The plot entails the spirit of Carmilhan, commander of a wrecked ship and drowned crew, who returns from the murky brine to seduce the heroine, Uda. In love, however, with the gallant Magnus, Uda inspires the monster's hatred for Magnus. The eerie play is a conglomeration of purple passages, which appeals to the child in everyone. Concerning diction, the play is one of Fitzball's outstanding examples of classic, rapid-fire stichomythia, as this example between Uda and Carmilhan will demonstrate:

C. Uda!

U. Who art Tho?

C. Carmilhan

C. The spirit of the wreck! What seekest thou?

C. Uda!

U. Me?

C. Aye!

With the piratical apparition of the ghost, Uda, another strong female, holds her own. The diction is rich in flavor, menace, and pressure. About the power of such a work, the *Athenaeum* acknowledged, "*Carmilhan* sounds more like a piece for the Easter holidays, and, after seeing it, we shall say that schoolboys would poll ten to one in its favor" (225). Even Fitzball's most didactic melodramas had a fairy-tale base to them; so *Carmilhan's* comes off as an example of an author lessening the blue-fire horror, the triad, and the theatre of the macabre to fit the escapism of so many children wanting the "Walt Disney" of their age, Fitzball.

However, with *The Crock of Gold!* or, *The Murder at the Hall: A MeloDrama in Two Acts*, Fitzball was back at his old tricks of scaring adults with the sensational triad hard at work. Opening at the City of London Theatre, in May 1848, this detective thriller was a contender for Grand Guignol immortality. Simon Jennings, like Caleb, is the incarnation of stage villainy, and one of the best character sketches drawn by Fitzball. Sadistically, he plots the murder of his aunt, Mrs. Quarles, in order the steal her gold, hidden in a crock. Hiding in the bedroom, he steals over the sleeping woman, stabs the dowager repeatedly, and takes the treasure. A character not unlike that of the heinous Bill Sykes in *Oliver Twist*, Jennings, to torment the old lady, sadistically echoes the last words said by his victim while she is thinking aloud in bed. A consummate villain, with no redeeming qualities at all, he is wonderfully evil. After the murder, he hides his ill-gotten gain by burying it. Fitzball still manages to give even a maniac a rationale: while committing the bloody deed, Jennings soliloquizes about why he is behaving so evily. His madness is cursed by heaven's thunder and lightning. Fitzball lets out all discretions throughout. The spectators thrilled to such mayhem on stage. Again, Fitzball had created a criminal of familiarity of a London underworld thriving with such monsters.

In his attempt to leave the country, Jennings is apprehended by the police. It is at this point that the "soap-operish" design of the play excitedly starts. On trial for murder, Jennings, in the witness box, faces the prosecutor's loud condemnations. Jennings screams to the court, "Liar—liar! I have never seen

you before. Never—never!" The *you* refers to his relative Ben, who has
suspected Jennings' misdeed in the first place. Again, Fitzball seems to borrow
a sequence from Dickens' *Oliver Twist,* which is Sykes' vision of Nancy's
ghost atop a roof, where he is planning his escape. He has killed *his* girl friend
earlier in the novel. As a result of the ghostly apparition, Sykes, in attempting to
flee, becomes entangled in his rope, falls from the roof, and hangs himself.
Jennings, in much the same way, condemns himself as the ghost of Mrs.
Quarles appears to him. In avenging herself, the ghost grips Jennings' throat.
The climax is at a frenzied pitch. While struggling with the invisible
strangulation, Jennings grabs the murderous knife and stabs himself. Stabbing
oneself was a customary way of suicide. The murderer, crazed and dying, yells:

Confusion! detected and convicted! Give me that knife! Ha, ha, ha! I'll not be dragged
back to a jail—die like a felon! NO—I defy you all. I escape. Take her fingers from my
throat. I did it, I her Nephew—in the dead of night! Gold—gold! Accursed avarice.
There she is again—with her pale, reproachful look whichever way I turn. I—I was her
mur. (Dies and Tableau) (*Crock of Gold* 20)

The Curtain Falls

With a courtroom scene reminiscent of a *Perry Mason* episode, in which
the culprit admits his duplicity, the ending of the play, with "THE CURTAIN
FALLS," recalls to mind the Universal horror films of the 1930s and 1940s,
wherein, after the villain had been dispatched, the credit "THE END" would
quickly appear. To be sure, Fitzball's plays had much that was cinematic about
them. Criminologically, Jennings is a powerful villain: a perpetrator of
femicide, his own aunt yet; a lunatic, without a doubt; and a villainously
charismatic rogue. Fitzball has thrust into his character all the passion and
habituation of a miscreat one might find in prisons, or, upsettingly, on the street
(Vedder, Koinig, and Clark 82). Jennings is as cunning a villain as was the
archetype of murderous insanity, Jack the Ripper, who was given literary
immortality in Belloc Lowndes' novel *The Lodger.* Jenning's schizoid
personality, at once deceptively kind, before the murder, and then flagrantly
perverse, in murdering his aunt, is worthy of comparison with some of
literature's most infamous criminals. The play is worthy of revival: it seems to
suggest, as a motif, the Aeschylean dictum of morality quelling passion.

Another play writhing in the macabre, particularly in the blue-fire
tradition, was *Thalaba, the Destroyer. A Melo-Drama in Three Acts.* First
presented at the ignominious Coburg Theatre on August 13, 1822, it was based
upon the romantic poet Robert Southey's "Roderick, the Last of the Goths."
The play was reckoned as "a fine strain of morality that runs through the

whole...of guilt, suffering, and repentance" (*Thalaba* 12). Of the frantic and rousing play, The *Spectator* wrote: "Demons and evil spirits superabound, and there is no lack of genius (on Fitzball's part). Thalaba was played by Miss Eliza Vincent, and animated statue of silver frost work in her suite of tinsel" (136) In the play, it is a villainess, who is the center of attraction. The plot concerns the sorceress Kawla, who, by the sultan's order, is to slay the rightful ruler, Hodeirah. Prince Rhalaba—a "breeches role"—is saved from the magician's clutches, as is another victim, by Ali, the servant. Kawla appears in fire when summoned by the wicked sultan, hence the blue-fire essence. By incantation, Kawla summons from hell the demon, Abdala, who is to murder Thalaba. The monster's attempts fail because a lighting bolt from Above strikes him. Heaven itself protects Thalaba, a popular Deus-ex-Machina device in historically classic theatre.

Obtaining a magic quiver through the intervention of his mother's ghost—a vision not unlike that paid Hamlet by his father's spirit—Thalaba wrecks havoc upon the villains. In a furious sequence of carnage, amidst a blazing fire in the palace, Thalaba stabs the sultan in the tower and thrusts a burning sward into Abdala. All is saved and the prince assumes his kingship. With a spectacle similar to the *Conan the Barbaran* sagas, this play has it all: exotic location, horrors aplenty, a sequence of Thalabals overcoming a dragon, and a fairytale mood and tone. As in *Hamlet*, Thalaba's course of action was to avenge his father's death by the sultan. With stirring music and dynamic action, the play was enjoyed by "D-K" to the point of praise: "It is the work of the ingenious Mr. Fitzball" (*Thalaba* 1). It will be recalled that Miss Vincent, a fine actress, was one of Fitzball's favorite persons, and, with "breeches roles" in vogue since Shakespearean characters, she had no difficulty in assuming the heroic part.

An obvious student of literature, Fitzball's adaptation of fine novels into drama was a studied diversion for him. With *Quasimodo: A Drama in Three Acts,* presented at the Covent Garden on February 2, 1836, Fitzball again, (as he had done with *Esmeralda; or, The Deformed of Notre Dame* at the Surrey Theatre on March 14, 1834), adjusted and transformed Hugo's 1831 novel about a deformed bell-ringer's unrequited love for a lovely gypsy girl into a play of powerful pathos. Oddly enough, Fitzball followed the plot of the novel fairly well, with the confrontation between the hunchback and the evil monk Frollo as the play's highlight. Although the actual combat between the two was not shown in the play, Quasimodo hurls the villain from the tower at Notre Dame after he has tried to rape Esmeralda. Fitzball poses the metaphysical question of morality: who is the actual beast, the hunchback or the monk? Ever so often, Fitzball would uncover a conundrum in his dramas that might tax the logic of the viewer. Usually though, the characters were either good or bad, with no leniency for interpretation.

With expert imagery, Frollo's death is narrated in the third act: "What was that fearful struggle! The hunchback tosses the monk form the very battlements unto the earth. Ugh" (*Quasimodo* 23). The *Ugh* implies the off-stage horror of seeing the corpse: as such, the audience could use their vivid imagination to enact the scene. Off-stage melodrama had the same imaginative effect that radio possessed for the viewer. With his propensity towards dramatic license, Fitzball changed the ending of the dramatized novel. Instead of dying with Esmeralda, as in the novel, Quasimodo, in a cliff-hanging finale, saves the gypsy from the gallows. She had been charged with the knifing of Captain Phoebus Apollo. Frollo had committed the crime. Quasimodo thrusts into the hands of her executioners an official pardon. Fitzball's reliance upon this "Deus-ex-Machina" device has the tradition of Euripides, who used the ploy often, as in *Medea* and *Iphigenia at Aulis*. However, in his struggle with Frollo, the hunchback has suffered a mortal stabbing.

In the sentimental ending, typical of Fitzball, the "beast-with-a-heart-of-gold" dies as a result of his injury, only after Esmeralda has been exonerated by clemency. The Hugo motif of unrequited love is maintained by Fitzball through the irony of the gypsy girl's love for the smug Phoebus. However, such a heart-wrenching conclusion is in keeping with melodrama's capacity to move the audience by emotion. The play, in my opinion, is one of Fitzball's best, even with the hurried resolutions.

The battle between the hunchback and the monk calls to mind a cinematic illustration, that of Lon Chaney and Brandon Hurst in the classic film of 1923. The play is outstanding because the macabre and the triad are combined with a certain sweetness concerning the monster's love for the girl. The protagonist's death, unlike that in most melodramas, brings about the moral. Usually, it is the villain's demise that spawns the lesson in the genre. However, such a dramatic altercation demonstrates Fitzball's careful versatility.

Continuing, there are three musicals, two burlettas, and an opera, which, hold a macabre fascination, by virtue of their respective dramatic sense of action and enchantment. Although minor works, Fitzball gave these "bread-and-butter" vehicles his typical flair. The *Phantom of the Nile* deals with the villainous Orchua, who attempts to sacrifice the heroine, Althea, to the gods. Nevertheless, he is foiled by Palinode, the hero. Althea, freed, rushes off to be united with Palinedo after Orchua is killed. The theatrical import of the play, beyond exotica, was its musical arrangement that caught the essence of Fitzball's musical fervor. The second play, *A Libertine's Lesson,* deals with the depression felt concerning aspiring love from a man-of-the world, Alfred. This opera concerns itself with Alfred's adventures with the sorceress Liska, who saves him from the evil robber Naddock. That these musicals are not overly lurid is granted. However, as was noted, Ftizball interpreted and expedited the macabre by degrees, thus sparing his audience the same kind of play night after night. In these examples, the eerie is used fancifully and gaily in the nether-world of magicians and witchcraft. Music was often used by Fitzball in the creation of such a fantasy world.

For the purist of the grotesque, however, the other burletta, *The Sea Serpent: or, Wizard of the Wind,* returns Fitzball to his sensational expertise. Suggestive of *The Tempest,* the play was produced at the Adelphi Theatre on September 23, 1831. The weirdly magical tone of Shakespeare's fantasy is captured on this idyllic island, where the natural and the supernatural become one. Similar to the Frankenstein tradition, the magician Novergade creates a monstrous sea serpent, which, upon escaping its confines, proceeds to destroy the community on the island. Part of Fitzball's morbid attraction was his presentations of mythologically-inspired demons, thereby giving his dramas an anachronistic shade. A servant, Inulkus, describes one of the beast's misdeeds when discovering a man "gash'd on by cruel fangs/ Slain by the serpent of the sea" (*Serpent* 15). The stage is now set for the Frankensteinian battle between creator and creation. Laments Novergade, "Serpent, approach; I drink thy cast of blood. We fall together" (*Serpent* 21). Dying, through the onslaught of heaven's lightning bolts, (the theological reference, again), the monster crushes its maker in its talons, just as the earth opens and devours them. For blue-fire excitement, *The Sea Serpent* was made to order. The serpent's death by Providence is strangely parallel to the film version of Maxell Anderson's play *The Bad Seed,* wherein charming, little Rhoda, a psychopathic killer, is struck by lightning in the end of the film. In the play, she lives, unsuspected by a world she is terrorizing, but film director Mervyn LeRoy felt that punishment from God would be a good ending for a devil's disciple. Heaven destroys the serpent for exactly the same reason. Novergade is a victim of his own intellect, as well as his own creation. Morality demanded the death of both entities. Though a burletta, Fitzball's play is not so much fluff; it is enthralling and spine-tingling adventure of the most frightening kind.

With a quintessence from Goethe's *Faust* and Patrick Hamilton's *Angel*

Street, Fitzball's *Robert the Devil; or The Devil's Son,* produced at the Adelphi Theatre on January 23, 1832, is a psychological thriller. Diabolically possessed, the evil Bertran attempts to drive Robert, Duke of Normandy, insane and then plans to seduce Robert's lady, Isabella. The ghost of Robert's mother warns her son to fight the scheme of Bertran. Fitzball's deference to Elizbethan and Jacobean tragic influences are obvious: the ghostly adviser, gothic intrigue, and devil possession. There are overtones of Gregory "Monk" Lewis' novel *The Monk,* which had to do with a cleric's possession, and *The Devil's Elixir* could also relate to this circumstance. At midnight, Betran comes to procure Robert's soul for the devil; Isabella's virginal loveliness and personal faith, however, help to disrupt Bertran's malicious intention. Foiled, Betran is attacked by the ghostly figure of Robert's mother, who sends the screaming villain into blue-fire perdition. The Chorus sings the benediction, "Let us be saved!" With insane, terrifying, and criminous loyalty, Bertran is enslaved to Lucifer and commissioned to procure Robert's soul. This morality play of good against evil has the evil in the form of a disciple of Lucifer himself, not in the guise of an ordinary villain. Fitzball's accent on this grim, psychological, and religious capacity is refreshing.

In *The Hunchbacks; or, The Sabre Grinders of Damascus,* presented at the Surrey Theatre on January 20, 1823, Fitzball showed his audience that the macabre could be used for striking symbolism, as well as for blatant fear. He demonstrated that deformity, a supposed sign of the fearful, did not necessarily have to be always so interpreted. Ibad the Cunning; Badekan the Selfish; and Syah the Simple were emblems of outward appearance being unrelated to inward aptitudes and attitudes. I have included this diversionary play to indicate once more Fitzball's multi-faceted uses of the macabre for reasons other than the shocking. The play has remnants of being a social-thesis drama, insofar as the plot concerns the adventures of these three freaks using their grotesqueness to befuddle a bigoted society. Fitzball's moral, at the conclusion, proves that "one may not indeed tell a book by its cover." Fitzball's outwardly macabre characters are actually experiential symptoms of new toleration. This play is one of the few in Fitzball's bizarre oevure which has such a metaphysical ring to it. For Fitzball, the macabre was not monolithic; rather, it was pliable and open to interpretation on the physical and emotional level. Blood-and-Thunder blue-fire was as much a symbol of social turmoil as it was a theatrical iridescence.

It may not be out of place in this sampling to mention Fitzball's contact with a classical play. In choosing Sophocles' *Antigone* (441 B.C.) as one of his projects, Fitzball presented the play at the Norwich Theatre on August 1, 1823. I have previously mentioned that both *Antigone* and *Agamemnon* were adapted by the dramatist as closet dramas; however, Fitzball's tedious adaptation emerged as acceptable theatre, although it played more in the vein of Addison's *Cato*. Fitzball maintained Sophocles' sequences of horror, crime, and madness, but they were void of Fitzball's typical frenzy. In truth, Fitzball seemed uncomfortable in staging his translation, as if he were blaspheming a sacrosanct treasure. Nonetheless, the audience, most of whom were unfamiliar with the Greek original, were pleased with the production, especially since all attending had been invited by Fitzball. In a word, it was a small, but appreciative house. Wrote Fitzball: "...it *is* to be disposed to excuse the liberties taken with it by a less worthy hand" (11:58). With *Antigone,* Fitzball's resilient self-confidence was at a low ebb, though he enjoyed venting his frustration as a tragedian on the classic. For a short while, Fitzball was among the greats in the melodramatic theatre. Always the poet-dramatist, Fitzball was pleased in reworking the Sophoclean classic: "I came first to break the bounds of Greek tragedy...by translation, paraphrase, or metaphrase, to use Dryden's phrases" (11:59). For all of Fitzball's efforts, *Antigone* fought melodramatization. Therefore, the melodrama failed, although Fitzball's translation reads well enough. In this, Fitzball's theatre of the macabre could not alter *Antigone's* ingrained tragedy. *Antigone* was Fitzball's resignation that blue-fire was not easily translated into plays unprepared for it.

If the master of blue-fire erred with *Antigone, The Black Hand: A Demon Play* put him back on track. Presented on September 19, 1834, at the Adelphi Theatre, the play featured the hellish monster Nocta. Ascending from "The Borders of the Burning Sea," the fiend plans to corrupt the symbols of faithfulness, Sadak and Azola, two lovers. In the frenzy of the misguided attack, after previous failed attempts, an earthquake occurs. The finale finds the lovers killed, but their purity in spirit (a sort of karma) has saved them for heaven. Another, unexpected earthquake sends Nocta back to hell, in crushing defeat. Several motifs and devices seem now pertinent to Fitzballian dramatic strategy. For one, the sea plays an important role in either producing or capturing monsters and villains. Secondly, theological faith is the refuge for the hero and heroine, even in death, as *The Black Hand* shows, and that sense of optimism was the hallmark of the play. And, thirdly, Fitzball's use of the "Deus-ex-Machina," many times in the form of a natural cataclysm, was extensive. *The Black Hand* also demonstrated the mass appeal for the monster play. Fitzball used monsters not as silly brutes, but as spectacular, fabulous things of dread.

Fitzball's demons were always cunningly attractive and fiercely challenging. *The Black Hand* remains a flawless wonder: thoughtful, straightforward, and frightening.

The next three plays will evidence Fitzball as his most experimental with the theatre of the macabre. These plays are void of his usual heavy-handedness, but laced with dark humor. A minor effort, *The Note Forger,* presented at the Drury Lane on April 20, 1835, is recalled for one reason: the play had one of Fitzball's best altercations of violence between the hero and the villain. The emotional line "Sword for sword! blood for blood! life for life!" defines the whole, emotional underpinning of the entire work (*Forger* 23). Of greater fantasy value was *Don Ouixote; The Knight of the Woeful Countenance and Humours of Sancho Panza; A Burlesque Musical.* Enacted at the Adelphi Theatre on January 9, 1833, this rambunctious, dark comedy was highlighted by Fitzball's gift for dialogue, which proved to be quite contemplative in the characters at hand. For all of us familiar with *Man of La Mancha* and Cervantes' novel, this exchange between the Quixote and Sancho has the rich flavor of both works. Says Quixote, "Sancho, let me advise thee how to read and write and become acquainted with grammar." Sancho relies, "Grammar! Who is he? Does he teach folks how to manage a government. I'll chop a few blocks of logic with him" (*Quixote* 30). With scathing satire, Fitzball attacked the pomposity of academia—probably a metaphor for dramatic criticism—with a tone not unlike Cervantes' own.

Based upon Mrs. Opie's work, *Giraldi; or, A Ruffian of Prague,* premiered at the Norwich Theatre in April 1820. Here, Fitzball was back at his old perturbation. A kind of lycanthrope, Giraldi changes into a bestial creature whenever he is upset. The affliction has become so dominant that he plots the murder of the heroine, Ethelind, and the child, Erest. In retrospect, the play is uncannily similar in the transformation rationale of that given in the film *I Was A Teenage Werewolf* (1957), in which emotional problems, not the traditional full moon, causes the man to turn into the werewolf. The film is mentioned to suggest that it used this Fitzballian source of transmorgification some 137 years later, and that Fitzball's theatrical dealings with the triad left a legacy for one of our modern conduits of the macabre, film. This could be an argument for Fitzball's cinematic prolepsis.

Pietro, the hero, kills the *loulpgarou* at the last, shocking moment before Giraldi can carry out his murderous intentions. The "Jekyll and Hyde" psychology displayed in the work lifts it above mere physical horror and terror. Laments Giraldi, "Curtains of darkness, veil the murderer's head/ And screen his hatred form every eye/ Save me from the wheeling Bat, Nights, favourite bird/ Which, shrieking, curses just like me...." (*Giraldi* 22). With the first play accentuating violence; the second, satire; and the third, abnormal psychology, Fitzball again showed his versatility, malleability, and capacity to experiment.

With an eagle as a villain, Fitzball's *The Dillosk Gatherer; or, The Eagle of the Cliff* opened at the Covent Garde Theatre on July 13, 1832. "D-K" suggests that the play was an adaptation of the short story "Three Courses and a Dessert" (*The Dillosk Gatherer* 1). The plot is simple, but unnerving. A child is abducted by a ravaging eagle. In hot pursuit, the parents must brave the cliffs of the giant bird. Just before the child is to be eaten, the father, Fergus, shoots the horrible carnivore. Though contrived, the play suited the matinee crowd's expectation for rugged thrills, inasmuch as they liked the gore and/or enjoyed being frightened (Bronson 254). Fitzball's affinity for birds as monsters-of-prey had peaked with Smith's diabolical Vulture some years before.

The Mill of the *Loire,* presented at the Adelphi Theatre on May 1, 1833, returns us to vintage Fitzballian hazardousness. A finely-etched villain, Theodore, has seduced Jacqueline, only to de done in, at last, by a rather bland hero, Paul. In the finale, the blackguard accidentally falls victim to the grainery's revolving wheel, as a fire bursts in the mill. Theodore, caught in the wheel's death-like grip, screams that he is a felon going to his end. The play ends with pure Fitzballian zestfulness: the grainery explodes into an inferno. Evil, criminous, and terrifying, Theodore, along with Mad Jack and Caleb, are prototypes in Fitzballian characterization. The play stresses the haunting environment around the old grainery, such as the dark skies and black forest, which gives the mill a dreadful aura. With Theodore menacing everyone, the diabolical set is made all the more sinister. Again, Fitzball's interest in his villains outweighed that interest for heroes.

With history certainly not safe in the artistic grips of Fitzball, *Joan of Arc,* given at Sadler's Wells Theatre on August 12, interprets the "Maid of Orleans" as victimized by the craftiest of brigands, Richerment and Chalons, who accuse Joan of witchcraft. In a powerful scene, Joan denounces her condemnation: "Assassin, hold!—he was in your power, and you would sacrifice him; but I in truth with heaven's vengeance appalled the tyrant and the murderer" (*Joan* 18). Toying with history, as he did with all literature he adapted, Fitzball presents Joan as a rebel against a usurper, Lord Bevais. Beginning in *media res* concerning Joan's career, all ends happily, with Joan being rescued by Charles just as her execution flames have started to lick the stake. Unusually complex and idealistic, Joan portends the heroine of the modern theatre to come. Against medieval gloom, the villains set the triadic tone before their comeuppance by Charles. The drama could easily play today as a melodrama retrospective. Not as a spoof of tragedy, the play, if revived, would demonstrate Fitzball's technical grasp of romantic tragedy, poetic diction, and theatricalism. By its legendary nature, *Joan of Arc*, in both the Shaw and Anouilh versions, seems to command a certain melodramatic calling, by the nature of a distinct heroine being embattled by villains. Fitzball's techniques did not hinder the essence and character of the heroine at all. The play, now long forgotten, is fine drama, though Fitzball's historicism does maintain his coy sense of dramatic license.

A captivating specimen of Fitzball's theatre of the macabre is *The Black Vulture*, a supreme monster drama, comparable to *The Flying Dutchman*. *The Black Vulture* is important because it entails Fitzball's definitive idea of the *Graustark*. That the play was a success, with management and audience alike, proved that Fitzball's mastery of the theatre of the macabre was insuperable and individual. The monster play is still a popular vehicle in theatre. The *Ascent of F6* by W.H. Auden and Christopher Isherwood was a type of inheritor of the monster plays left by Edward Fitzball and other writers of Blood-and-Thunder horrors. The interpretation of demons and monsters as physical-cum-psychological entities was a remnant of Fitzball's astuteness, as *The Black Vulture* indicates. Presented on October 4, 1830, at the Adelphi Theatre, *The Black Vulture* was a successful culmination of Fitzball's ideas about grotesquerie on the stage and in the spectators' minds. The chilling drama welded the two as one. Against the background of 0. Smith's magnificent performance as the winged devil, the play quickly became a prototype for the monster drama. For the first time, the villain was a demonic bird, a damned and hellish creation of the devil himself. Heretofore, the monster play had been pretty much confined to gothic terror or to pacts with Satan. *The Black Vulture* was an inspired menace from the likes of mythological monsters. Again, Fitzball's monster could very well have set the theatrical and imaginative precedent for filmic monsters, such as *Rodan* and/or the ornithic giant (supposedly a roc) in *The Giant Claw*. The low budget horror film *The Vulture*, with a monster half-man and half-vulture, seems a direct descendant. Obviously, Fitzball's influence superseded his own art and certainly his own era, if one bothers to interpret him at all. Excelling himself in the play, Fitzball quickly gives the bird its ominous character in a coachman's remarks: "I've seen the black vulture, which preys on the ladies of those sworn to death on the wheel" (*Vulture* 3).

In the plot, Ision, the monster's keeper, is a servant of hell and permits the fiend to kidnap a child of the King of the Mountains because the ruler has sought to confiscate his text of black magic and enjoin its teachings. Again, a fairy-tale environment, replete with monster and magical book, emerges as a controlling metaphor. In true Fitzballian fashion the heavens roar with thunder and lightning—a blue-fire symbol—as the vulture appears, screeching, to the servitude of Ision. The creature takes the child deep into the mountain retreat, but the hero, Gedolyne, and the heroine, Janthe, follow the monster, all the while praying to the Ozinda, the spirit of light, for assistance. Entering the creature's liar, Gedlyne and Janthe meet the vulture, but, before it can destroy them and the child, Ozind (the "Deus-ex-Machina" figure) intercedes to strike the vulture and Ision, the monster's guardian. In a wonderfully exciting spectacle of a finale, the vulture and Ision are consumed in a fiery death, which Ozinda causes. The hero, heroine, and child escape the conflagration, which also destroys the magical wheel, that had been used for the extraction of gold from the mountain.

Illogical and gay, the play makes sense—as does any horror theatricality—only within its dramatic confines. As a burletta—and not even that musical form was immune to Fitzball's antics—the play uses music, again, for emotional effect. However, the theological directive of the play is intriguing. Ozinda has the essence of Zoroastrianism, inasmuch as Fitzball has characterized a spirit of light, correlative to that ancient religion's Ormazd; and one of darkness, Ision, relative to the religion's spirit, Ahriman. Of course, theological overtones abounded in melodrama. In fact, Fitzball's better drawn villains, Gortzburg, Bertran, and the like, always had about them an obsequiousness with hell and darkness. To say that Fitzball consciously infiltrated his horrors with doses of a 3,000-year-old religion may be stretching even an eisegesis a bit far, yet his depiction of characters along those lines merit speculation. Since melodrama was mostly a drama of symbolism, allegory, and metaphor, Fitzball's vulture is at once physical dread and, at the same time, a cathartic vehicle for the audience. Through his blue-fire aesthetic, Fitzball forged not only horror, but happiness, as well.

Another play which checked Fitzball's mystery play prowess was *The Traveler's Room,* presented at the Surrey Theatre on November 1, 1847, at a running time of 85 minutes. The usual running time for a good melodrama was about 90 minutes. Somewhat of a potboiler, the play, nonetheless, used the macabre to full effect. In the plot, the satanic Brune stabs—it is now obvious that this technique was the most popular way of doing away with an undesirable—a traveler in order to rob him. Ghoulishly, Brune rolls a rock onto the corpse to bury it. Unlike in *Jonathan Bradford*, Fitzball here seemed little interested in details, his hack obligation to manufacture plays in quick order an obvious reason. The liveliest scene occurs in the pending execution of Brune. Rather than hang, the culprit, in a sequence as that from Jennings' desperate act in *The Crock of Gold*, grabs a knife and kills himself. The play was a minor effort, a "B" film in cinematic terms, if you will. Nonetheless, Fitzball colors Brune well: he is an insane, grimacing villain. We must never lose sight of the fact that, for Fitzball, the sensational triad was a tangible item. The feeling of terror was usually commensurate with an act of horror. This was the philosophy behind his best efforts. In short, Fitzball let the public see the monster first before he considered the emotional reactions.

Of unique interest to the sensational triad was the domestic drama. In this category of melodrama, the lachrymose and lugubrious attitudes of those in distress was a direct result of the sensational triad in Fitzballian fare. Perhaps the macabre played a minor role therein, but crime and madness (jealousy, deceit, and infidelity) were causations for the plot. Some members of Fitzball's public may not have understood the actions of a Gortzburg in wanting the soul of a monk, but all members of that audience could empathize and sympathize with a victim of divorce, infidelity, or unrequited love. They could also understand "crimes of passion" and the brinks of insanity to which a lover could be driven. Fitzball's classic "tear-jerker" was *Alice May; or, The Last Appeal*, which premiered at the Surrey Theatre on June 23, 1852, starring the fine actress Miss Coveney as Alice. The play had all the syrupy, sentimental circumstances of any good *Harlequin Romance*. More realistic in plot and, to an extent, in acting, than were his Grand Guignol extravaganzas, Fitzball packed the play with emotionalism and cathartic trappings. Present were even an evil landlord and tearfully long monody.

The evil landlord Louden evicts honest Mathew and his little family from their tawdry apartment because he has another tenant who is willing to pay more rent for the room. Enraged, Mathew murders the scoundrelly Louden, but Neville, Alice's friend and employer, is blamed for the crime. However, Mathew, unable to live with his guilt, confesses his misdeed, just before Neville is to be hanged. This spectacular declaration is made before Alice and her husband, farmer May. Alice May is a goodly woman, a typically compassionate heroine, who gives succor to those suffering human misery. Again, Fitzball has used the cliff-hanger as a stunning device. Resulting from his painful remorse, Mathew falls into Alice's arms, dying, thus bringing to an end Neville's terror and Alice's long, long angst. Of course, the domestic drama punctuated the "long suffering woman" and Fitzball's play was exemplary of that slant. Through the standard mechanics, Mathew, whose wife has died after their eviction, has stabbed himself, thus the reason for his collapse. In a death scene, magnificently filled with angels, reparation, repentance, and exalation, Mathew softly exculpates his innermost thought to the caring Alice. The dialogue is an inspirational example of melodrama's flamboyance, since "dying speeches" were specialties in the genre. It suggests the inspirited eloigning of Little Eva in *Uncle Tom's Cabin*.

Alice: Pray for mercy, and you will be forgiven.

Mathew: Forgiven! Alice, shall I? William, good-by...Pray for me, Alice (Music rises). Hush! That's my wife's voice. She comes for me. There are my children holding out their little hands for me. Neville, the one I saved, holds his hand to help me over. I am forgiven. Ha! Ha! Ha! May last appeal is heard. (Dies) (28)

With its grammatical eccentricities, emotional expletives ("Ha! Ha! Ha!"), and enfolding hallucinations, this death scene, for all of its schmaltz, which our jaded society might find amusing, was the ingredient that indeed made melodrama forever sentimental and empathic. One must always see art in its historic circumstance before judging its contemporary value. Fitzballian melodrama was emotionally exaggerated, charged by the deepest of feelings within a given character, within a given play. The other domestic drama, *Christmas Eve*; or, *Dual in the Snow*, had that same romantically haunting measure to it. There is a gentle, haunting aura about Alice May. This was done to assume a nostalgic and tender texture. For all of Mathew's crime, morality, in the last instance, rests with him. Louden was the source of evil. *Alice May* is important to this study, in that Fitzball has strategically turned the tables on the moral question. In the usual melodrama, the sensational triad was the province of the villain. Yet, in *Alice May*, the murder was perpetrated against the villain, who, hypocritically, lived a socially acceptable lifestyle, and whose crime of eviction, for the sake of avarice, caused the death of a family. Therefore, with blood on his hands, Mathew shows honor in avenging his family and in exonerating Neville. Mathew's crime was justified in melodrama's dream world: Mathew reaches to heaven in atonement.

In Fitzball's topsy-turvy world, where all kinds of physical and spiritual manifestations occur, Disher gives a key to appreciating melodrama's charm: "Melodrama must be judged for what it is. Shuffle those dog-eared penny plays and penny dreadfuls long enough and the pattern of a fairly recent, but forgotten life takes place" (4).

Chapter V
Fitzball: A Final Appraisal

Of the numerous plays studied in this discourse, one demanding trait of Fitzball rings true: he knew the process by which a practicing playwright could make sensational drama accessible to the people, emotionally and commercially, and make an aesthetic contribution at the same time to his art. It is an ability that has escaped many a playwright over the centuries. Possibly, in this final analysis, R.G. Collingwood's statement about one of art's functions is applicable:

There is a hedonistic theory of art:...that even if the function of art is to give "delight" still this delight is not pleasure in general but pleasure of a particular kind. The artist as purveyor of amusement art makes it his business to please his audience by arousing certain emotions in them and providing them with a make-believe situation for these emotions. (81)

This philosophical attitude was Fitzball's driving force and a reason for his success. He was aware of his vocation, as a hack, and, as such, he had to be conscious of the kind of drama wanted by the working-class constituency in his playhouses. An understandable drama was imperative, he theorized in his autobiography, for the "practical author," which he was:

...a practical author means a playwright who looks beyond his steel pen, and requires a foolscap. It is not quite essential, as Dickens has it, that he should write for the washing tub; but it is absolutely necessary that he know that there is such a commodity...in a theatre where he may be engaged to write. (11: 260-1)

Artistic imagination, combined with a practical understanding of the mechanics of the theatre, for Fitzball, was the theorem for dramaturgic, strategic prosperity. Proud of this idea, he would declare, "I must certainly, for the last thirty years, at least, have been the most practical author on the boards" (11: 386) As has been made apparent, not all theatrical personnel agreed with Fitzball's dramatic ideologies. The critic Daniel Terry once prevented the Adelphi from running Fitzball's Indian play, *Omala*, because of its verbiage, which he considered self-indulgent and pompous. Not to be dissuaded, Fitzball merely put it on at the Olympic (1: 133). In art and in life, Fitzball was quite resilient. Fitzball prided himself as a playwright of the people, a folk dramatist, whose lurid dramas struck a chord of popularity and interest in the common man The whole aspect of popular culture defined Fitzball as practitioner and as theorist of the stage. Without briefly fathoming the nuances of what constitutes popular culture, into which theatre was originally born as a harbinger of that phenomenon, one cannot appreciate the aesthetic makeup of Fitzball in the first place. Leo Lowenthal suggests Fitzball in these remarks.

> Great works of literature enable us to study the way in which people live out their social roles. To consider literature in a sociological context immediately brings us the problem of the reliability and typicality of its data. For whom does a writer speak? Does he have in mind, for example, only himself and a limited elite who are his readers? How far beyond this group do his insights extend? By and large, the great dramatists and novelists have only been read by a small minority, while the majority were exposed mainly to mass-produced and very largely escapist material. Certainly, all literature whether first or second rate, can be interpreted sociologically...Goethe felt that the specific function of art is to stimulate productive imagination. "All pleasures, even the theatres," Goethe wrote, "are only supposed to distract...." (xii-iii)

This declaration by Lowenthal defines Fitzball's artistic directive: he took macabre sensationalism, through ideas (horror, crime, and madness) which all could comprehend, if not in art, then certainly through a tumultous society, and diverted the fearful into a theatrical pleasure. From this creation, Fitzball enticed the mass audience and, therefore, alienated an elitist press, for the most part. The critics looked upon theatre as a privileged institution; Fitzball looked upon it as a public amusement, where art and moralizing could merge.

It must always be remembered that Fitzball amenably served the function of a "generic, social playwright." If not offering overt social thesis in protest over abject conditions of his day, he did offer the best of escapism. And such a response was validated. Entertainment's main target has always been pointed towards the psychological amelioration of a people victimized by poverty, illiteracy, toil, and hopelessness. Immigrants to London, often from Eastern Europe, as well as from other areas in the United Kingdom, had only the theatre—and one usually segregated in their squalid neighborhoods—as an entertaining respite. In our modern, crumbling cities, many cinemas—counterparts to the playhouses of old—yet maintain this demographic and social faculty. To his credit, Fitzball, seeing this plight, and appreciating his audience's uncouth demeanor, euchered this sadness by his magic insouciance. David Meyer has pointed out that the function of such escapism is that "popular theatre originates with and is controlled by the popular audience through the dynamics and ethos of their society" (263). Fitzball consistently followed that populist directive, even if occasionally confounded by it, whenever his audiences rejected a particular play.

Fitzball as Bourgeois Escapism
It has been observed that the bourgeois reader fancied amusement, but that he also wanted information along with the entertainment (Lowenthal 48). In conjunction with this reflection, Cervantes once wrote, "Nothing, in fact, more truly portrays us as we are and as we could be than the play and the players" (Corrigan 1). Relevant to Fitzball, these maxims were, indeed, brought together, inasmuch as Fitzball issued information about man's morality through his theatrical divagations. Walter Kaufmann has deduced that tragedy concerns immense suffering which, it is hoped, will cause a cathartic and empathetic reaction in the viewer. Thus, implied Kaufmann, moral sanity may return to mankind through seeing the ravages caused by immorality and evil (98). Such has been the dream of philosophy and serious art forever. In Fitzballian horrors, this tragedian claim is manipulated strongly. For all the theatrical harangue in his plays, Fitzball touted morality as a most serious choice for his patrons to consider. The sensational triad had, indeed, a psuedo-tragic and compassionate aesthetic beneath it. As the *Illustrated London News* aptly and conclusively said of *Marmion:* "...[it had] great capabilities for scenic display and pageantry" (392). This well summarizes the Fitzballian charisma above all else.

In the final judgment of Fitzball, one must recall his place in time and the vogue of melodrama: "In the gaslight era, the supernatural took hold of the public imagination, and British authors quickly dominated the field of horror" (Kanfer 76) . In the midst of this macabre plethora, Fitzball's works might be noticed as so much *kitsch,* a gauche kind of fluff. *Kitsch* and *fluff* were indeed part of Fitzball's hack-repertoire. Even if he had been the finest dramatist ever, he could not have given his audience a steady diet of dramatic intellectuality and remain employed. Echoing Goethe's sentiments, Fitzballian kitsch, if you will, was merely a coloration for public attraction. With the so-called serious playwrights scrambling for showcases, Fitzball knew that kitsch, a term misunderstood critically, was theatre's solvency. As William Hammel notices about popular art, kitsch is often a necessity. As such, Fitzball is vindicated for his indulgences into mass-escapism.

Although much on "kitsch" is concerned with humorously freakish literature, the concept of "kitsch" is helpful in any study of popular literature…a word apparently of Russian in origin, *kitsch* means vulgar showoff, and it is applied to anything that took a lot of trouble to make and is quite hideous. It is paradoxical stuff, kitsch. It is terribly ingenious, and terribly ugly…and yet it has one of the qualities of good art—which is that, once seen, it is not easily forgotten. of course it is found in all of the arts…. Kitsch is well known in drama. Perhaps you may think that this a depraved taste. But really it is an extension of experience. (47-55)

Fitzball's role as a cult dramatist, or a dramatist who appealed to a certain, aesthetic mentality, used kitsch methodically. The kitsch elaboration drew the public into the playhouses, where Fitzball's hypnotic bravura kept them. This is underscored by Fitzball's remark about the value of the average theatregoer:

…to listen to moralising language to see the voices of mankind pictures as in a glass… and punished as they deserved…and this in practical illustrations of life as it absolutely exists. (11: 407-8)

Didactic melodrama, even with a kitsch trajectory, was a sign of Fitzball's artistry, his concern for mankind, and his hope for happiness through the happy ending syndrome of his plays. Blood-and-Thunder, therefore, had more than spectacle. Fitzball's heroes, though temporarily *dislocated* from normalcy by the villain's subterfuge, always returned in victory. They personified hope in their championship, just as tragic heroes personified failure by their *harmatia* (tragic flaw).

That people cannot bear too much reality and, consequently, are in a necessary quest for fantasy, rather than for reality, confirms all that has been written here about Fitzballian art. Fitzball's dramaturgic philosophy, with this moral as its objective, substantiated the necessity for human willpower. If one notices, Fitzball's most dynamic heroes are inundated with self-motivation and tremendous willpower. These were their weapons against corruption. Hammel sees popular art as that salvation; in he indirectly speaks to Fitzball's artistic soul:

The growth of a large popular audience, increasingly accessible through the mass media, caused in turn a demand for artists to satisfy its cultural needs. To these artists success lay not in pleasing the rich patron and his small, aristocratic, cultural circle, but in satisfying an increasingly broad "popular" audience. The popular artist had to make his own tradition by investigating his market, calculating its desires, and evolving devices (many of which he adapted from folk art) for reaching it. He became a kind of professional who created for profit the kind of art the public wanted. The appearance of the popular artist tradition, therefore, derives from a shift—initiated in the eighteenth century and completed during the nineteenth—from the patronage of the arts by the restricted upper class to the support offered by a huge, virtually unlimited, middle class audience, within the context of great technological, social, and political change. modern mass society was fully formed by the middle of the nineteenth century. Popular culture developed with it. (9)

Fitzball's imploring of the masses for artistic and economic solvency was no different from the Elizabethan dramatist soliciting support from the realm, as The Lord Chamberlain's men did. Kurt Anderson defends that entity, known as popular culture, as a rassmatazz, wanted by the public in any entertainment that is "quick, vivid, and exuberant." It is pop culture's merit—and Fitzball's merit in popular drama—to be vital and have a "give-'em-what-they-want" mentality for survival. The free market has spawned pop culture, which is, in effect, the free market idea itself. Requiring no tutelage or special sensibility—which Fitzball's patrons surely had little of—pop culture is unlike other art. It does not even require close attention for the Objective Correlative to grow and to prosper among the masses. Anderson asserts that the function of pop culture is to welcome all kinds of folk, regardless of their social position, into the common aesthetic. Fitzballian drama and theatre operated under that humanitarian edict (Hammel 68-9). All pop art is revolutionary art, in its ideas and in its final form: it must be because of its interest in average people. In fact, Fitzball's first dramaturgic principle was to inspire his patrons with his *playful* plays. James Smith summarizes the rationale behind Fitzball's theatrical shenanigans in an historical context:

Between 1800 and 1900 the essential elements of popular melodrama did not change. But not even an uneducated audience will pay good money to see the same play every night for a century. Melodramatists had to invent variations. They incorporated waterfalls, mechanical magpies, human monkeys...performing dogs to rescue drowning children, dig up bodies, and sink their fangs into murderer's padded throats. They ransacked newspapers, novels, poems, history books, and atlases; they cribbed from their colleagues in France, Germany, and America; they staged last week's invention, yesterday's catastrophe and this morning's trial at the Old Bailey. Above all, they invented new scenery, new characters, and new theatrical effects. By turns, melodrama became gothic, brigandish, exotic, military, navel, domestic, regional, historical, romantic, criminal, urban and plain posh. (38-9)

One is able to see quickly melodrama's outrageous legacy left to vaudeville, burlesque, and silent films in its milking of the weird and the bizarre as entertainment: for early twentieth-century entertainment was no more than an almost verbatim transposition of nineteenth-century melodrama. As an aside, showing quickly that Fitzball did not create in a vacuum, it is interesting to note, regarding melodrama's international penchant for "borrowing dramatic ideas" wherever it could, that Fitzball's social-thesis play *Nitocris* (1855) was written some four years before Dion Boucicault's antislavery epic, *The Octoroon; or, Life in Louisiana* (1859). Also, Boucicault's *The Poor of New York* (1857) touted the same repudiation of crime, miscreants, and social decay found in Fitzball's crime sagas. Without his flair for blue-fire sensationalism, Fitzball could have been keenly compared to Boucicault, in that they both relied upon all sorts of melodramatic tactics for the desired, cathartic pondering in their audiences. Melodrama, for all of its theatrical aggrandizement, may have been the most democratic of genres.

Fitzball knew that no class had a monopoly on culture, since theatre, from the Greeks of antiquity, urged everyone to attend plays and even made special arrangements for that reason. Moreover, the person who believed that "high-toned art" would, in and of itself, make him more intelligent would, ironically, miss the pleasure of culture as a whole. Kurt Anderson has written, "Pop culture is, after all, populist culture, too" (Hammel 74). Fitzball rationalized well that the six elements only had validity in the basis of erecting drama; they would be avoided as just another literary criticism, or as so much restrictive dogma, if they became misguided, as was the case with the French Academy of seventeenth-century France. In all of Fitzball's works, these words of the critic David Daiches ring true: "Passion, sensation, and pleasure are, under the proper conditions, good and helpful things, conductive to knowledge and love" (96). For Fitzballian drama, moral knowledge and the love of that knowledge are the conquering forces; they are the forces ingrained in melodrama as a genre. The legacy of that attitude dominates the melodramatic media of today in popular and commercial preeminence. As Daiches has remarked, artistic conventions are based upon public consent:

No individual poet can himself create all his own conventions, for conventions must be based on some degree of public consent; yet he must bring them alive in his own way, or they remain mere conventions and not means of bringing imaginative life and scope to a necessarily limited work. (187)

This entire study has been an interpretation of Fitzballian conventions, evoked in their most uncanny procedures. Fitzball was an artist pleased in expressing social conventions within the conventions of melodrama; his artistic passion was a resurgence of the romantic idealism of virtue victorious over the monsters in man's collective soul. In essence, he delighted "to contemplate similar volitions and passions as manifested in the goings-on of the Universe and habitually impelled to create them where he does not find them" (Daiches 92). Perseverance was perspicuous and pertinacious to Fitzball's moral trust in melodrama's portrayal of man's gallantry against evil. Fitzball's three *P's*, *perseverance*, *perspicuousness*, and *pertinaciousness*, honestly summarize his goal in drama.

In summarizing Fitzball's dramaturgic prowess, we may assert that his plays are artificial, because of reasons made apparent in this study; that they are histrionic, because of the Delsartian alliance with melodrama; that they are emotionally exasperating, because of Fitzball's implementation of the classic, cathartic principles of Aristotle (the arousal of pity and fear in the audience for empathic purposes); and that they are scenically grandiose, because Victorian theatre commanded such a scenographic elaboration, expressed by Fitzball's expertise in blue-red-fire discharges.

Beneath all of these characteristics lay Fitzball's amusing approach, not to the thesis of a play, but to its theatrical execution. He sported with theatricalism to make a philosophical point with the viewer. Early into the twentieth-century sensationally triadic plays were common on Broadway. A case in point was Crane Wilber's popular *The Monster* (1922), which provided DeWolf Hopper one of his greatest roles, that of the crazed Dr. Ziska. Lon Chaney would magnificently recreate the part in the 1925 film. One can see Fitzballian devices aplenty in the drama: trap doors, sliding panels, eerie sounds, and stark blue-fire terror and horror, as the hero and heroine battle the demonic Ziska for escape. Audiences, for 112 performances, wailed in sheer horror as the pair sought a cliff-hanging flight from the villain. The advertisements read, "Will the sadistic fiend have his way with these two, or will they manage to escape in time" (Bronner 315). It was Fitzballian chaos all the way.

In this summation of Fitzballian sensationalism, one tenet should be addressed, even if briefly, for it does not involve theatre directly: Fitzball's legacy to the modern modes of his theatre of the macabre, which are, of course, television and film (the horror film essentially). It is my contention that examples from these media owe a debt to this forgotten champion of an entertainment now acknowledged as a commercial cornerstone of these industries. This will also put Fitzball into a contemporary perspective, which will disengage him from being just another anachronistic dramatist. A deliberation by Carl Jung seems poignantly applicable to the dark, psychological metaphors that characterize so much of Fitzball's works and to that of the sensational media event, whether film, television, or theatre:

The poets' work is an interpretation and illumination of the contents of consciousness, of the ineluctable experiences of human life with its eternally recurrent sorrow and joy... Whatever its particular form may be, the psychological work of art always takes its materials from a vast realm of conscious human experience from the vivid foreground of life.... It is a primordial experience which surpasses man's understanding, and to which he is therefore in danger of succumbing. (Ghiselin 211-2)

Fitzball in Modern Sensationalism

In the "Shaping-reshaping-the eternal spirit's eternal pastime," the artists of the macabre prick man's perennial absorption in the fanciful, albeit terrifying, manifestations of what the macabre is in relation to human sorrow and joy (Ghiselin 212). The experience of discovering that absorption is an anodyne through theatre and film. Fitzball's horrors were integrated into his opalescent, fairytale world of enchantment, just as in the above examples show. Carlos Clarens declares the same reason for the popularity of the horror film as was given for the upsurge of Fitzballian sensationalism: troubling times and the human and artistic response to them.

It would seem logical to suppose that troubled art is born out of troubled times...there seems to be inside of us a constant, ever-present yearning for the fantastic, for the darkly mysterious, for the cocked terror of the dark...art works that stir the black hue in human experience have a steady unvarying coherence in their emblems and embodiments...we are meant to be frightened...and fear is still a powerful instrument and the most intense reaction to an experience. (xiv)

This insinuation for the horror film's rationale is the same for the sensational plays of Fitzball. Both entities share the morality play essence, good battling evil, and the composition that fear is basic to mankind's world and fancy. The nature of Fitzball's manner of horror exploitation, if you will, has become so dominant in film, internationally, that *Time* had on its front cover, for July 28, 1986, a promotional photo of the monster and star, Sigourney Weaver, in James Cameron's *Aliens,* a sequel to the 1979 blockbuster film. The film's premise and monster—to a degree, excepting the differences in special effects now and in nineteenth-century theatre—have an uncanny reminiscence to *The Black Vulture.* Both art works dealt with the sensational triad in the conviction that horror entertainment is at once confrontational and evasive. Wrote Richard Sticker: "The wit of the picture lay in its relocation of that classic device of the horror genre: a monster stalking the spaceship's endless corridors, picking off victims one by one. *Aliens* never forgot that its basic business is escapist" (58). Beyond entertainment, *Aliens,* like *The Black Vulture,* offered moral conviction and victory, in the face of execrative fear. Its relationship to Fitzball, more than this, lay in the use of blue-fire types of chilling excitement: pyrotechnic explosions, a ghastly monster-villain, and an atmosphere of claustrophobic horror. In *The Devil's Elixer* and *Dutchman*, there was the gruesome closeness of a monastery and an eerie ship. In *Aliens*, a rocket ship-station becomes the gothic enclosure. Another similarity lay in both being, in Booth's reference to melodrama, "good box office" with art appealing to people's emotions rather than their intellect (*Villain* 18). The horror film and Fitzballian drama share yet another facet: their fears are the kind experienced by mankind most in his life. This is not to say that we see gigantic vultures and hideous creatures from outer space; it is to say that melodrama, in all of its inherited media forms, paints a villain and a hero. And, in life, the melodramatist asserts, we meet people, situations, and decisions which are, to us, either good or bad. Melodrama merely concretizes and enhances symbols of these feelings. The horror film and Fitzballian horror share, for all of their bombast and affectation, the melodramatic purpose of delighting and impressing the audience (Carlson 2145). Fitzball knew that the actor's gait, gesture, and grimaces were an "interpretation or expression of the emotion depicted" (Ruckmick 198). The horror film capitalized on this presentational emotion to unparalleled heights.

Another similarity that the horror film, in particular, adapted from Fitzball's specific direction was the type of audience in attendance. Before film became thoroughly democratic in its offerings—meaning, before fewer films were made for more and more people—it addressed what Fitzball had helped create in his minor theatre clientele: the shirtsleeve audience, or those from the blue-collar, working-class, social depository (Turner and Price 9). Again, these comparisons, either directly or presumed, retreat back to man's conception of fantasy. Lyall Watson has said that oftentimes man cannot distinguish between reality and dreams (306). If horror entertainment does nothing else, from its historic (Fitzball) or modern (Cameron) perspective, it is to make the dream world, where the theatre of the macabre may be real in all of its impossible processes, tangible and genuine. Fantasy becomes concrete, in essence. Bruno Bettelheim, in his fine text *The Uses of Enchantment,* explores the ramifications and implications of fantasy and fairytale literature upon the psychological and aesthetic nature of mankind. His conclusions have an discernible impact on just how entertainment of the bizarre affects man's cognizance of reality. Bettelheim's remarks are important in this concluding chapter because Fitzball and his modern artistic counterparts deal almost exclusively within that cognitive dissonance. To understand Fitzball, and his legacy to modern sensationalism, the rationale behind the literature of the fantastic is warranted, at least on the theoretical basis:

In child or adult, the unconscious is a powerful determinant of behavior. When the unconscious is repressed and its content denied en route to behavior, then eventually the person's conscious mind will be partially overwhelmed by derivatives of these unconscious elements.... But when the unconscious material is to some degree permitted to come to awareness and whirled through in imagination its potential for causing harm is reduced; some of its forces can then be made to serve positive forces. The fairy tale, from its mundane and simple beginning, launches into fantastic events...At the tale's end the hero has mastered all trials and despite them has remained true to himself, or in successfully undergoing them has achieved this true selfhood...In fairy tales, unlike myths, victory is not over others but only over oneself and villainy. (127-8)

Lastly, the horror film and Fitzballian drama are, of course, not the same. Time and technology have superseded this synonymous identity. I have compared the two genres for one, simple reason: the horror film, from its composition, goal, and aesthetic being, is unmistakably grounded in the type of macabre sensationalism penned by Fitzball. The cultural ambiance of audience and social factors are overtly similar. Fitzball's sensationalism is a type of dramatic enjambment unto the horror-adventure movies, melodramas all. For this reason, Fitzballian horror, crime, and madness are easily transposed into movie art, again excepting technical conventions. The heroes are basically furtive and the villains basically evil and gruesome. The nurturing of melodrama has changed, but not its nature.

In finalizing popular culture, to which Fitzball and his legacy belong, Horace Newcombe has summed up the issue promptly:

But in examining the popular arts, even from the aesthetic point of view, we should keep in mind that the discovery of excellence is not our primary task. Cawelti puts it this way: ...In distinguishing invented structures from formulas we are trying to deal with the relationship between the work and its culture, and not with its artistic culture. (223)

Fitzball and Modernity

If Fitzball were alive today, he would be a writer of movies, not of film or cinema, and of television soap operas. His drama was to theatre what movies are to cinema. The distinction is in perception and working confines, not necessarily in artistic judgments, of which Fitzball was unjustly a victim. Pauline Kael has written that movies fit the way man feels. And that this feeling has come about because the "schoolbooks" have lied about how one should exist in the real world. "Good movies," she says, "make you care, make you believe in the possibilities again." Movies make the average viewer care about the principle dramatic elements: acting, the scenery, the story, et al. The movies, she goes on, tap man's emotions, in a way that high culture cannot. In short, "movies took their impetus from the peep show, the Wild West Show, the music hall—from what was coarse and common, not from the desiccated imitation European high culture" (Combs and Mansfield 414-8). Fitzball is conterminously revealed by these insights.

Edward Fitzball was a playwright, in essence, who looked at theatre the same way that a "B" film director looks at cinema, or a writer of romance novels looks at a *Gone With the Wind*. With Fitzball, his vocation of hack did not deter his artistry, his intellect, or his concern. Fitzball's plays, while decidedly illogical and fantastic (they were written to be fantastic, in any event) were outlets for the beleaguered of his society. Fitzball's absurdist drama of enchantment gave the viewer, and the observant critic, a journey into the unknown where demons, fairies, and heroes flourished in a morality play of stature. There the universe was gauged not by science, but by special effects on stage, a throwback to the liturgical drama.

Fitzball's world has about it a type of absurdism which warrants investigation. Martin Esslin's seminal *The Theatre of the Absurd* seems to speak to Fitzball's prophetic, theatrical tendencies:

The theatre must not be just a means to make the bourgeois comfortable, it must also frighten him, turn him into a child again. Said Yvan Goll, "The simplest means is the grotesque, but without inciting to laughter. The monotony and stupidity of human beings are so enormous that they can be adequately represented only by enormities. Let the new drama be an enormity." (324)

Fitzball cannot be termed an absurdist because, even within his dream world of monsters and villains, there are also heroes and heroines, thus, hope and victory. Fitzball is unconcerned with the preoccupation of spiritual annihilation, as are the absurdists; he is unconcerned because he has faith, whereas the absurdists have permitted the world to rob them of theirs. Fitzball's *enormous* plays permit everything to be larger-than-life. Aristotle's dramatic elements are distended to great lengths in a world unconcerned with limit. The play's point-of-attack for Fitzball is aimed at that annihilation which has vexed the absurdists. For Fitzball, the villain is tangible; so, whenever that tangibility is downed, virtue then is free rightfully to reign. His spectators could, in their simple ways, identify with that message. Of course, the melodrama was steeped in an *Horatio Alger* reference and frame-of-mind, but that simplistic moral was food for thought for those aching in life. The absurdists, in hardly any way, are able to defeat life's enemies, physical or otherwise. The latter's sense of uselessness and defeatism is the differentiation between Fitzballian and modern, absurdist fantasy.

The dramatic examples given in this work have dealt with Fitzballian sensationalism as a folk-theatre. For all of the extravagance, impulsiveness, and magnanimity, Fitzballian dramas were, as *explications de texte,* an art for public consumption, a surfeit of adaptations, originals, legends, and music, all of which combined to produce curios of madcap theatrics and dramatic vistas, having a surreal-romantic quality about them. Holman has defined folk drama as any drama dealing with themes of human nature in a rather unsophisticated way. He has traced its lineage from the Greek theatre, to the Medieval liturgical play, and to such modern works as Marc Connelly's *Green Pastures.* In folk drama, the customs, language strictures, and environmental dimensions of a particular folk are stressed (204). To be sure, Fitzball could never be accused of being not a populist, although he did lament over the audience's rejection of *Andreas Hofer* and *Nitocris* as being too intellectual. Nevertheless, he assuaged his spectators lack of perception with such oddities as *The Last of the Fairies* (1852), *Harlequin and Humpty Dumpty* (1850), and the infamous burlesque, *Zazezizozu* (1836), among others during his long career. Fitzball emerges as a baroque theorist and avid practicer of viable theatricalism. An example was his casting of Frederick Vining in the lead of his tragedy, *Edwin,* because the actor had fame as a portrayer of regal gentlemen and fops. Fitzball used anything, or anyone, thought good for his purposes (Boas 260).

The plays thus examined indicate that indeed Fitzball was a systematic playwright for the following reasons. First of all, the plots followed the levels of the dramatic pyramid, as demonstrated in *Jonathan Bradford.* Fitzball's dramatic structure pursued a combination of the climactic-episodic form: the plot began early in the story and moved through numerous episodes; the time covered was a relative short span, although *Edwin* went on for some length, while the average Fitzballian drama was 90 minutes, the length of the feature film to come; there was an abundance of scenes in his notable plays, a clear characteristic of melodrama; there were several characters in the plays who gave the viewer a sense that the play had a certain breadth: the more characters, the bigger the play in importance and epic quality; and, finally, the scenes of action usually followed a cause-and-effect continuum, even though Fitzball would inject a scene with something of a dramatic *non sequitur* for effect, such as the "Deus-e-Machina" device.

Secondly, Fitzball forms a world where contradictions in reality have a place. Anything may happen in Fitzball's dramatic environment; hence, his love for special effects, the spectacular, and the supernatural. He develops his microcosm to be adaptable to any logic that mirrors it. In short, Fitzball's schemata is answerable to no rule of composure, save the moral and stylistic demands of the genre. Thirdly, aspects of the sensational triad are in almost all of his extant plays. Fitzball had an inclination for furious action and violence. Thus, metaphorically, he was reflecting his era's social and psychological turmoil. His plays are never enervated; rather, they are always persistently active, often to the point of exhaustion. Fourthly, Fitzball's plays always accent, whether they be supernatural or natural, the human condition and human spirit. The theatre of the macabre and the sensational triad all surround an essence of humanity. Even the abject horror in *The Demon of the Wolf's Glen,* in which the cunning Count Rudolph is pulled into hell by his accomplice, Zamiel the Demon, does not exclude the hope for mankind to rally, morally and intellectually. And, fifthly, as *The Fatal Blow* will show, Fitzball's plays are filled with ironic and unexpected (almost Hitchcockian in nature) twists and convolutions. When the sixteenth-century poet Marino wrote, "Astonishment's the poet's aim and aid; Who cannot startle best had stick to trade," he must have been presaging The "Terrible" Fitzball's blue-fire plots (Van de Bogart 139). *The Fatal Blow* is a final testament to this assessment.

The plot of *The Fatal Blow* is as follows. Michael Goltz, the father, is a Lear-like character, befuddled about his station in life and about what he thinks life owes him. His accomplice son, Brune, is a cutthroat, pure and simple. Together, they waylay and kill a traveler for his gold, not knowing that the victim is the son of the elder Goltz and, subsequently, Brune's brother. Callously, Brune remarks that the dead look sleeping, but, in addition, are not dangerous. Ferdinand, an officer and resemblant to the killed Herman, requites a confession from Brune, who then stabs himself to death. Goltz, in custody, attempts suicide by swallowing a knife, which lodges in his throat! One may find himself stammering over the stark preposterousness of it all, but, recalling Fitzball's system, such an act in a drama was not out of the realm of implausible stage reality. As long as the dramatic activities suited the thought behind the work, they met Fitzball's capricious criterion.

As a finale to Fitzballian drama, *The Fatal Blow* accentuates the type of theatrical riot that would make an excellent black comedy. The macabre activities and the formation of the sensational triad in the play are incredulous, Fitzballian gambols. Murdering a brother and son, whose corpse is not recognized by its killers, and swallowing a knife in a botched suicide attempt, because the dagger becomes lodged in the throat, are the black, comedic capers that a playwright such as Fitzball would pull. Such a frenzied play would be the stuff which Fitzball's audiences would enjoy thoroughly. Fitzball's knack for successful, dramatic experimentation was a qualitative and quantitative measure of his success: give the patrons exploitation that meets a synesthesia in the theatrical experience. Fitzball's frustrations about being a respected tragedian, with having some of his plays fail receptively, and feeling sometimes that his vocation as a hack was demeaning and limiting, were always short-lived in the wake of public popularity. In summation, Fitzball knew how to create diversion with intelligence, artistry, and style. He had the gift of *class*. Richard Meyers has written this about exploitation entertainment, which calls to mind Fitzballian sensationalism. It has much to say about human psychology:

...throughout history, the most civilized sorts have otherwise entertained themselves in the most bestial of manners. Whether it was the Roman Coliseum where Christians were thrown to the lions and gladiators fought to the death of France's Grand Guignol Theatre where realistic dramas of mass murder were enacted, everyone from the upper crust to the groundlings were left screaming for more. The truth is that "exploit" means "to utilize, especially for profit." (xiii)

Fitzball in Conclusion

As a dramaturge, Fitzball elevated drama for the masses through his artistic versatility as poet, musician, and theorist. His aesthetic of the sensational triad stimulated both the emotions and thought of his audiences. His lurid and exciting plays made solid entertainment as well as moral commentary. His public was the "shirtsleeve audience" who saw sensationalism as the gate to Fitzball's theatrical garden. That he was subject to controversial appraisals by his critics and, consequently, ignored by theatre history, and, knowing the qualms of criticism anyway, it is enough to vindicate him as a talent and prophet for current styles in popular entertainment. More than a relic, his melodrama, as has been suggested, seems quite contemporary in the various modes of entertainment; which today stress fantasy, thrills, and chills in the eternal morality—and melodramatic—play of good against evil. The tastes that attacked Fitzball would be those praising him today. His sensationalism is now rampant in artists of repute.

Even with his brand of theatricalism reflected in Andrew Lloyd Webber's musicalized theatre of the macabre, *The Phantom of the Opera*, and in the eerily fantastic *Starlight Express*, the precocious Fitzball is likely to remain forgotten. The Blood-and-Thunder stylistic began to die, as a distinct form, when the stage melodrama began declining during the early twentieth century. With the coming of realism as a theatrical, dramatic, and actorish style, the moral absolutes in melodrama's dramatic range became vague and inapplicable in the sight of psychological and educational deductions, themselves, for the most part, inconclusive and fickled in offering genuine directives for a world bewildered by itself. For all of its dogmatic bombast, melodrama, with Fitzball leading one of its forms, was an innocent form. After a world war, that innocence died quickly and continues to have dirt heaped upon its grave with each grim, succeeding decade.

However, melodrama, if not in its pure stage sense, remains, commercially, public entertainment's most viable form through the outlets of film, television, and theatre. Moreover, Fitzball's harrowing sensational triad is not defunct, or his theatre of the macabre outlived. They have merely taken different forms in ways unimagined by "the master of blue-fire deviltry." Therefore, each time we shriek in the dark, with happy and terrified delight, at the monster on stage, or cheer the hero's derring-do against the villain, we are paying a sort of social and cathartic homage to the twinkling and madcap artistry of "The *Wonderfully Terrible* Fitzball."

Works Cited

a' Beckett, Gilbert. "The quizziology of the British drama." *Punch* (1869): 4.

Actors by Midnight. (September 1838): 5.

Adams, W. Davenport. *Dictionary of Drama.* London: Chatto and Windus, 1904.

Aldritch, Virgil C. *Philosophy of Art.* Englewood Cliffs: Prentice Hall, 1963.

Altshuler, Thelma, and Richard P. Janero. *Responses to Drama,* New York: Houghton Mifflin Co., 1967.

Aristotle. *Theory of Poetry and Fine Arts.* Trans. S.H. Butcher. New York: Dover Books, 1951.

Arnheim, Rudolph. *Toward a Psycbology of Art.* Berkeley: U of California P, 1966.

Athenaeum. (April 1835): 262.

Athenaeum. (May 1852): 570.

Bailey, J.0., ed. *British Plays of the Nineteenth Century* New York: Odyssey P, Inc., 1966.

Baker, H. Barton. *The London Stage.* London: W.H. Allen and Co., 1889.

Ball, Edward. *The Revenge of Taran.* London: C. Chapple, 1821.

Barry, Jackson G. *Dramatic Structure.* U of California P, 1970.

Beckerman, Bernard. *Dynamics of Drama.* New York: Alfred A. Knopf, 1970.

Bentley, Eric. *The Playwright as Thinker.* New York: Harcourt, Brace and World, Inc., 1967.

Bettelheim, Bruno. *The Uses of Enchantment.* New York: Vintage Books, 1977.

Bettman, Otto L. *The Good Old Days—They Were Terrible.* New York: Random House, 1974.

Boas, Frederick S. Introduction. *The Players Library.* London: Faber and Faber, Ltd., 1950.

Bonesana, Caesar. *An Essay on Crime and Punishment.* Philadelphia: A. Walker, 1819.

Booth, Michael. *English Melodrama.* London: Herbert Jenkins, 1965.

_____., ed. *Hiss the Villain: Six Melodramas.* New York: Benjamin Blom, Inc., 1964.

Bordman, Gerald. *The Oxford Companion to the American Theatre/New York:* Oxford UP, 1984.

Boulton, Marjorie. *The Anatomy of Drama.* London: Routledge and Kegan Paul, Ltd., 1960.

Brockett, Oscar. *History of the Theatre.* Boston: Allyn and Bacon, Inc., 1982.

_____. *The Theatre: An Introduction,* New York: Holt, Rinehart and Winston, 1979.

Brook, Peter. *The Empty Space.* New York: Atheneum Books, 1969.

Brophy, Philip. "Horrality—The Textuality of Contemporary Horror Films." *Art and*

Text (September 1985): 13.

Bronner, Edwin J. *The Encyclopedia of the American Theatre: 1900-1975.* New York: A.S. Barnes and Co., Inc., 1980.

Brosnan, John. *The Horror People.* New York: New American Library, 1976.

Buss, Arnold. *The Psychology of Aggression.* New York: John Wiley and Sons, 1961.

Byrne, M. St. Clare. "Early Multiples Stages in England." *Theatre Notebook.* London: Theatre Studies, 1954.

Carlson, Marvin. *Theories of the Theatre.* Ithaca: Cornell UP, 1984.

Checkland, S.G. *The Rise of Industrial Society in England. 1815-1885.* New York: St. Martin's, 1964.

Chesney, Kellow. *The Anti-Society: An Account of the Victorian Underworld.* Boston: Gambit, 1970.

Cirlot, J.E. *A Dictionary of Symbols.* New York: Philosophical Library, 1983.

Clarens, Carlos. *An Illustrated History of the Horror Film.* New York: Capricorn Books, 1967.

Clark, Barrett H. *European Theories of the Drama.* New York: Crown Publishers Inc., 1965.

Cleaver, Dale G. *Art: An Introduction.* New York: Harcourt, Brace, and Jovanovich, Inc., 1977.

Cohen, B. Bernard. *Writing About Literature.* Glenview: Scott, Foreman and Co., 1963.

Combs, James E., and Michael W. Mansfield, eds. *Drama in Life: The Uses of Communications in Society.* New York: Hastings House, 1976.

Coombes, H. *Literature and Criticism.* New York: Pinguin Books, 1977.

Collingwood, R.G. *The Principles of Art.* New York: Oxford UP, 1966.

Corrigan, Robert W. *The World Of Theatre.* Glenview: Scott, Foresman and Co., 1979.

Coville, Walter J., Timothy Costello, and Fabian L. Rouke. *Abnormal Psychology.* New York: Barnes and Noble, 1960.

Crawford, Jerry L. *Acting in Person and in Style.* Dubuque: Wm. C. Brown Company, 1980.

Crews, Frederick, ed. *Psychoanalysis and Literary Process.* Cambridge: Winthrop, 1970.

Cross, Gilbert. *Next Week East Lynn.* Lewisburg: Bucknell UP, 1977.

Daiches, David. *Critical Approaches to Literature.* New York: W.W. Norton and Co., 1956.

Daniels, Les. *Fear. A History of Horror in the Mass Media.* London: Granada, 1975.

Davidoff, Henry, ed. *Pocketbook of Quotations.* New York: Pocket Books, 1968.

Day, Martin S. *History of English Literature; 1160-1837.* Garden City: Doubleday and Co., 1963.

_____. *History of English Literature. 1837-Present.* Garden City: Doubleday and Co., 1964.

De Quiros, C. Bernaldo. *Modern Theories of Criminality.* Boston: Little, Brown, and Co., 1912.

Disher, Maurice. *Blood and Thunder: Mid-Victorian Melodrama and Its Origin.* London: Frederick Muller, Ltd., 1949.

Douglas, Drake. *Horror.* New York: Collier Books, 1966.

Dramatic Magazine. (January 1827): 317.

Dramatic Magazine. (November 1830): 99.

Duerr, Edwin. *The Length and Depth of Acting.* New York: Holt, Rinehart, and Winston, 1962.

Dukes, Ashley. *The Drama.* New York: Henry Holt and Co., 1927.

Dukore, Bernard F. *Dramatic Theory and Criticism.* New York: Holt, Rinehart, and Winston, 1974.

"Edward Ball." *British Museum General Catalogue of Printed Books.* Vol. 10. London: Trustees of British Museum, 1965.

"Edward Fitzball." *Encyclopedia Britannica.* 1911 ed.

Egri, Lajos. *The Art of Dramatic Writing.* New York: Simon and Schuster, 1960.

Ellis, Havelock. *The Criminal.* London: Walter Scott, 1890.

Esslin, Martin. *The Theatre of the Absurd.* Garden City: Anchor Books, 1969.

Everson, William K. *The Bad Guys: A Pictorial History of the Movie, Villain.* New York: Cadillac, 1964.

Examiner. (May 1822): 436.

Examiner. (April 1869): 262.

Fairchild, Henry Pratt, ed. *Dictionary of Sociology and Related Sciences.* Totowa: Littlefield, Adams, and Co., Inc., 1965.

Figaro in London. (November 1840): 180.

Finch, Robert. *How to Write a Play.* New York: Greensburg, 1948.

Fitzball, Edward. *Thirty-five Years in a Dramatic Author's Life.* 2 vols. London: T.C. Newby. 1859.

Foucault, Michel. *Discipline and Punishment.* Trans. Alan Sheridan. New York: Vintage Books, 1979.

Fox, Vernon. *Introduction to Criminology.* Englewood Cliffs: Prentice Hall, 1976.

Fraser, John. *Violence in the Arts.* New York: Cambridge UP, 1974.

Gassner, John, and Edward Quinn, eds. *The Reader's Encyclopedia of World Drama.* New York: Thomas Y. Crowell, 1969.

Ghiselin, Brewster, ed. *The Creative Process.* New York: St. Martin's, 1980.

Gielgud, John. Foreword. *The Entertainers.* New York: St. Martin's, 1980.

Golden, James, Gordon F. Berquist, and William E. Coleman. *The Rhetoric of Western Thought.* Dubuque: Kendall/Hunt, 1983.

Greenwood, Ormerod. *The Playwright.* London: Sir Issac Pittman and Sons, 1950.

Grose, B. Donald, and 0. Franklin Kenworthy. *A Mirror to Life: A History of Western Theatre.* New York: Holt, Rinehart and Winston, 1985.

Hall, Vernon, Jr. *A Short History of Literary Cirticism.* New York: New York UP, 1963.

Hamilton, Cicely. *The Old Vic.* London: Jonathan Cope, Ltd., 1926.

Hanunel, Willaim, ed. *The Popular Arts in America.* New York: Harcourt Brace and Jovanovich, Inc., 1977.

Harper, Ralph. *The Path of Darkness.* Cleveland: Case Western Reserve UP, 1968.

_____. *The World of the Thriller.* Cleveland: Case Western Reserve UP, 1969.

Hartnoll, Phyllis, ed. *The Oxford Companion to the Theatre.* London: Oxford UP, 1967.

Harvey, Paul Sir. *The Oxford Companion to Classical Literature.* London: Claredon P, 1966.

Hatlen, Theodore W. *Orientation to the Theatre.* New York: Appleton Century Crofts, 1962.

Heilman, Robert B. *Tragedy and Melodrama.* Seattle: U of Washington P, 1968.

Hill, Douglas, and Pat Williams. *The Supernatural.* New York: Signet Books, 1965.

Hill, Knox C. *Interpreting Literature.* Chicago: U of Chicago P, 1966.

Hobbes, Thomas. *The Leviathan.* Ed. A.R. Walker. New York: The MacMillan Co., 1904.

Hofstadter, Richard, and Michael Wallace. *Violence in America: A Documentary History.* New York: Vintage Books, 1971.

Holman, C. Hugh. *A Handbook to Literature.* New York: Odyssey P, 1972.

Hook, Sidney, ed. *Art and Philosophy.* New York: New York UP, 1966.

Hull, Raymond. *How to Write a Good Play.* Cincinnati: Writer's Digest Books, 1963.

Hume, Robert D. *The London Theatre World: 1600-1800.* Carbondale: Southern Illinois UP, 1980.

Huss, Roy, and T.J. Ross, eds. *Focus on the Horror Film.* Englewood Cliffs: Prentice Hall, 1972.

Hutchinson, Tom. *Horror and Fantasy in the Movies.* New York: Crescent Books, 1974.

Illustrated London News and Sketch. (June 1848): 392.

llustrated London News and Sketch. (March 1869): 251.

Kanfer, Stephen. "King of Horror." *Time* 14 (1986): 83.

Kaufmann, Walter. *Tragedy and Philosophy.* New York: Doubleday Books, 1968.

Kennedy, George A. *Classical Rhetoric and Its Christian and Secular Tradition from Ancient to Modern Times.* Chapel Hill: U of North Carolina P, 1980.

Kenney, C.L. *A Memoir of Michael Willaim Balfe.* New York: DeCappo P, 1978.

King, Basil. *The Conquest of Fear.* Garden City: Doubleday, Page, and Co., 1922.

Kitto, H.D.F. *Form and Meaning in Drama.* London: Methuen and Co., 1959.

_____. *Greek Tragedy. A Literary Study.* London: Methuen and Co., 1954.

Lanham, Richard A. *A Handist Of Rhetorical Terms.* Berkeley: U of Califorina P, 1968.

Loban, Walter, Margaret Ryan, and James Squire. *Teaching Language and Literature.* New York: Harcourt, Brace, and World, Inc., 1969.

London Times. (October 1836): 3.

Lovecraft, Howard Phillips. *Supernatural in Literature.* Reprinted in E.F. Bleiler, ed. New York: Dover Books, 1973.

Lowenthal, Leo. *Literature, Popular Culture, and Society.* Englewood Cliffs: Prentice

Hall, 1961.

Lucas, F.C. *Tragedy.* New York: Collier Books, 1962.

Mander, Raymond, and Joe Mitchenson. *The Theatres of London.* London: Pitman P, 1975.

Mank, Gregory Willaim. *It's Alive. The Classic Cinema Saga of Frankenstein.* New York: A.S. Barnes, 1981.

Mannheirm, Herman. *Pioneers in Criminology.* Montclair: Patterson Smith, 1972.

Marston, John W. *Our Recent London Actors.* London: Sampson Law, 1888.

Marx, Milton. *The Enjoyment of Drama.* New York: F.S. Crofts and Co., 1940.

Mathews, Brander. *A Study of Drama.* New York: Riverside P, 1910.

Mayer, David. "Towards a Definition of a Popular Theatre." *Western Popular Theatre.* New York: Methuen and Co., Ltd., 1977.

McCalmon, George, and Christian Moe. *Creating Historical Drama.* Carbondale: Southern Illinois UP, 1965.

Medved, Harry and Michael. *Son of the Golden Turkey Awards.* New York: Villard Books, 1986.

Merton, Robert K., and Robert Nisbet. *Contemporary Social Problems.* New York: Harcourt, Brace and Jovanovich, Inc., 1971.

Meyers, Richard. *For One Week Only: The World of Exploitation Films.* Piscataway: New Century, 1983.

Millon, Theodore and Renee. *Abnormal Behavior and Personality* Philadelphia: W.B. Saunders Co., 1974.

Minot, Stephen. *Three Genres: The Writing of Poetry, Fiction, and Drama.* Englewood Cliffs, 1971.

Moses, Montrose J. *The American Dramatist.* New York: Charles Scribners Sons, 1910.

Murray, Gilbert. *Euripides and His Age.* New York: Henry Holt and Company, 1913.

Nagler, A.M. *A Source Book in Theatrical History.* New York: Dover Books, 1952.

Nash, Robert Jay. *Almanac of World Crime.* New York: Bonanza Books, 1986.

Nettler, Gwynn. *Explaining Crime.* New York: McGrawHill. 1972.

Neuburg, Victor E. *Popular Literature: A History* New York: Penguin Books, 1977.

Newcombe, Horace. *T.V.: The Most Popular Art.* Garden City: Anchor Books, 1974.

Nicoll, Allardyce. *A History of English Drama, 1600-1900.* 6 vols. Cambridge: Cambridge UP, 1955. (This provides a listing of Fitzball's dramas.)

O'Connor, William Van. *Climates of Tragedy.* Baton Rouge: Louisiana State UP, 1943.

Page, Curtis Hidden. "The Romatic Emancipation." *Lectures of Literature.* Freeport: Books for Libraries P, Inc., 1911.

Patrick, David, ed. *E.K. Chambers Encyclopedia of English Literature.* 2 vols. London: W.R. Chambers, 1902.

Peacock, Ronald. *The Art of Drama.* New York: The MacMillan Co., 1957.

Penzoldt, Peter. *The Supernatural in Fiction.* New York: Humanities P, 1965.

Pick, John. *The West End.* Eastbourne, East Sussex: John Oxford, 1983.

Pike, Luke Owen. *A History of Crime in England.* 2 vols. Montclair: Patterson Smith, 1968.

Pollack, Sir Frederick, ed. *Macready's Reminiscences and Diaries.* New York: MacMillan And Co., 1875.

Punch. (July 1841): 36.

Rabkin, Eric S. *The Fantastic in Literature.* Princeton: Princeton UP, 1976.

Rahill, Frank. *The World of Melodrama.* University Park: Pennsylvania State UP, 1967.

Rice, Charles. *The London Theatre in the Eighteen-Thirties.* London: Society for Theatre Research, 1950.

Roberts, Vera Mowry. *On Stage. A History of Theatre.* New York: Harper and Row, 1962.

Roose-Evans, James. *London Theatre. From the Globe to the National.* Oxford: Phaidon, 1977.

Rosenfeld, Sybil. *A Short History of Scene Design in Great Britain.* Totowa: Rowman and Littlefield, 1973.

Ross, Ralph. *Symbols and Civilization: Science, Morals, Religion, Art.* New York: Harbinger Books, 1962.

Rowell, George. *Theatre in the Age of Irving.* Oxford: Basil Buckwell, 1981.

_____. *Victorian Dramatic, Criticism.* London: Methuen and Co., Ltd., 1971.

_____. *The Victorian Theatre:* 1792-1914. London: Cambridge UP, 1978.

Ruckmick, Christian A. The Psychology of Feeling and Emotion. New York: McGrawHill, 1936.

Sands, Mollie. *Robson of the Olympic.* London: Society for Theatre Research, 1981.

Schickel, Richard. "Help! They're Back." *Time* 128 (1986): 54-58.

Shank, Theodore. *The Art of Dramatic Art.* Belmont: Dickenson Publishing Co., 1969.

Shawn, Ted. *Every Little Movement. A Book About Francois Delsarte* New York: Dance Horizons, 1954.

Skinner, Otis. "Good Diction on the Stage." *The Emerson Quarterly.* (March 1929): 34.

Smiley, S. *Playwrighting.* Englewood Cliffs: Prentice Hall, 1971.

Smith, James. *Melodrama.* London: Methuen and Co., Ltd., 1973.

Sobel, Bernard, ed. *The New Theatre Handbook.* New York: Crown, Inc., 1959.

Spectator. (August 1822): 136.

Spectator. (September 1822): 946.

Spectator. (April 1825): 345.

Spectator. (October 1836): 1055.

Spectator. (October 1855): 1053.

Spector, Robert O., ed. *Seven Masterpieces of Gothic Horror.* New York: Bantam Books, 1970.

Stephen, Sir Leslie, and Sidney Lee. *Dictionay of National Biography.* London: Oxford UP, 1900.

Stevenson, Robert Louis. "A Penny Plain, Twopence Colored." *Memoires and Patriots.*

London: Chatto and Windus, 1877.

Symonds, J.A. Introduction. *Webster and Tourneur*. New York: Hill and Wang, Inc., 1966.

Thalbitzer, S. *Emotion and Insanity*. New York: Harcourt, Brace, and Co., Inc., 1926.

Theatrical Inquisitor. (1819): 259.

Thompson, David. *England in the Nineteenth Century*. New York: Penguin Books, 1977.

Thompson, G.J.S. *The Mystery and Lore of Monsters*. New York: The Citadel P, 170.

Thompson, G.R., ed. *The Gothic Imagination: Essays in Dark Romanticism*. New York: Washington Square P, 1974.

Tobias, J.J. *19th Century Crime in England: Prevention and Punishment*. New York: Barnes and Nobel, 1972.

_____. *Crime and Industrialized Society in the 9th Century*. New York: Schocken Books, 1967.

_____. *Crime and the Police in England: 1700-1900*. Gill and MacMillan, Ltd., 1979.

Trewin, J.C. *The Edwardian Theatre*. Oxford: Basil Blackwell, 1976.

_____. *The Pomping Folk in the Nineteenth-Century Theatre*. London: J.M. Dent and Sons, Ltd., 1968.

Turner, George E., and Michael Price. *Forgotten Horrors. Early Talkie Chillers from Poverty Row*. New York: A.S. Barnes and Co., 1979.

Van De Bogart, Doris. *Introduction to the Humanities*. New York: Barnes and Nobel, 1968.

Vedder, Clyde B., Samuel Keening, and Robert E. Clark, eds. *Criminology: A Book of Readings*. New York: Henry Holt and Co., Inc., 1953.

Verdac, A. Nicholas. *Stage to Screen*. New York: Benjamin Blom, 1949.

Watson, Layall. *Supernature*. Garden City: Anchor P, 1973

White, H.A. *Sir Walter Scott's Novels on the Stage*. New Haven: Yale UP, 1927.

Whitmore, Charles Edward. *The Supernatural in Tragedy*. Cambridge: Harvard UP, 1915.

Wilson, A.E. *East End Entertainment*. London: Arthur Barker, Ltd., 1954.

Wilson, Edwin. *The Theatre Experience*. New York: McGrawHill, 1985.

Wilson, Garff B. *Three Hundred Years of American Drama and Theatre*. Englewood Cliffs: Prentice Hall, Inc., 1973.

Wimsatt, Willaim K., Jr., and Cleanth Brooks. *Literary Criticism: A Short History*. New York: Alfred A. Knopf, 1966.

Wischhusen, Stephen, ed. *The Hour of One: Six Gothic Melodramas*. London: Gordon Fraser, 1975.

Wolf, Leonard. *Monsters*. San Francisco: Straight Arrow Books, 1974.

Wright, Wilmer C. *A Short History of Greek Literature*. New York: American Book Co., 1907.

Young, Paul T. *Emotion in Man and Animal*. New York: Robert E. Krieger, 1973.

Appendix: A
Handlist of Fitzball's Plays

Section One

The following list, based upon Allardyce Nicholl's bibliographical reference, will be composed of two sections: 1) sketches of plays judged as representative of Fitzballian dramaturgy and/or the sensational triad in his theatre of the macabre, and 2) titles of plays either redundant in dramatic scope or unavailable for reading. The titles of these plays will indicate the versatility of Fitzball's style, strategy, and theatricalism. Also, several plays will be synopsized which were not so sketched in the body of the work. This was done to confirm that Fitzball produced exemplary plays having traits of interest beyond the theme herein. The theatres and dates of the dramas' debuts will follow the title. With this methodology, the plays will be neither alphabetized nor sequenced. In addition to a synopsis of the sketched dramas, other pertinent information may be added to insure a more comprehensive overview of the drama when warranted.

Mary Glastonbury, at the Surrey, on September 9, 1833. Exciting drama of two women struggling to escape a lustful and pernicious villain, in order to save the life of an injured man, by way of the spooky moors. It combines eerie horror and crime and heroine strength, uncommon for melodramatic females. It has merit in characterization.

Margaret's Ghost; or, The Libertine's Ship, at the Victoria, on October 14, 1833. One of Fitzball's best-drawn ghost stories of a murdered wife returning to destroy her reckless, guilty husband aboard a blazing ship. A twist has the spectre as an appropriately justified avenger, in the Blood Revenge tradition of English tragedy.

Haunted Hillk, at the Adelphi, on July 12, 1831. The evil smuggler Caleb kidnaps Suzette and is killed in the rescue by her lover, Oakum, in one of Fitzball's best examples of pyrotechnical blue-fire, by an explosion on the ship. Fitzball's play is distinguished by fine tour-de-force acting in 0. Smith and T.P. Cooke and the excellent incarnation of the triad in the person of the wicked Caleb. It is blue-fire excellence.

The Earthquake; or, The Spectra of the Nile, at the Adelphi, on December 8, 1828. A holiday extravaganza epic about an *Arabian Night* adventure in which magic is used by Fitzball to a wonderfully escapist epitome. This saga is a portent of the filmic wonders to come, in such an example as *The Seventh Voyage of Sinbad*, in 1957. It is a children's delight and a telling reminder of Fitzball's interest in sheer, adventuresome fantasy.

Carmilhan; or, The Drowned Crew, at the Covent Garden, on April 20, 1835. A typical macabre play, in which the penny-dreadful acumen of Fitzball shines, as the monstrous ghost, Carmilhan, lusting for Uda, is destroyed by her beloved Magnus (notice the pun for *great*). While typically Fitzballian, the play is reminiscent of a neat, Disneyesque fantasy.

The Crock of Gold; or, The Murder at the Hall, at the City of London, deals will the villainous Jennings murdering his aunt for her funds and stabbing himself, in court, upon seeing her ghost. The hallmark lies in the frenzied courtroom pitch, inaugurated by Fitzball, as the madman dies in a gloriously awful denouement. Fitzball's triadic personification in Jennings somehow predicts the thrills of a *Perry Mason* situation in the court scene.

Thalaba, the Destroyer; or, The Burning Sword, at the Coburg, on August 11, 1823, has a sorceress, Kawala, ordering the demonic Abdala to destroy Thalaba. In a true Fitzballian rousing adventure, the macabre monster play ends with the heroine, played by Miss Vincent, dispatching evil. It is a finely-etched example of juvenile adventure.

Ouasimodo; or, The Gipsy Girl of Notre Dame, at the Covent Garden, on February 2, 1836. This is a wonderful operatic revision of the Hugo novel which, in some ways, maintains a precedent to the film versions of the classic novel, especially in the confrontation between the bellringer and his master, the evil Friar Follo. Esmeralda's salvation from execution by the doomed hunchback is a climactic gem. The triad with a dash of sentiment thrown in, is handled with concern by Fitzball. *Esmeralda* was Fitzball's first version, at the Surrey, on April 14, 1834.

The Libertine's Lesson, at the Adelphi, on October 8, 1827. This opera shows that Fitzball's penchant for magical fantasy did not have to be gruesome, or disturbing, aesthetically. The robber Naddock is foiled by the sorceress Liska in his attempt to undo her lover, Alfred. While this work is not sensationally triadic as are many of the plays herein listed, it does indicate that Fitzball was versatile in creating sensationalism in any guise, even in opera.

The Sea Serpent; or, Wizard of the Wind, at the Adelphi, on October 3, 1831. This burletta likewise shows that Fitzball could incorporate music as a dramatic ploy in a *Frankensteinian* method, inasmuch as this burletta was actually a terrifying tale of a dragon's attack upon mankind, until God destroys it and its creator, the magician Novergade. Thus, the bromide of "leaving things in nature untampered" is erected to a thrilling conclusion. This play is wonderfully spectacular and made to order as blue-fire.

Robert the Devil; or, The Devil's Son., at the Adelphi, on January 23, 1832, in association with Mr. Buckstone. This typical sensational triad gem has a devilish disciple in want of Robert's soul. However, Robert's ghostly mother and beloved, Isabella, destroy Bertram's wickedness, that throws him into hell. This is an exemplary, Fitzballian morality drama.

The Hunchbacks; or, The Sabre Grinders of Damascus, at the Surrey, on January 20, 1823. This is a Fitzballian social-thesis attempt to use the grotesque, in human deformity, as unrelated to the normalcy in the soul. Perceptively, the macabre is used for a moral acceptance of people different from other men in the "brotherhood of mankind."

Antigone; or, The Theban Sister, at the Norwich, in February 1821 and revived at the Surrey on August 11, 1823. Fitzball adapted the Greek classic as a closet drama, while maintaining a good sense of poetry, in all of the triadic circumstances therein. *Agamemnon* was read, as a closet drama, in 1876, four years after Fitzball's death. It seems to be the last rendition of his dramas.

The Black Hand: A Demon Play, at the Adelphi, on September 29, 1834. This is typical Fitzballian abandonment to the triad as the demon Nocta, while killing the hero and heroine, Sadak and Azola, fails to win their souls. In a theologic statement, Fitzball sees secular sensationalism as impotent to crush man's divine place in the universe. It is a philosophically-oriented work.

The Note Forger, at the Drury Lane, on April 20, 1835. This run-of-the mill triadic drama is distinguished by the battle between good and evil being emotionally exhausting. The villain is caught tormenting his acquaintances and is vanquished by the hero.

Don Quixote, The Knight of the Woeful Countenance and Panza: A Burlesque Musical, at the Adelphi, on January 9, 1833. This satire attacks the triadic ingredient of madness in human folly.

Giraldi, or, A Ruffian of Prague, at the Norwich, in April 1820. This is an eerie play about lycanthropy, wherein Giraldi kills when transformed and is killed by Pietro before the beast slays a baby. The triad is at its height as a suspenseful tool and as shocking fun.

The Dillosk Gatherer, or, The Eagle's Nest, at the Covent Garden, on July 13, 1832. An eagle kidnaps a child, is pursued, and killed. The key lies in spine-tingling, last-minute desperation in the quest.

The Mill of Loire, at the Adelphi, on May 1, 1833. A standard Fitzball shocker is distinguished by a fine, triadic heavy, Theodore, who "steals the show" from a bland hero, Paul. The fiery death of Theodore is starkly terrific.

Joan of Arc, at Sadler's Wells, on August 12, 1822 and revived at the Drury Lane on November 30, 1837. Fitzball saw this as blue-fire excitement with Joan being persecuted by three well-drawn villains, who are vexed before they can burn her by the hero, Charles. Joan was seen by Fitzball as a rebel. His opinion became somewhat of a prototype for the future renditions of Joan.

The Black Vulture; or, The Wheel of Death, at the Adelphi, on October 10, 1830. This is superlative sensational triad with O. Smith's monster battling the heroes unto death. The play has everything that is Blood and Thunder greatness. It is representative Fitzball.

The Fatal Blow, at the Surrey, on November 1, 1847. This play is ironic, sensational fun about wanton crime and the accentuated madness in the two villains, Michael and Brune, killers of their relative.

The Flying Dutchman; or, The Phantom Ship, at the Adelphi, on January 1, 1827. With one of Fitzball's greatest monsters, Vanderdecken, this eerie play is about the ghost's attempts to seduce the heroine and the wonderful battle to the end with the hero that follows.

Jonathan Bradford; or, The Murder at the Roadside Inn, at the Surrey, on December 12, 1833. Fitzball's masterpiece, which ran 200-400 times, throws the audience into the chilling clutches of the triad personified, Macraisy and his bouts with the hero, Bradford. It is a psychological and theatrical melodramatic gem of thoughtful verisimilitude.

The Devil's Elixir; or, The Shadowless Man, at the Covent Garden on April 20, 1829. Fitzball's contribution to the Faustian motif, with a monk attempting to impersonate his brother, so that he may lustfully partake of life, only to discover that strong faith is enough for him to overcome his plight, in destroying his demonic master, the magnificent Gortzburg. It is an excellent, triadic form of the highest melodramatic art.

The Traveller's Room, at the Surrey, on November 1, 1847. A standard mystery yarn about murder, robbery, and the villain Brune's downfall. It is a minor effort that, nonetheless, makes the triad evocative.

Alice May; or, The Last Appeal, at the Surrey, on June 23, 1852. Fitzball exploits the ultimate, sentimental, soap-operatic, and lachrymose play about Mathew killing the evil landlord, Louden, to save his family, who die anyway; and his eventual restitution, upon dying himself, in the arms of the emotionally empathetic employer and friend, Alice. It portends and signifies the best of triadic shmaltz.

Christmas Eve, or, A Duel in The Snow, at the Drury Lane, on March 12, 1860. A standard play, based upon a painting seen by Fitzball, about a climactic duel between a cad and hero, who both die in the new snow of Christmas Eve. The Captain is a fine, triadic villain, encompassing all auras of horror-terror, crime, and madness.

Nitocris; or, The Ethiope's Revenge, at the Drury Lane, on October 8, 1855. This play, with Edward Smith as the Ethiope, is interesting because Fitzball attempts to attack slavery, as a social problem, and the consequences of a slave who avenges himself on those hurtful to him. The play fails as socially important, but, as melodrama, it is noticeable.

Der Freischutz: or, The Demon of the Wolf's Glen, at the Surrey, on September 6, 1824. This is a rousingly frightening play about a demon's rule over humans until he is challenged by the hero, Casper. As such, Zamiel, the demon, and his human servant, Count Rodolph, are cast into hell in an exciting conclusion. This is one of Fitzball's better efforts in the macabre triad.

Paul Clifford, at the Covent Garden, on October 28, 1835. Fitzball's adaptation is from Bulwer Lytton's novel about a "Robin Hood-like" hero of the oppressed in eighteenth-century England. Fitzball's love for rugged adventure is stressed here, with accent on action and derring-do. Fitzball changed the novel's ending, in that Clifford is discovered to be the lost son of the judge. This play was typical of the melodramatizing of the classic anagnorisis, or recognition of the truth at the last minute.

Harlequin and Humpty Dumpty; or, Robbin De Bobbin (Subtitle sometimes omitted in surveys), at the Drury Lane, on December 26, 1850. Ingratiating fable, in combination of commedia dell arte and expressionistic style, which Fitzball uses as a confluence for such diverse elements as biblical characters (i.e. Gog and Magog as animated trees), nursery rhyme plots (Humpty flies to the moon and catches a dragon), and a Frank L. Baum type of atmosphere. While not macabre in the traditional sense of the triad, this fairytale drama was performed, for children, in keeping with the Yuletide season. While this children's play is wonderfully fantastic, it does, still, show the wild imagination for the eerie had by Fitzball, who evidences here a type of fantasy that a Steven Spielberg would cinematize.

Zazazeizozu; or, Dominoes. Chess, and Cards, at the Covent Garden, on April 4, 1836. This merry burlesque dealing with Chinese customs was to have been H.M. Milner's hack work at the Covent Garden. When he died unexpectedly, Osbaldiston entreated Fitzball to pen this madcap farce. The play is important as a predecessor to the type of playlet sketches and humor that Vaudeville and Burlesque would enjoy at the turn-of-the-century. Said Fitzball of this work, which he loathed as inartistic: "...with my hod or mortar, the drudge and stopgap of many a high sounding failure, when salaries could not else have been paid" (1: 104).

Robin Hood; or, the Merry Outlaws of Sherwood, at Astley's, on October 8, 1860. This was the right adventuresome and equestrian spectacle for the theatre famous for its "horse shows." Fitzball sprinkled the usual plot of Robin's "robbery-of-the-rich-for-the-poor" with as much action and gala as possible. The play boasted Fitzball songs and Rebecca Isaacs as Allan a' Dale, a fine "breeches" role.

The Phantom of the Nile: A Burletta, at the Surrey, in 1826. This piece of Far-Eastern exotica—the action occurs in Egypt—concerns itself with the evil Orchus who, in attempting to gain wizardry in the black arts, plans to sacrifice the fair heroine, Altheas. She is saved and he is killed by the heroic Palinedo: "Tyrant, at your peril, touch not the life of Althea." It is a good example of Fitzball's penchant for exoticism.

Walter Tyrrel, at the Covent Garden, on May 16, 1837. Historicizing (Geschichtlich) by his often-used method of exchange—as Fitzball did in changing the locale of *The Pilot* from America to England—the playwright transposed Walter Tyrrel, from being the traditional murderer of England's King William (Rufus) in the eleventh-century, to being a Saxon hero, who is persecuted by the villain, Rufus. History and identities were to Fitzball merely parts of his theatrical puzzle. Before dying, Tyrrel manages to slay Rufus with the same arrow the latter had used in killing Tyrrel's father. In an attempt at tragedy, yet again, Fitzball has Tyrrel going mad after Rufus' death, when he learns that his beloved Editha has been slain earlier by Rufus. Opting for John Vandenhoff to play the lead, Fitzball settled for the fine Edward Elton when the former left for America: "We had 'Walter Tyrrel' and no 'Walter Tyrrel' to put into the part" (11: 101).

The Miller of Derwent Water, at the Olympic, on May 2, 1853. A social-thesis play—and one nearest that appellation in Fitzball's corpus—the drama deals with a miller's protest against the monopoly of a greedy plutocrat. Faced with ruin, the miller is saved by his son's help, thereby concluding the play in Fitzball's usual melodramatic style of "a happy ending." However, the play is well written and, as theatre, the acting roles are highlights.

The Pilot; or, A Tale of the Sea, at the Adelphi, on October 31, 1825. Based upon Cooper's 1823 novel, the first of a trilogy (*The Red Rover* and *The Waterwitch,* the other two sea sagas), Fitzball altered the American setting to that of Britain during the American Revolution. Mr. Terry as The Pilot (Gray in Cooper's novel) leads the nautical fight against the upstart Americans, with Long Tom Coffin (Cooke) a tar delight. As was mentioned, the play was a national success, as the title page indicated: "…As Performed with Unanimous Applause." *Pilot: A Nautical Burletta* 1) It is high sea adventure, and Fitzball's skills as a numancia (nautical) dramatist are stressed.

False Colors; or, the Free Trader, at the Covent Garden, on March 4, 1837. A tedious nautical drama made palatable by T.P. Cooke's tar and the fiery sinking of a ship on stage. Fitzball wanted it to be more "nautical than The Pilot scene" (11: 88).

Azael; or, The Prodigal of Memphis, at Astley's, on November 3, 1851. This equestrian play is reminiscent of John Howard Payne's 1825 melodrama, *Mazappa,* wherein the hero is tied to a racing horse, as a sacrifice to the Egyptian diety, Isis. The tragic quality of the play pleased Fitzball, even though the Astley aura of equestrian theatre subordinated drama for continuous action.

Uncle Tom's Cabin; or, The Horrors of Slavery (three versions) at the Olympic, Grecian, and Drury Lane, on September 20, October 25, and December 27, 1852. An obvious social-thesis play based on the classic novel, Fitzball had the play end happily with Tom's enfranchisement. Fitzball's application of the triad to slavery was artistically deft. With all of its spectacle, the play is neither trite nor escapist.

The Red Rover, at the Adelphi, on February 9, 1829. Based upon the 1827 sea novel by James Fenimore Cooper, this high adventure concerns the exploits of a regal pirate, "The Red Rover" (Richard Yates), who ravages the British seas until he is "blown to smithereens" by the Navy. The "Robin Hood" syndrome is re-structured by Fitzball, in that The Rover is mercenary for himself, yet courteous to women. It is one of Fitzball's most famous sea dramas. T.P. Cooke plays a tar with aplomb.

The Floating Beacon; or, The Norwegian Wreckers, at the Surrey, on April 19, 1824. This nautical play has the sensational triad as eminent and identifiable. Frederic (Mr. Rowbotham) is besieged by piratical outlaws (among them, 0. Smith) and threatened with death. He discovers, by way of the peripeteia, that a strange woman, aboard the lightship, is his lost mother. Before being killed by the villains, who rob shipwrecked victims, Frederick and Mariette are rescued by Jack Junk (Mr. Gallot) and his marines, who kill the villains and burn the lightship. Fitzball's Deus-ex-Machina device of Junk and the sailors is well deployed, thus making this play a good example of nautical-gothic theatre.

The Inchcape Bell; or, The Dumb Sailor Boy, at the Surrey, on May 26, 1828. This tediously written play is about a mute boy discovered to be the lost son of Sir John Trevanly. The boy is rescued from pirates and reunited with Trevanly. The play does boast some well-etched characters, such as the comic servant Becky, her suitors, and the heroic tar, Tom Taffrail. The play is standard high-sea adventure.

The Innkeeper of Abbeville; or The Ostler and The Robber, at the Norwich, in March 1822 and revived at the Surrey on May 13, 1822. This domestic drama concerns Clauson, landlord of the Quartre Inn, and his condemnation to death for the murder of a guest, Baron Idenberg, who, in actuality, was killed and robbed by the evil Dyrkile. Standing in front of the firing squad, with no reprieve coming, as in the similar *Jonathan Bradford,* by way of Macraisy's confession, Clauson is missed by the bullets, while Dyrkile, fighting with the servant Zyrtillo, falls into the deadly line-of-fire himself. To increase the suspense, Fitzball let Loise, Clauson's daughter, swoon before the reprieve comes to Clausen to Dyrikile is a great triadic villain, and the play could easily be revived with interest.

Father and Son; or, The Rock of La Charbonniere, at the Covent Garden, on February 28, 1825, and revived as *Antoine: The Savage*, at the Coburg, on August 4, 1828. Fitzball mentioned that whenever the "bloody handkerchief" was brought onto the stage, audiences gasped and that the play's theme, the corrupting power of money, was objected to by George Colman, the then Director of Play Censoring at the Lord Chamberlain's Office. Complained Fitzball, "It is a price of points and there is a point in it which cannot be got over with the public…cowardly assassination" (1: 221-2). Here, the triad had a distinctly social purpose, not mere blue-fire terror.

The Daughter of the Regiment, at the Surrey, on December 12, 1847. Andreas, a gallant soldier, returns to Tyrol, some 12 years after the Battle of Marengo, to discover his beloved Madlaine is in the army. Thinking her dead, Andreas had joined other fronts of battle, but, upon releasing her disguise, he discovers that she has not been killed. The lovers are reunited. Though a trite rendition of the "disguised lover," the play has not the qualities of the triad; rather, the play targets the strength of love to conquer war and separation. This theme was very much a Ftizballian motif.

Waverly; or, Sixty Years Since, at the Adelphi, on March 8, 1824. With a type of Dickensian tone, Fitzball's lively adaptation of Scott's *Waverly* (1814), the first of 32 romantic novels, centers upon the treachery of Fergus against Captain Waverly and the Royal Army of Scotland. Though a rebel in the cause of freedom, Fergus is caught and hanged for treason. However, Fergus is not drawn as a villain; rather, he is a believer in his cause of insubordination. His ascent to the gallows is reminiscent of Carton's death in *A Tale of Two Cities*.

Omala; or, Settlers in America, at the Olympic, on October 1, 1825. This three-act drama about the relationship between the British and the Indians of newly-claimed America is distinguished by its reflection of the vogue of writing Indian plays in nineteenth-century America. Omala is the son of Pultawa and confronts the arriving British with reserved help. It is discovered that Orilla, thought to be an Indian, and beloved of Omala, is the lost daughter of Governor Etheringord. Though contrived with a stretched "discovery scene of Orilla's true identity," the play smacks of John Augustus Stone's *Metamora*, the 1829 "Noble Savage" play for the American actor, Edwin Forrest.

The Momentous Question, at the Lyceum, on June 17, 1844. This conventional domestic "soap-opera" concerns Rachael Ryland's marriage to the rogue and poacher, Robert Shelley. Though his love has been unrequited for Rachael, James Greenfield, a gamekeeper, seeks to comfort her inspite of Robert's philandering. They fall in love. In a stirring finale, Robert is shot to death by the authorities after committing a crime. Robert dies in Rachel's arms in much the same manner as the sequence in *Alice May*. Robert is more of a misunderstood and confused scamp than a consummate villain.

The Children of the Castle, at the Marylebone, on November 23, 1857. Sir Alif has kept the Lady Mabel and her children prisoners after usurping the position of his cousin, Lord William, a crusader in Palestine. As a despot, Alif has wrecked ruin for his own greed. Alif, found out as a villain and kidnapper of Mabel and her daughters, Alice and Christiline, is beset by the Hermit in a sword fight. The Hermit turns out to be Lord William, who, being disguised and protected from Alif by his friend Oliver, kills Alif, and the family is reunited. Fitzball injected a proper amount of the melodramatic inclination for "disguises" and "last-minute recognitions" to maintain enjoyment. Alif is a fine heavy, and the gothic atmosphere is well tuned. William is seen as The Hermit and then, continuing the masquerade, as The Figure. Before-Mabel in the denouement. Fitzball was careful not to reveal William's identity until the exact time. The "Hermit" and "Figure" are not in the *Dramatis Personae,* thus adding to the mysterious elements in the play.

Edwin, Heir of Cressingham: A Tragedy, at the Norwich, in 1817. Wrote Fitzball of this, his first tragedy: "Tremblingly alive to all the fears and anxieties of those who like me, appear before so awful a tribunal as the Public, I submit my Tragedy to them 'with all its imperfection on its head' " (*Edwin* 1). Based upon Jane Porter's *The Scottish Chiefs* (1810), a forerunner to the romantic novels of her childhood friend, Walter Scott, the play concerns itself with the exploits of Edwin, King of Northumbria, who ruled over Scotland (Edinburgh bears his name) and all of the United Kingdom, or what there was of it in the seventh-century. He fell to Prince Penda of Mercia (now central England) in 633. Fitzball captures the fervor of the time again, in exploiting dramatic licensing to the hilt—by having Edwin a "Macbeth-like" king and Lady Margaret a "Lady Macbeth" in her psychological mannerisms. The play is filled with political, social, and emotional intrigue. The piece, in keeping with Fitzball's Greek tragedy adaptations, reads more as a closet drama than as an acted play.

Tom Cringle; or Mat of the Iron Hand, at the Surrey, on May 26, 1834. The exciting adventure saga is pure Fitzballian delight and sensationally triadic in the villain, Mat of the Iron Hand. The gothic atmosphere of storms and castles gives the play a relishingly dark tone. Leading a marauding gang of thugs, Mat has terrorized the countryside, by land and by sea; however, Tom Cringle, his nemesis, confronts him in a frantic showdown in a gloomy mansion. Cringle has killed one gang member, Black Walter, in attempting to free the heroine, Elizabeth. Going mad, Mat, grabbing his handy knife, rushes Cringle, who shoots him to death. The Marines, in hiding, come out to arrest the other gangsters. With the "Wreckers" and Mat downed, Tom embraces Fanny, another heroine, victimized by Mat. Fitzball's emphasis xzcklon characterization and suspense is well crafted.

Section Two
  The following play titles are those in Nicholl's compendium. Included are plays unsketched, but otherwise read; and those unavailable. Herein, only the titles, playhouses, and dates of debuts will be listed.

Bertha; or, The Assassins of Istria, at the Norwich, March 8, 1819.

Edda; or, The Hermit of Warkworth, at the Surrey, May 29, 1820.

Ugolino; or, the Tower of Famine, at the Surrey, December 26, 1821.

The Innkeeper of Addbeville: or, The Ostler and the Robber, at the Norwich, March 1822, and the Surrey May 13, 1822.

The Fortunes of Nigel; or, King James I and His Times, at the Surrey June 25, 1822.

The Treadmill; or, Tom and Jerry at Brixton, at the Surrey, 1822.

The Barber: or, The Mill of Bagdad, at the Surrey, 1822.

Peveril of the Peak; or, The Days of King Charles II, at the Surrey, February 2, 1823.

Prince of Persia; or, the Demon of the Flood, at the Sadler's Wells, May 19, 1823.

Laurette; or, The Forest of Unterwald; at the Surrey, August 11, 1823.

Iwan; or, The Mines of Ischinski, at the Surrey, September 22, 1823.

The Fire-worshippers; or, The Paradise of the Peris, at the Surrey, April 19, 1824.

The Floating Beacon; or, The Norwegian Wreckers, at the Surrey, April 19, 1824.

William the Conqueror; or, The Days of the Curfew Bell at the Coburg, May 17, 1824.

The Burning Bridge; or, The Spectre of the Lake, at the Surrey, August 16, 1824.

The Koeuba; or, the Indian Pirate's Vessel, at the Surrey, October, 4, 1824.

Wardock Kennilson: or, The Outcast Mother and Her Son, at the Surrey, October 25, 1824.

Mr. Chairman, at the Adelphi, April 1826.

Nelson; or, The Life of a Sailor, at the Adelphi, November 19, 1827.

The Robber's Bride, at the English Opera House, July 15, 1829.

Les Deux Nuits; or, The Night Before the Wedding at the Covent Garden, November 17, 1829.

Ninetta; or, The Maid of Palaiseau, at the Covent Garden, February 4, 1930.

The Maid of the Oaks, at the Vauxhall, June 1830.

Adelaide; or, The Royal William, at the Vauxhall, July 23, 1830.

The Libertine of Poland; or, The Colonel of Hussars, at the Coburg, October 11, 1830.

The Sorceress, at the Adelphi, August 4, 1831.

Der Alchymist, at the Drury Lane, March 20, 1832.

Nina, The Bride of the Galley Slave, at the Adelphi, March 26, 1832.

Andreas Hofer, The Tell of the Tyrol, at the Surrey, June 11, 1832.

The Magic Fan: or, The Fillip of the Nose, at the Vauxhall, June 18, 1832.

The Bottle of Champagne, at the Vauxhall, July, 27, 1832.

The Sedan Chair, at the Vauxhall, August 27, 1832.

The Maid of Cashmere, at the Drury Lane, August 16, 1833.

The Soldier's Widow; or, The Ruin of the Mill, at the Adelphi, May 4, 1833.

The Felon of New York, at the Surrey, August 24, 1833.

Lekinda; or, The Sleepless Woman, at the Adelphi, September 30, 1833.

Esmeralda; or, The Deformed of Notre Dame, at the Surrey, April 14, 1834.

The Lord of the Isles; or, The Gathering of the Clans, at the Surrey, November 20, 1834.

The Young Courier; or, The Miser of Walden, at the Strand, December 1, 1834.

The Last Days of Pompeii; or, The Blind Girl of Tessaly, at the Victoria, January 6, 1835.

The Siege of Rochelle, at the Drury Lane, October 29, 1835.

Inheritance; or, The Unwelcomed Guest, at the Covent Garden, November 24, 1835.

The Carmelites; or, The Convent Belles, at the Covent Garden, December 3, 1835.

The Bronze Horse; or, The Spell of the Cloud King, at the Covent Garden, December 14, 1835.

The Assurance Company; or, The Boarding School of Montesque, at the Covent Garden, April 30, 1836.

The Wood Devil, at Sadler's Wells, May 9, 1836.

The Rose of the Alhambra, at the Covent Garden, May 12, 1836. Fitzball acted a minor role in this drama.

The Sexton of Cologne; or, The Burgomaster's Daughter, at the Covent Garden, June 13, 1836.

The Hindoo Robber, at the Covent Garden, September 29, 1836.

Mutual Expense; or, A Female Travelling. Companion, at the Covent Garden, October 11, 1836.

Zohrab the Hostage; or, The Storming of Mezanderan, at the Covent Garden,

February 28, 1837.

False Colours; or, The Free Trader, at the Covent Garden, March 4, 1837.

The Eagle's Haunt, at the St. James, May 5, 1837.

The Negro of Wapping; or The Boat-builder's Novel, at the Garrick, April 16, 1838.

Diadeste; or, The Veiled Lady, at the Drury Lane, May 17, 1838.

The Outpost, at the Covent Garden, May 17, 1838.

Oconesto; or, The Mohawk Chief, at the Royal Pavilion, September 3, 1838.

The Maid of Palaiseau, at the Drury Lane, October 13, 1838.

The King of the Mist; The Miller of the Hartz Mountains, at the Drury Lane, April 1, 1839.

Scaramuccia; or The Villagers of San Ouintion, at the English Opera House, August 23, 1839.

Keolanthe: or, The Unearthly Bride, at the English Opera House, March 9, 1841.

The April Fool, at the Olympic, May 17, 1841.

The Robber's Sister; or, The Forge in the Forest, at the English Opera House, June 7, 1841.

Hans of Iceland, at the Covent Garden, September 27, 1841.

Charlotte Hanwell; or, Sorrow and Crime, at the Sadler's Well, January 10, 1842.

Ombra; or The Spirit of the Reclining Stone, at the Surrey, February 22, 1842.

The Trooper's Horn; or, The Goblin of the Chest, at the Lyceum, May 9, 1842.

Jane Paul; or, The Victim of Unmerited Persecution, at the Victoria, May 16, 1842.

The Miller's Wife, at the Victoria, August 22, 1842.

The Owl Sisters; or, The Haunted Abbey Ruin, at the Adelphi, September 29, 1842.

Alma, at the Adelphi, November 7, 1842.

Mary Melvyn; or, The Marriage of Interest, at the Adelphi, February 20, 1843.

The Queen of the Thames; or, The Anglers, at the Drury Lane, February 25, 1843.

The Ranger's Daughter, at the Olympic, February 27, 1843.

Ondine; or, The Maid, at the Adelphi, October 7, 1843.

La Favoita, at the Drury Lane, October 18, 1843.

Home Again; or, The Lieutenant's Daughters, at the Lyceum, November 28, 1844.

The Fairy Oak, at the Drury Lane, October 18, 1845.

Maritana, at the Drury Lane, November 15, 1845.

The Crown Jewels, at the Drury Lane, April 16, 1846.

The Desert; or, The Imann's Daughter, at the Drury Lane, April 5, 1847.

The Wreck and the Reef, at the Surrey, May 24, 1847.

The Forest Maiden and the Moorish Page, at the Surrey, May 31, 1847.

The Maid of Honour, at the Drury Lane, December 20, 1847.

Marmion; or, The Battle of Flodden Field, at the Astley's, July 12, 1848.

Quentin Durward, at the Covent Garden, December 6, 1848.

Corasco; or, The Warrior's Steed, at the Astley's, February 12, 1849.

The White Maiden of California, at the Astley's, April 9, 1849.

Alhamar the Moor; or, The Brother of Valencia, at the Surrey, April 9, 1849.

The Prophet, at the Astley's, October 1, 1849.

The Four Sons of Aumon; or, The Days of Charlemagne, at the Astley's, April 1, 1850.

Alonzo the Brave and the Fair Imogene, at the Princess's, December 26, 1850.

The Cadi's Daughter, at the Drury Lane, January 27, 1851.

Azael the Prodigal, at the Drury Lane, February 19, 1851.

Hans von Stien; or, The Robber Knight, at the Marylebone, August 11, 1851.

Vin Willoughby; or, The Mutiny of the Isis, at the Marylebone, August 25, 1851.

The Greek Slave; or, The Spectre Gambler, at the Marylebone, November 20, 1851.

The Last of the Fairies, at the Olympic, March 4, 1852.

The Secret Pass; or, The Khan's Daughter, at the Surrey, May 31, 1852.

Peter the Great, at the Astley's July 26, 1852.

The Field of Terror; or, the Devil 's Diggings, at the Olympic, August 11, 1852.

The Rising of the Tide, at the Marylebone, January 24, 1853.

Amakosa; or, *Kaffir Warfare,* at the Astley's March 28, 1853.

Berta; or, The Gnome of the Hartzberg, at the Haymarket, May 26, 1855.

Raymond and Agnes at the Manchester, 1855, and at the St. James, June 11, 1859.

The Lost Ship; or, The Atlantic Steamer, at the Marylebone, March 17, 1857.

The Husband's Vengeance; or, The Children of the Castle, at the Marylebone, November 23, 1857.

Pierette; or, The Village Rivals, at the Hull, March 6, 1858.

Auld Robin Gray, at the Surrey, April 19, 1858.

The Lancashire Witches, at the Lyceum, July 17, 1858.

The Widow's Wedding, at the St. James, October 1, 1859.

Lurline, at the Covent Garden, February 23, 1860.

The Gipsy Girl; or, The Cottage of Roses, at the Edinburgh, September 7, 1863.

She Stoops to Conquer, at the Covet Garden, February 11, 1864.

The Magic Pearl, at the Alexandra, September 29, 1873.

The Barber of Seville n.d.

The Marriage of Figaro, n.d.

Pascal Burno, n.d.